Dignified & Efficient

The British Monarchy in the Twentieth Century

Dignified & Efficient

The British Monarchy in the Twentieth Century

Charles Douglas-Home
Completed by Saul Kelly

First published in Great Britain in 2000

Claridge Press
Horsells Farm Cottage
Brinkworth
Wilts SN15 5AS
www.claridgepress.com

Copyright © Jessica Douglas-Home and Saul Kelly

Cover design: Projections
Cover photograph: PA Photos

Index compiled by Douglas Matthews

Printed by Antony Rowe Ltd

CIP data for this title is available from the British Library

ISBN No: 1-870626-52-4

History

Contents

Preface

Charles Douglas-Home was editor of *The Times* from March 1982 to October 1985, when he resigned two weeks before his death from bone marrow cancer at the tragically early age of 48. Before he died he was working on a book which sought to describe the role which the Sovereign plays in the modern British constitution. He wanted to show how that role has developed in the twentieth century, with special emphasis placed on the generally unknown part played by the Private Secretary to the Sovereign.

Using evidence gathered from public and private archives and interviews with former officials, Charles Douglas-Home sets out to explain how successive Sovereigns in the twentieth century have exerted their influence and prerogative powers during constitutional crises and in more normal times. His purpose was to demonstrate that the constitutional monarch continues to have a role to play in our democratic system of government. As such, it forms a useful, if belated, contribution to the ongoing debate on the Monarchy.

Charles Douglas-Home wrote two-thirds of the manuscript of this book before his death, getting as far as the end of the Second World War. It is clear, from his surviving notes, that he intended the story to be carried up to the present day. In accordance with his intention, I have written new chapters on the end of George VI's reign from 1945-52 and Elizabeth II's reign from 1952 to the present. I hope these are in character with the rest of the book. With regard to the chapters covering the period from the reign of Edward VII to George VI and the Second World War, I have revised these in the light of recent research and my own findings. I have also reduced them in number and rearranged some passages in the text in order to make his account of the British Monarchy in the Twentieth

Century clearer and easier for the reader to follow. The conclusion is based on an article on the Crown and the Commonwealth written by Charles Douglas-Home the year before he died. I have provided footnotes where necessary. In preparing this book for publication, I have only done what Charles Douglas-Home would have done in the way of editing the manuscript. I hope he would have been pleased with the result.

I would like to thank Jessica Douglas-Home, David Pryce-Jones and the Trustees of the Charles Douglas-Home Trust who commissioned me to do the work and financed it. On behalf of Charles Douglas-Home, I wish to acknowledge the assistance he received in researching this book from the staffs of the libraries and archives mentioned in the footnotes. I am also grateful to the holders of copyright material for permission to quote it in the text.

Saul Kelly

Cambridge
March 2000

1

Edward the Enhancer

Monarchy adjusted remarkably quickly to the twentieth century. When Queen Victoria died in 1901, after nearly 64 years on the throne, her son, King Edward VII, was already nearly sixty himself. But he was not as ill-prepared for the takeover as has been so commonly assumed. As Prince of Wales, he carried out public and social functions on her behalf. Towards the end of his mother's reign he had been given access to Cabinet papers and Foreign Office despatches; he was kept informed by Ministers about affairs of State, and he himself corresponded with Ministers and government officials. Above all, through his family's connections with most of the crowned heads of Europe and his yearly travels on the Continent, he had an intimate knowledge of European affairs. Thus, he gained valuable experience and knowledge of the business side of a constitutional monarchy. Edward VII had obtained, therefore, the essential political knowledge on which to base any change in the forms of his position, and a constitutional understanding as a basis for adjusting to the changes when they did occur. The changes in the style and conduct of the monarch which occurred during King Edward's reign mostly reflected the difference in personality between son and mother and their differences in taste — both political and private.

The Queen's authority had derived from three things: the tradition of the office, her length of service, and her own personality which, even in her dotage, could claim integrity of a kind through the fearless expression of opinions and strong prejudices, and a native almost peasant cunning about the limits of her power. Edward VII inherited the office without that lengthy experience and without that kind of personality. However, he had a certain shrewdness. He did not squander his inheritance. If anything, because his dealings with politicians were less tinged with passion and emotion than were those of his mother, he enhanced the dignity and efficiency of his office within the body politic.

With his great love of display (as seen at Queen Victoria's funeral, the annual State Opening of Parliament and the Coronation) and his intuitive understanding of the people's need to see their sovereign, Edward VII was able to symbolise power to a far greater extent than his reclusive mother, 'the Widow of Windsor'. His refurbishment of the royal palaces and spectacular revival of Court life gave the Monarchy a style and glamour which it had lacked since the days of George IV. King Edward and his consort Queen Alexandra made the Monarchy interesting and, by doing so, personalised the government and the nation. Thus, as the nineteenth century political commentator, Walter Bagehot, had foreseen, they fulfilled a modern need in an increasingly impersonal age.

Alexandra, with her intense love for her children, also gave the Monarchy that air of mutual devotion which was to become so important for the institution, while Edward, with his very human weaknesses for women, horses and food, made the Monarchy real in the sense of making it part of everyday life. Edward VII deepened the hold of the Monarchy in Britain by his appeal to all classes and because of the increasing tendency of many to see the Throne as a reassuring symbol of continuity at a time of rapid and uncertain change both at home and abroad. This explains the widespread sense of grief felt at his death and the rapid sanctification of his memory which, in contrast to the nineteenth century, made criticism of royalty seem tantamount to disloyalty. By carrying out the dignified aspects of his role with such aplomb, Edward VII made the Monarchy popular and more accessible. Thus, he added important new elements to the legacy left by his mother and father, who had made the modern monarchy respectable and identified it with the nation as a whole.

With regard to Edward VII's political role in the efficient working of the constitution, many Edwardians believed that his high public profile meant that he exercised great influence on domestic and, particularly, foreign affairs. In fact the King's power was less than it appeared. Encouraged by the mid-Victorian delusions of his constitutional advisers, Lord Knollys (his Private Secretary) and Lord Esher, Edward VII failed in his attempt to play the political role his mother and father had filled in the mid-nineteenth century. His reign saw the further erosion of the royal prerogatives of mercy, the dissolution of Parliament, the selection and dismissal of ministers, the cession of territory, the declaration of peace and the appointment of bishops, colonial governors and judges.[1] His death prevented him from being forced to exercise extensively the last great prerogative: the creation of peers. But that does not mean, as one commentator concluded a generation ago, that 'Edward VII exercised little or no influence on the "high politics" of his reign.'[2]

Edward VII may not have been as dedicated to unremitting paperwork as his mother and his successors had been. But he kept himself informed about government policy and made his views well-known. He did this not only through regular audiences accorded the Prime Minister and the Foreign Secretary and by social meetings with ministers, but also through his seven well-placed and trusted advisers. The latter included his Private Secretary, Lord Knollys, his military and constitutional adviser, Lord Esher, his naval adviser, Sir John (later Lord) Fisher, his diplomatic adviser, Sir Charles (later Lord) Hardinge, the anti-German Portuguese Minister in London, Luis de Soveral, and his financial adviser, Sir Ernest Cassel. Finally there was his mistress, Mrs George Keppel.

As the character of his advisers indicates, the King was certainly more interested in foreign and defence matters than he was in domestic, Irish, colonial or Indian affairs. It does not follow, however, that he concentrated on the former spheres at the expense of the latter. The momentous political events at home, in Ireland, in South Africa and India prevented this. He may have been 'bored', as one observer put it[3], by the sectarian dispute over the great reforming Education Act of 1902, but he closely followed the 'Tariff Reform' issue which split the Unionist government. He was intimately involved in resolving the Cabinet crisis of September 1903, when five ministers resigned, and gave his much-needed support to the weakened Prime Minister, Arthur Balfour, in the last two years of his government. Although a Free Trader by instinct, the King advocated the appointment of a Royal Commission to investigate the whole Tariff issue; a suggestion which was rejected by Balfour.[4]

---

[1]   Sir Sidney Lee, *King Edward VII* (Macmillan, London, 1927), Vol 2, pp 38-44.

[2]   Frank Hardie, *The Political Influence of the British Monarchy, 1868-1952* (Batsford, London, 1970), p 93.

[3]   *Ibid.*

[4]   Peter Fraser, *Lord Esher* (Hart-Davis, MacGibbon, London, 1973), pp19-20.

The King deplored as politically and socially divisive the Liberal government's legalisation of picketing under the Trades Disputes Act, the Education Bill, and moves to tax the rich, to give women the vote and abolish the hereditary element in the House of Lords. His interest in Ireland was not simply limited to his opposition to Home Rule.[5] Following a successful visit to Ireland in 1903, which was of great assistance to the Balfour government at a time when they were pushing the Irish Educational and Land Bills through Parliament, the King 'personally intervened in appointments at the Irish Office and he insisted on inserting a paragraph with a description of the Irish tour in the next King's speech'.[6] Moreover, the King tried, but failed, to prevent the resignation of the Irish Secretary, George Wyndham, as a result of a crisis in the Unionist government over the involvement of his Catholic Under-Secretary, Sir Alexander MacDonald, in the recently-established Irish Reform Association.

The King's interest in South Africa did not cease with the end of the Boer War. He supported Lord Milner's policy of reconstruction and regarded the importation of Chinese labour, which the Liberal Opposition castigated as 'Chinese Slavery', as 'a necessary measure'.[7] Like Milner, he opposed the grant of self-government to the ex-Boer Republics of the Transvaal and the Orange Free State and regarded as premature the establishment of the Union of South Africa (he reluctantly agreed to the appointment of the 'hopeless' Home Secretary, Herbert (Lord) Gladstone, as the first Governor-General of South Africa). He was a supporter of the other great proconsuls, Lord Cromer in Egypt (he tried unsuccessfully to persuade him to become Foreign Secretary in the 1906 Liberal Government, in preference to Sir Edward Grey) and Lord Curzon in India. He was sympathetic to Curzon in his disputes with the Balfour government over Younghusband's expedition to Tibet and with Kitchener over constitutional control of the Indian Army which forced Curzon to resign his viceroyalty. Briefed by Curzon, he unsuccessfully opposed the Liberal government's first attempt at responsible government in India (the Morley-Minto reforms) and the appointment of the first Indian, SP (later Lord)

---

[5] Hardie, *Political Influence*, p 94.
[6] Keith Middlemass, *The Life and Times of Edward VII* (Weidenfeld and Nicolson, London, 1972), p128.
[7] Hardie, *Political Influence*, p 87.

Sinha, to the Viceroy's Council. But he did persuade the Liberal government to back the Government of India and institute a new Press Law to crack down on sedition in India. He thought a soldier was needed as Viceroy and proposed that Lord Kitchener should succeed Lord Minto. He was overruled by the Secretary of State for India, John Morley, who insisted on a civilian and secured the appointment of Sir Charles Hardinge (the King thought his diplomatic adviser should stick 'to his last').[8]

Encouraged by Lord Esher, the King took seriously his constitutional position as head of the Army and the Navy (officers were commissioned by and owed allegiance to the King). There may even have been an attempt to extend royal power in service politics. Edward VII used his considerable social influence within the officer corps to support the appointment of reformers in the overhauling of the services following the Boer War and the rise of Anglo-German antagonism. His consistent support for Sir John (later Lord) Fisher in his successful drive (in the face of considerable opposition from within the Navy led by Lord Charles Beresford) to modernise and redeploy the fleet in order to face the German threat was of critical importance in ensuring that Britain had a proper naval defence in 1914.[9] Edward VII played an important part also in ensuring that the British Army was capable of sending an expeditionary force abroad, at short notice, as it did after the outbreak of the First World War. He helped to secure the removal of two incompetent Secretaries of State for War, St John Brodrick and Arnold-Forster, and the appointment of a third, Haldane, who instituted the necessary reforms in the Army. The influence which the Monarchy had in Army and Navy affairs, and the potential for its expansion, was to be clearly demonstrated during the Curragh Incident in March 1914 (see Chapter 2) and the First World War (see Chapter 3).[10]

[8] Simon Heffer, *Power and Place. The Political Consequences of King Edward VII* (Weidenfeld and Nicolson, London, 1998), pp153, 199-203, 208, 295-6.

[9] See Arthur Marder, *From the Dreadnought to Scapa Flow. The Royal Navy in the Fisher Era, 1904-1919, Vol1* (Oxford University Press, London, 1961), p 100; Sir Philip Magnus, *King Edward VII* (John Murray, London, 1964), p 277; Ruddock F. Mackay, *Fisher of Kilverstone* (Clarendon Press, Oxford, 1977), pp 393-4, 398.

[10] See John Gooch, 'Adverserial Attitudes; Servicemen, Politicians and Strategic Policy in Edwardian England, 1899-1914', in Paul Smith (ed) *Government and the Armed Forces, 1856-1990* (Hambledon Press, London,1996), pp 55-6; John Gooch, *The Plans of War. The General Staff and British Military Strategy, c.1900-1916* (Routledge and Kegan Paul, London, 1974), Chap 2; Edward M Spiers, 'The South African War' in his (ed) *The Army and Society, 1815-1914* (Longman, London, 1980).

It has been said that Edward VII's 'role in military and naval affairs was greater and more beneficial than his role in diplomacy'.[11] But this is based on a misperception of the King's role in international affairs. It is true that Edward VII was not the power in international relations that Esher and his French and German contemporaries, and some historians, have claimed.[12] But the role he played and the influence he had on the European scene was not as neglible as Balfour, Lansdowne (Unionist Foreign Secretary from 1900-5) and Grey, and various historians have made out.[13] The King may have played no direct part in the formulation of Britain's European policy but that was primarily due to the fact that he agreed with the Entente policy with France and Russia pursued by his ministers as the best way of blocking Germany's expansionist ambitions. Thus, a major dispute over policy never arose (if the King had opposed this or an alternative policy, he might very well have undermined it). As has been pointed out, he had certain powers which enabled him

> to influence the course of British foreign policy, and to play a positive role in the cultivation of Britain's relations with the European powers ... The King made a unique, and important contribution to the creation and maintenance of both the Anglo-French and Anglo-Russian Ententes by using his charm, his authority and his unrivalled network of contacts to help government policy. He was supported in his efforts by a group of friends [the "Hardinge Gang" comprising Sir Charles Hardinge, Sir Francis Bertie and Sir Arthur Nicolson], whose careers he in turn promoted, who were, in the main, and with much justification, suspicious of German intentions ... by the time of the King's death, in May 1910, thanks in part to his own efforts, Britain was in a much stronger position, diplomatically and militarily, to resist German aggression than it had been at the start of his reign.[14]

It has been said that 'during Edward's reign royal influence was more

[11] J A Thompson and Arthur Mejia, Jr, *The Modern British Monarchy* (Doubleday, New York, 1971), p 36.

[12] *Ibid*, p 33; Gordon Brook-Shepherd, *Uncle of Europe. The Social and Diplomatic Life of Edward VII* (Collins, London, 1975), pp 49-60; for the revised view see Roderick Reid McLean, 'Monarchy and Diplomacy in Europe, 1900-1910', Unpublished PhD thesis, Sussex University, 1996, p 92.

[13] Thompson and Mejia, *Modern British Monarchy*, pp 34-5.

[14] McLean, 'Monarchy and Diplomacy', pp 140-1.

apparent than real . . . '[15] As has been shown above, however, despite the destruction of 'virtually all the vestiges of royal power and . . . the direct bases of royal influence'[16] Edward VII made use of the monarchy's remaining ability to influence politics in a subtle and indirect way. Brighter and more energetic than many historians have given him credit for, Edward brought his knowledge and prestige to bear in many spheres of government in an effective way through his circle of trusted advisers. As such, he played a part in the efficient working of the constitution which complemented his dignified role. This was to be highlighted during the constitutional crisis at the end of his reign.

The King's Private Secretary, Lord Knollys, wrote to the Lord Chamberlain, Lord Althorp,[17] on 14 September 1909: 'It seems not improbable that before long we may be plunged into the gravest political and constitutional crisis that there has been since 1832.' He was right. The crisis of 1909-11 racked the body politic like nothing since 1832, and like nothing afterwards. Its outcome dictated the broad shape of the British constitution in the twentieth century which has not been fundamentally affected by the Irish settlement, the dismantling of Empire, the abdication, or two world wars. Today, devolution, the possibility of a three party system if proportional representation is adopted by the Westminster Parliament, and/or the abolition of the House of Lords may again summon the same kind of demons from the deep, to threaten the very foundations of the throne.

The crisis in 1909-11 concerned the House of Lords. The Liberals had been in a permanent minority in the Upper House since the Home Rule split of 1886 (when those Liberals opposed to Gladstone's policy of Home Rule for Ireland left the party and later formed a coalition with the Conservative Party dedicated to the preservation of the Union). When the Liberals returned to the Commons with a landslide victory in 1906 they set about creating more peers, in the hope of reducing their enormous disadvantage. Edward VII did not like it; and the gap was anyway too large to be bridged by anything other than saturation tactics. The Lords,

---

[15] Thompson and Meija, *Modern British Monarchy*, p 38.

[16] *Ibid.*

[17] The grandfather, on his mother's side, of Charles Douglas-Home.

impervious, carried on treating Liberal legislation with contempt.

In 1909, however, this state of armed neutrality between the Houses of Parliament turned into what threatened to be a war to the death. The first budget of the radical Liberal Chancellor of the Exchequer, Lloyd George, was rejected by the Lords. Such a challenge — involving the denial of supply to the government, and thus going to the very heart of the question of Parliamentary sovereignty — was one which the Liberal Prime Minister, Herbert Asquith, felt he had to meet head on rather than with the shrugged shoulders that had characterised Liberal attitudes to the reverses they had previously received from the Lords. True, the House of Lords had a perfectly legal right to reject a budget; and the official opposition, led by Balfour, had sound economic arguments for so doing. Both these aspects soon became overshadowed by the great constitutional implications which necessarily grew out of a Liberal conviction that the powers of the Lords would have to be curtailed, and that given that the Upper House itself had the current power to prevent this, it had to be politically coerced into using its unrestricted power for the last time to limit its absolute veto power. The only way that this could be done, given the unlikelihood of the Lords assenting to it, was to swamp, or to threaten to swamp, the Upper House with sufficient Liberal peers to overcome the large Conservative majority. This would involve asking the King to use his prerogative to threaten a mass creation of peers (as William IV had reluctantly agreed to do in 1832, if it had been necessary to ensure the passage of the Great Reform Bill).

The argument between the parties thus spilled over into a constitutional one which inevitably embroiled the King. While Liberals and Conservatives had been content to use existing procedures to pursue their struggle, the position of the Monarch remained and gave him a base from which to influence the course of the struggle in time-honoured ways, but protected him from the glare of decision making. However, the moment it appeared that the Liberals did not any longer want to play by the existing rules, even by bending them, but actually to change them, the Monarchy was confronted by the prospect of having to agree to an Act which would alter the whole structure of relationships that together formed the Crown in Parliament and had been the accepted kernel of the British constitution for hundreds of years.

The first warning shot had been fired by Sir Henry Campbell-Bannerman's government in 1907. He introduced a resolution that 'the power of the other House should be so restricted by law as to secure that within the limits of a single Parliament the final decision of the Commons should prevail.'[18] The resolution was intended to warn the Lords that a conflict between the two Houses would raise grave constitutional issues and would ultimately involve the prerogative of the Crown. For better or worse, the warning seemed to go unheeded in the Lords. A new Education Bill was badly mauled, then dropped. The same fate befell a Plural Voting Bill, and a Land Valuation Bill — all three measures which had been clearly heralded by the Liberal victory in the 1906 election.

When the Lloyd George budget was thrown out by the Lords on 30 November 1909, Asquith had little alternative but to seek a dissolution of Parliament. He moved a resolution in the House of Commons to the effect that the action of the House of Lords was 'a breach of the Constitution and an usurpation of the rights of the Commons.'[19] Even before Asquith opened his general election campaign, in which he was thought to have implied that he had received advance guarantees from the King that a sufficient number of peerages would be created to force a Parliament Bill (restricting the Upper House's veto) through the Lords, should the Liberals win the election, Lord Knollys had sent him a letter saying that such an eventuality — involving the creation of five hundred new peers — would practically 'be almost an impossibility, and if asked for would place the King in an awkward position'.[20] In fact, as a moderate Liberal, Knollys felt even more strongly than that. He felt that swamping the House of Lords so obviously in the Liberal interest would perhaps terminally undermine the hallowed impartiality of the Monarchy, as well as conniving at the constitutional destruction of the second House as it had functioned hitherto. Indeed at one moment he felt that the King should abdicate rather than give his consent to such a measure.

On Edward VII's instructions, Knollys followed up this letter by descending on No 10 Downing Street on 15 December and informing the Prime Minister's Private Secretary, Vaughan Nash, and therefore Asquith, that 'the King had come to the conclusion that he would not be

---

[18] John Wilson, *CB. A Life of Sir Henry Campbell-Bannerman* (St Martin's Press, New York, 1973), p 563.

[19] Bruce K Murray, *The People's Budget, 1909-10: Lloyd George and Liberal Politics* (Oxford University Press, London, 1980), pp 232-3).

[20] Lee, *Edward VII*, Vol 2, p 670.

justified in creating new Peers (say 300) until after the second general election ... The King regards the policy of the Government as tantamount to the destruction of the House of Lords and he thinks that before a large creation of peers is embarked upon or threatened, the country should be acquainted with the particular project for accomplishing destruction as well as with the general line of action as to which the country will be consulted at the forthcoming Elections.'[21] In other words, the King was setting out some principles which he felt should be followed before a victorious party at an election could claim a mandate for constitutional change, viz — that such a change must be specified in its election programme, along with all the general material. And in that first election, no such specific proposal for House of Lords additions had been made, though the Liberals had, in all conscience, made their definitive intentions for House of Lords reform fairly clear in the Campbell-Bannerman resolution of 1907.

The result of the general election in January 1910 was that the Liberals lost 104 seats to the Conservatives, and their majority was reduced to two (the Liberals had 275 seats to the Conservatives' 273) — though their overall parliamentary position was secured by the support of 82 Irish Nationalists and 40 members of the Labour Party — giving Asquith a working majority of 124 over the Conservatives. Asquith had to reveal to the House of Commons on 21 February 1910 that he did not have the guarantees from the King which he had alluded to in December 1909. He sought to limit the danger to his own political position by enunciating the new doctrine that: 'To ask, in advance, for a blank authority, for an indefinite exercise of the Royal Prerogative, in regard to a measure which has never been submitted to, or approved by, the House of Commons, is a request which, in my judgement, no constitutional stateman can properly make, and is a concession which the Sovereign cannot be expected to grant.'[22] These words were later to return to haunt him. The Irish Nationalists, upon whom the Liberals depended to keep them in power, were not prepared to shelve the question of the reform of the Lords, which was

---

[21] J A Spender and Cyril Asquith, *Life of Herbert Henry Asquith, Lord Oxford and Asquith* (Hutchinson, London, 1932), Vol 1, p 261.
[22] *Ibid*, p 273.

necessary in order to secure the passage of the Irish Home Rule Bill through Parliament.

By April, Asquith's Cabinet had stiffened his resolve. He decided immediately to proceed with the reform of the House of Lords, passing three resolutions which would have the effect of depriving the Lords of veto power over money bills, while the veto over other bills would be only suspensive; enabling any non-money bill to pass into law after its third passage during successive sessions, regardless of a continuing veto; and reducing the duration of a Parliament from seven to five years. These resolutions were embodied in the Parliament Bill laid before the House of Commons on 14 April 1910.

Mr Asquith warned his supporters in the Commons that if the Lords rejected the Parliament Bill 'we shall feel it our duty immediately to tender advice to the Crown as to the steps which will have to be taken if that policy is to receive statutory effect in this Parliament.' He added that 'if we do not find ourselves in a position to ensure that statutory effect will be given to this policy in this Parliament, we shall then either resign our offices or recommend a dissolution of Parliament. And let me add this: that in no case would we recommend Dissolution except under such conditions as will secure that in the new Parliament the judgement of the people as expressed in the election will be carried into law.'[23] He would not be drawn to explain what he meant by these utterances but the implication was clear. The King would be asked to guarantee before the general election that if the government were returned, he would agree to create the necessary number of peers to ensure passage of the Parliament Bill.

Lloyd George's budget passed the Commons on 27 April by a majority of 93. The next day it was accepted by the House of Lords without a division. If the Lords thought they had acted constitutionally by obstructing the Budget once, and then deferring to the House of Commons after the people had made their wishes plain by returning the Liberals to power, albeit with a much reduced majority, they were mistaken. The passage of the Budget merely meant that the great constitutional debate which was about to begin did so with no secondary issues to cloud it. It was, and was

---

[23] *Ibid*, p 299.

intended to be, a straight exercise in readjusting the balance of power in favour of the Commons, at the expense of the Lords. The Liberals expected the Crown, through its use of the prerogative, to throw its weight decisively in favour of the Commons.

Ten days later King Edward died. Up to that moment, it was clear that, advised by Lord Knollys, he had jibbed not at the actual proposals of the Parliament Bill but at the idea that it should become law through a saturation creation of peers, which was seen by the Palace as a frivolous abuse of the Royal Prerogative, and therefore to be avoided. There was always the alternative of refusing Asquith's advice on peers, accepting his resignation, putting Balfour, the Conservative leader in, and granting him a Dissolution. That course would have threatened to create irredeemable hostility between the Liberals and the Monarchy. The former option might have brought conflict between the Tories and the Monarchy, but with one important difference — the Tories would never become irreconciliable with the Monarchy. Republicanism was a Liberal bolthole, not a Tory one. If one course or the other had to be taken, after an election, therefore, it seemed likely that the King would be advised to accept the lesser risk, and create the peers; since to take the greater risk, and give the Tories a dissolution, would not advance matters if the subsequent election returned a Liberal government pledged to make demands of the Prerogative. Before this question could be chewed over, however, King Edward had died. It was left to the new King to pick up the pieces.

2

Interventionist Monarch

George V was born in 1865. He was thus forty-four when he acceded to the throne. He had spent fifteen years of his life in the Navy which endowed him, not only with a taste for the politics of the Senior Service, but a bluntness and an honesty — almost painful honesty — which became the hallmark of his reign. He was not as cut off from public affairs as some have maintained, since he had carried out representative duties on behalf of both his grandmother (e.g. his official visit to Ireland in 1897) and father (e.g. his extended tour to the Antipodes in 1901). Although he was only allowed access to a limited supply of State Papers in 1901, from 1903 onwards he saw all Foreign Office papers.

In 1894 he had been instructed by Mr J R Tanner of St John's College, Cambridge, in the law and practice of the constitution. Tanner induced him to read and analyse some of Bagehot's *The English Constitution* and there is a notebook in the Royal Archives at Windsor with his (George's) summary of the duties of a constitutional monarch.

In the notebook he wrote: 'The existence of the Crown serves to *disguise* change and therefore to deprive it of the evil consequences of revolution.'[1] He was echoing one of Bagehot's favourite views of the role of the monarch. In fact, according to John Gore (the biographer of the King's private life), George *never* learnt the meaning of the British constitution to the satisfaction of his private secretary, Sir Arthur Bigge (who became Lord Stamfordham

---

[1] Harold Nicolson, *King George V. His Life and Reign* (Constable, London, 1952), p 62.

in 1911). But then Bigge was a hard man to satisfy. Gore actually suggested that it was not until 1901 that George began to do something to repair the gaps in his knowledge of English and Constitutional history in order to attain 'the normal educational standard of the average public schoolboy at leaving age. These gaps had not yet been repaired, that standard not reached, when he came to the Throne . . . He was still methodically plodding on with his education when his reign was half over.'[2] But Gore's over-emphasis on the gaps in George V's education misses the point. The tour the Prince and the Princess of Wales undertook to India in 1905-6 engendered in George a vision of the importance and responsibility of a Democratic Sovereign which provided that bedrock of constitutionality so necessary in the years of strain which lay ahead.

At the start of his reign, therefore, we observe a man of forty-four years, who was better equipped for the hard task ahead than many been supposed. Above all, it was his honesty, integrity and the impregnable devotion not just to a general idea of duty, but to the specific preservation of his office, which helped him to preserve it during a nearly twenty-six year reign which saw the extinction in Europe of five Emperors, eight Kings and eighteen minor dynasties.

Sir Harold Nicolson, in his official biography, describes George, when Prince of Wales, as remaining 'aloof from the internecine quarrel' between Lord Charles Bereford and Sir John (Lord) Fisher over British naval policy. 'He strove to approach the problem, with all the technical controversies which it aroused, in an impartial spirit.'[3] Nicolson also describes George, when King, as having 'a constant desire . . . to act strictly in accordance with the duties and responsibilities of a constitutional monarch'.[4] This meant that he could express his views in the most forthright manner, but all decisions were left entirely in the hands of politicians. That certainly became true for George V in the last half of his reign, but only after a fierce baptism of fire in the constitutional crises of 1910-14, and then after the First World War and the Russian Revolution, which for different reasons, seemed to cause a profound, almost radical transformation in the way the King carried out his duties. Certainly in 1909, when he was Prince of

---

[2]   John Gore, *King George V. A Personal Memoir* (John Murray, London, 1941), p 7.

[3]   Nicolson, *George V*, p 178.

[4]   Nicolson, *George V*, p 107.

Wales, the evidence of his pressure on Fisher, the First Sea Lord, to resign his office hardly fits Nicolson's description of constitutional propriety.[5] The serious dangers which faced him as King may have had some influence on his later capacity to distinguish between forthright expressions of opinion (proper) and the use of his position to influence decisions in accord with his opinions (improper).

This involvement in the squabbles about naval policy may have been caused by his social contact with, or more probably earlier professional friendships for, naval officers who were near the top of their service. It became serious at his Accession, however, because throughout the saga of naval argument which permeated the Admiralty from 1905 until 1916, George took the side of those who believed that the Liberal governments were fundamentally ignorant of, and careless with, the nation's security needs. George, first as Prince of Wales, later as King, associated himself with these sentiments. So when he became King he brought with him an underlying prejudice — that of the simple naval officer — against the Liberal leadership for its inadequacy in matters naval, which must have sat uneasily with his punctilious and perfectly correct approach to Asquith's other policies.

So the auguries were mixed when this dogged, opinionated naval officer ascended the Throne in 1910. It should not be imagined, however, that he was entirely on his own. Had that been the case, he might easily have caused a disaster before he had time to pick wise counsel. As it is, one of his earliest difficulties was caused by divided counsel, owing to the fact that he inherited Lord Knollys, his father's private secretary, but also brought with him his own private secretary, Sir Arthur Bigge (Lord Stamfordham). It was not until this unfortunate diarchy was resolved in favour of Stamfordham, with Knollys' resignation in 1913, that the King's footwork became somewhat more sure. But in 1910 the contrasting characters of Knollys and Bigge, and the King's unfortunate decision to retain two private secretaries, got him off to a bad start.

Sir Arthur Bigge had been Queen Victoria's Private Secretary from 1895 until her death, succeeding the veteran Sir Henry Ponsonby in the

---

[5]   Marder, Vol 1, p 92; A Marder (ed) *Fear God and Dreadnought. The Correspondence of Admiral of the Fleet Lord Fisher of Kilverstone. Vol II Years of Power, 1904-1914* (Jonathan Cape, London,1956), pp 255-6.

office. When Edward VII succeeded to the Throne he transferred Bigge to George, Duke of Cornwall and York, and appointed in his place Sir Francis, later Lord, Knollys (who had served him as private secretary since 1870). This was a technical demotion for Bigge, but a fortuitous one, since it ensured his return to Buckingham Palace when George V succeeded his father in 1910. On the other hand, if Bigge had stayed on to be Edward VII's Private Secretary, he might well have found himself replaced in 1910 by a man who had been grooming George, Prince of Wales, for the Throne. As it was, Bigge, the Olympian figure among royal private secretaries, had been able to educate his royal master for nine years before he was exposed to the rigours of constitutional monarchy. However, for the first three years of George V's reign they had Knollys to contend with, and that was clearly a difficulty.

Knollys obviously felt that Bigge's stewardship between 1895 and 1901 had been inadequate, and that the position of the Monarch had been eroded by a combination of the Queen's failing powers, the politicians' exploitation of that decline, and Bigge's lack of vigilance. Knollys had tried to reassert the Sovereign's position, certainly over ministerial consultation, but his battles to reposition his Master in the dominant and pervasive role that Victoria had occupied were undermined by the passage of time, and by the fact that a new generation of Ministers and more government business inevitably meant that the Sovereign was involved in less routine matters and only the important issues.[6]

There was another side to Knollys which was most unsympathetic to Bigge and the new King. Knollys was a prominent, active, and apparently unabashed supporter of the Liberals. Edward VII, though less obviously Liberal in his sympathies, had involved himself most particularly in Army and Navy affairs (as we have seen) and was quite strenuously in support of the reformers, in which area he obviously used Knollys as an active intermediary. The future King George V, and *his* Private Secretary, Sir Arthur Bigge, were not naturally close to the Liberals, and even less so when the question of military and naval reform was used as the measurement. For both reasons, therefore, Bigge and George V would have had reason to regard Knollys with reserve. Their instincts were to be

---

[6] Magnus, *King Edward* pp 351-2.

sadly confirmed during the resolution of the House of Lords crisis.

Following the Accession of King George V, the politicians agreed to suspend their constitutional struggle over the House of Lords and to attempt, by means of a constitutional conference, to find an agreed settlement between the parties. By November 1910, it was clear that agreement could not be reached. Asquith, with the approval of the Cabinet, asked the King not just for another dissolution, but 'contingent guarantees' that in the event of the Liberal government being returned and the continued refusal of the Conservative-controlled House of Lords to surrender the absolute veto, he should use his prerogative to ensure that sufficient peers were created to pass the Parliament Bill limiting the powers of the Upper House.

Although the King took the view that he was obliged to act on the advice of his ministers, he was against giving a hypothetical promise. He believed that this would compromise his political neutrality by supporting the election programme of the Liberal Party. He preferred to wait until a situation requiring the exercise of his prerogative actually arose and then to decide how to act, being guided, as usual, by the advice of his ministers. No part of the prerogative, particularly so sensitive a use of it as was proposed by the Liberal government, should have formed part of a hypothetical understanding between the Sovereign and one of the country's political parties. This threatened to compromise his all-important constitutional position of political neutrality. But the Liberal government refused to accept the King's arguments. It had not only been committed by Asquith in April to securing these guarantees, but it did not trust the King to use his prerogative in their interest because of his incautious remarks while Prince of Wales about Asquith being 'not quite a gentleman' and questioning how anyone could serve under 'that damn fellow Lloyd George'.[7]

The two royal private secretaries, Knollys and Bigge, then engaged in a struggle for the new King's soul. It will be remembered that Knollys had told George V's father, Edward VII, that it would be better to abdicate than to accept a request for guarantees on the creation of peers. In a reversal of this position, Knollys now invoked the memory of Edward VII,

---

[7]　Vernon Bogdanor, *The Monarchy and the Constitution* (Clarendon Press, Oxford, 1995), p 67.

whom George V revered so much, to suggest that the late King would surely have given the guarantees and that no alternative government was available. This was not strictly true, since Balfour had indicated to Knollys and Esher at the Lambeth Palace conference a few days before the old King died, that he would be prepared to accept office if the Liberals resigned. Bigge thought Knollys' remark unfair, if not improper, and countered with the suggestion that he would have given the opposite advice to Queen Victoria, and she would have accepted it. Bigge argued forcefully that it was both improper, and for that matter unnecessary, to extract hypothetical guarantees from the King, who could have been relied upon to act on the Advice of his ministers to create peers if and when such advice had to be tendered.

Faced with Knollys' determination and under heavy pressure from Asquith and Crewe (the Liberal leader in the House of Lords), the King reluctantly agreed on 16 November 1910 to give the contingent guarantees. But he insisted that they be kept secret and that the Lords should be given a chance to debate the Parliament Bill before Parliament was dissolved for a second time and a general election held. In retrospect it seems that Knollys and Esher were guilty of, at best, a gross piece of incompetence, at worst a most unseemly triumph of political interest over loyalty and duty to their King.

The outcome of the second general election held in December 1910 was very similar to that of the previous January: the Liberals losing three seats to the Conservatives' one. The House of Lords crisis ran on until August 1911. In the end, the activities of the Parliament Bill's diehard opponents, led by Lord Halsbury and Lord Willoughby de Broke, made it necessary for Asquith to reveal his ultimate weapon — the King's canned agreement to saturation peerages should the Lords throw out the Bill. Balfour and Lansdowne, who led the opposition in the Lords, were told by Knollys on 19 July, and this was confirmed by Asquith in writing the next day.

Bigge went to see the King to complain that the assumptions that they had been asked to make on Balfour's likely refusal to accept office the previous November had been wrong. It appeared now that Balfour *would* have accepted office. Knollys wrote to Esher to refresh his memory, recalling that the two of them had dined with Balfour and his private secretary, J S Sandars, at the time. The two Conservatives, Knollys recalled, said that if Balfour had been sent for 'he would have pointed out the almost insurmountable difficulties which he would have to encounter owing to the certainty, practically, that at the Dissolution he would be unable to obtain a majority.'[8]

Esher received another missive from Knollys on the same day, which revealed something of the strains then permeating the Household. He said:

> The Tories are as usual stupid and perfectly out of hand at least some of them headed by Salisbury, Selborne and Lord Halsbury and have revolted against Balfour and Lansdowne, behaving very badly to them both. I cannot myself see how a creation of a certain number of Peers can be avoided, but possibly it may not exceed 40 or 50. I am of course speaking quite confidentially but the King has exhibited a mania for seeing people on the situation and in this he is backed up by Bigge. Putting aside the ministers he has seen six people and wanted today to see a 7th Ld Halsbury who would not however come. I only hear of it after the matter has been settled and I am therefore powerless. He is remaining in London on account of the crisis, but I think it would be a very good thing if he were to leave as it is impossible to say who he will next send for.[9]

Knollys complained a few days later to Esher about Bigge coming to him to say that 'the King is in a pretty mess' with much more of the I-told-you-so variety. Knollys found it 'difficult to remain silent' and surprised Bigge by saying that 'if I had to give the same advice over again. I should certainly do so'.[10]

Knollys might have been writing of the Conservatives in that dismissive way, but Bigge (who had been made Lord Stamfordham in the Coronation Honours List) was taking them more seriously. Lord Salisbury was one of the six visitors of whom Knollys had complained. In Stamfordham's view the discussion might have left things unclear. He wrote to Salisbury:

> In this blood-heat political temperature it is most important that there should be as few misunderstandings as possible and, so far as the King is concerned, we must endeavour to guards[sic] against any more. But I understand that when you saw the King the question you submitted to His Majesty was — 'Is it the case that Your Majesty has undertaken to

---

[8] Churchill College, Cambridge: Esher Papers, 10/52, Knollys to Esher, 25 July 1911.

[9] CCC, Esher Papers, 10/52, Knollys to Esher, confidential, 25 July 1911.

[10] Esher Papers, 10/52, Knollys to Esher, 28 July 1911.

create an unlimited number of Peers and so swamp the House of Lords with a permanent Liberal majority.' The King replied 'Certainly not — I have only promised to make sufficient to pass the Parliament Bill not one more nor less.' If the opposition appeared with all its force, Stamfordham warned, this would force the King to create a minimum number 'which would be not unworthy of the name *unlimited*. We must remember that the Bill will have to pass.[11]

Salisbury replied with thanks, referring to the King's wish imparted to him, to pass on 'his acute desire that the Unionist Party should not consider him as unfriendly'.[12]

Certainly, when the King heard that he had been, not deceived, but simply not made aware of one vital and relevant fact, he was very angry. So was Bigge. So was Balfour, who never trusted Knollys again. It was effectively the end of Knollys, though he lingered on until 1913. The great Stamfordham era had begun. George V recovered his balance, and went on to consolidate his office. But the Knollys-Bigge affair demonstrated vividly how the Private Secretary can, by giving his advice or withholding it, make or mar a monarch.

Fortunately, the King seemed to escape the tremendous public row over the Parliament Bill which occurred in the summer of 1911. The Commons erupted on 24 July and had to be adjourned. Conservative censure motions were defeated in the Commons but passed in the Lords on 7 August. After the direst and most explicit warning from Lord Morley (reading a statement agreed with the Palace) about the 'creation of Peers sufficient in number' to meet any combination of opposition, the Bill was only passed by a majority of seventeen. It was a great relief, the King noted in his diary, to be 'spared any further humiliation by a creation of peers'.[13]

In a final letter on the subject to Esher, written on the Royal Train as he journeyed north for the shooting season, the King admitted:

It is indeed a great relief to me that the Bill has passed without the odious necessity of the creation of Peers. I don't think I should ever have got over the great humiliation to myself. The more I think of it the more I am

---

[11] Hatfield House: Salisbury Papers, 4M/70/77. Stamfordham to Salisbury, 28 July 1911.

[12] Salisbury Papers, 4M/70/81, Salisbury to Stamfordham, 29 July 1911.

[13] Nicolson, *George V*, p 159.

convinced that I was very unfairly treated and put in a false position without being able to defend myself. I am sure you can realise all I have gone through these last months, the worry and anxiety was a great strain on me.[14]

The constitutional crisis over the Parliament Bill exposed George V, at the very start of his reign, to the gravest political dangers. The saga revealed the fact that, whether politicians liked it or not, the Sovereign remained a kind of referee of the constitution, so that when its other constituent parts ceased to work properly together, only the Monarch held the key to unblocking the impasse and creating a new settlement. It put the Monarchy in a very important position, but a very dangerous one. By their nature constitutional changes tend to be disputatious, even divisive, because they occur not through the emergence of a reasonable consensus, but because existing structures no longer reflect the balance of forces within the constitution. The House of Lords crisis in 1910 was a case in point. The equality of the Lords with the Commons, standing unchallenged for centuries, had gradually been undermined from 1832 onwards, as the Commons first of all reformed itself and then started broadening the electoral system, expanding public education to the point where it could — even without the women's vote — legitimately claim an infinitely stronger representative personality, and therefore democratic base, than could the House of Lords. But only the King, in a crisis of conflict between the two Houses, could facilitate the act which categorically reflected the surrender of power by the Lords. Had all the Lords ganged up against all the Commons, it might not have been so difficult for the King to side with the Commons. What made him so uncomfortable was the fact that, in acting on the advice of his Ministers, he was appearing to alienate almost half his subjects, led by the official opposition, who claimed that he was, by acceding to Ministerial advice, not at all upholding the constitution in accordance with his vows, but actually subverting it. No charge could have more disturbed such a worried and dutiful man as King George V, but in the end he perceived where his duty, however painful, lay.

The crisis also had its unfortunate side effects. Coming so soon in George V's reign it gave him if not a false, at least a very dangerous sense of his own political importance. He had been important in the crisis —

---

[14] CCC, Esher Papers, 6/5 The King to Esher, 13 August 1911.

crucially so, especially in a matter of the prerogative which remained hallowed ground, not to be trespassed on, or taken for granted by politicians. By the time he died, all sorts of emollient and moderating influences had worked on George V to bring home to him the limitations of his office, along with the fact that his greatest contribution was likely to be in the forceful expression of opinion, and the constancy of his presence within the Prime Minister's counsels.

In 1911 his only experience had been as an active, controversial, interventionist monarch, a role forced upon him, perhaps, by the exigencies of the political situation, but nevertheless a reality. He survived the crisis, bruised, but seemingly of the view that he could have survived it better if he had trusted to his own instincts. Moreover, although Asquith had made every allowance for the new King, and had developed a warm relationship with him, there was more than a sense in which George V regarded Asquith, and possibly Sir Edward Grey, the Foreign Secretary, as exceptional Liberals. He viewed the other members of the Cabinet with great suspicion, particularly Churchill and Lloyd George, who were destined for the rest of his reign to feature more prominently than Asquith.

So his early blooding at the hands of the House of Lords may have induced him to feel that the state of the country — its instability, the Home Rule crisis, the suffragette movement, and so on — justified a more dirigiste approach from the Throne. Perhaps nothing so explicit went through his mind, and it was, instead, just a reflection of his natural instincts, combined with the thrust of the Monarchy, and the reflexes of his courtiers, which pitched him further into the battle than was wise. It was not as though he had sought this prominence, not as though he had initiated anything even as respectable as his father's constant pressure for military reform. It was the politicians who had come to him, to invoke him, to compensate for their inability to play the game any longer according to the old rules. They needed his sanction for new rules, or else a categorical refusal to change them. They needed to know where he stood. Reluctantly, he showed where he stood. Very well then, he would be less reluctant next time. If he was going to be at the mercy of politicians, in the humiliating way he felt he had been, then he must see that he was on top of the game.

Shortly after George V ascended the Throne he received a memorandum from Lord Rosebery, the former Prime Minister. 'The King has to start without the advantages of his father and with a clean slate', he wrote, 'but with this great advantage, that he had served in the Navy, and that he had known the Empire and has expressed his interest in the empire by memorable words and deeds.' Lord Rosebery advised him to make his mark within the next two years.[15] Amid all the jangle of constitutional argument, George V was already convinced that his special contribution would be to do for the Empire what Edward VII had done for Britain in Europe. He told Lord Esher at the time that he intended to visit India again, the next year, to crown himself at the Durbar, and to visit every Dominion. 'These are bold projects,' noted Esher. 'There will be difficulties with Ministers. Still he may find a way.'[16] In the end, war, illness, age, all baulked him. But he managed to go to India, and it provided the bedrock involvement in imperial affairs which fueled him for the next twenty-five years. No Viceroy, no Governor-General, could sit down at his desk and conduct his quasi-regal business without the faint feeling that the beady naval eye above the bristly beard was peering didactically down on him.

Lord Esher was right. There were difficulties with Ministers over the proposed visit to India; but the King surmounted them. He put his proposal to Asquith, the Prime Minister, and then to Lord Morley, the Secretary of State for India. They were both rather taken aback, and Morley retreated cautiously into that time worn bureacratic foxhole — the question of cost. However, the Cabinet rather hesitantly agreed to the King's idea in November 1910, and the Palace were able then to get on with the planning directly with the Viceroy.

The King had been overwhelmed by the experience of his previous visit to India in 1905, and had remained intimately and emotionally involved in the affairs of the sub-continent ever since. It was to be a life-long interest. The Morley-Minto reforms of 1909 had started to advance slowly the idea of representative institutions in India, under the watchful, unconvinced gaze first of Edward VII, then of his son. They both felt that the character of India revealed a pattern of allegiance to princes and chieftains which was unwisely overlooked both by the nationalist movement and by those British statesmen who gradually yielded to it. In a sense, the King's influence was therefore often exercised expressly to redress this

---

[15] Nicolson, *George V*, p 140.

[16] Oliver, Viscount Esher (ed), *Journals and Letters of Reginald, Viscount Esher* (Ivor Nicholson and Watson, London, 1938), p 17.

imbalance. India, under the Viceroy, was clearly a most appropriate setting in which to exploit prerogative power, since it was a vast tangle of many interlocking prerogatives already. The Raj was essentially underwritten by the coercive authority of British power, acquiesced in by many — willingly or unwillingly — welcomed by others — the Princes — as a means of underwriting their own lesser powers and prerogatives. The King felt then, not without justification, that the Viceroy sat at the apex of a pyramid of powers and Royalties which needed some symbolic figurehead to which they could all defer. That pinnacle was the Viceroy, yet he was after all only an emanation of the King. So although British policy was worked out by the Viceroy's Council, acting on major issues in concert with the Secretary of State for India, the India Council and the Cabinet in London, there was also endless scope for the King's influence to be brought to bear.

This triangular relationship of the King, Viceroy and Secretary of State put most of the burdens on the Viceroy to see that it did not break down. He had his difficulties since on basic issues of policy the Cabinet's wish must obviously prevail, though the man on the spot, and such an eminent spot as that, would obviously expect most of his views to be taken, not just into account, but as the dominant element in any appreciation. This was, of course, the opening for the King Emperor, since he was at liberty to correspond directly with the Viceroy, not just about honours, appointments, military matters — all quintessentially obsessive subjects for every occupant of the Throne — but across the whole range of policy as well. This direct line of contact between the King Emperor and the Viceroy was disliked in Whitehall, for obvious reasons. The Secretary of State felt he was His Majesty's principal adviser for Indian affairs and that the Viceroy was a servant of the government. As early as August 1910, Sir Arthur Bigge noted to Lord Minto that Morley, the Secretary of State for India, much disliked his writing directly to the King.

'I did not know the Secretary of State objected to my writing to HM but I strongly suspected it,' Minto replied. 'But really it is out of the question that I should not do so.'[17] They had already had one passage of arms in which the King became a lightning conductor over Morley's appointment

---

[17] National Library of Scotland (NLA) Minto Papers (MS 12787), Minto to Bigge, September 1910.

of a member of the Viceroy's Council without first consulting the Viceroy — let alone the King. Minto, to Bigge, maintained that 'the authority of the King Emperor is so direct towards India itself, that the King would be fully and constitutionally justified, when such appointments are submitted to him, in asking for the Viceroy's opinion and in being largely influenced by it in his decision.' The Viceroy complained bitterly about Morley's interference in everything. 'Morley is so sensitive as to his own position that he would certainly, if he knew it, take exception to any wide expression of opinion to the King.'[18]

Nevertheless Morley was a man to be reckoned with. The choice of successor to Minto was then being considered. Everybody — the King, Asquith, Haldane, Balfour — all wanted to send Kitchener. Only Morley objected. Bigge told Minto that they even tried to argue as their trump card that Kitchener was the 'dying wish of King Edward', but even that failed to sway the redoubtable Secretary of State.[19] His nominee was Hardinge; and Hardinge became Viceroy. This might explain a waspish note which Knollys sent Hardinge later in the year when the Mintos, on their return, lunched with the King and the Queen. 'She [Lady Minto] was much down I hear on Morley, but he defended him. I have never cared much about her, as I always thought she was rather a little cat.'[20]

Morley had met the Kitchener lobby head-on. In a Cabinet memo he said: 'It is argued that the new Viceroy should know India and its government. This reverses the standing principle that it is of supreme advantage to place at the head of the government of India a fresh mind, trained in public business and national affairs, but without special Indian experience. More than ever is a fresh mind, unwedded to administrative practice maxims, and points of view, desirable today when the Government of India is confronted by a fresh system [the Morley-Minto reforms] and something of a fresh India.'[21]

Immediately Hardinge arrived in India plans for the great Royal visit proceeded. The King was full of suggestions; some good, some others

---

[18] Royal Archives, Windsor (RA), PS/GV/A6a/20, Minto to Bigge, 5 July 1910.

[19] NLA, Minto Papers (MS 12727), Bigge to Minto, 17 July 1910.

[20] Cambridge University Library (CUL), Hardinge Papers, 104/3, Knollys to Hardinge, 15 December 1910.

[21] RA, PS/GV/N473/1, Morley memo, 5 June 1910.

better left aside. In December 1910 he mooted merging the two states of Bengal into a Presidency, like Bombay and Madras, to mark his visit — thus repairing Curzon's partition of Bengal which aroused great bitterness. The King thought 'this would flatter the Bengalis very much, allay discontent and stop sedition, and would be well worth the extra cost to the country; think this over, I have not mentioned it to a soul yet.'[22]

By a different post, the same month, Bigge had to trouble the Viceroy with a more trivial thought — the King's wish to shoot. Everybody had suggested that His Majesty should repair to Nepal so as not to descend to the level of other mortals. But the King wanted to shoot duck at Bhurtpore. 'Everyone who knows the country,' pleaded Bigge, 'feels that, were the whole of Native India almost trembling with emotion at the prospect of the actual appearance of their great "divinity", to hear that His Majesty had been seen in wading boots up to his waist in a *Jeel*, shooting duck, there would have been a great danger of their idol being, if not shattered, at all events, seriously shaken!! No one has yet told His Majesty their views on this point, though I myself have questioned the advisability of it to him . . . Minto, Crewe, Lawrence and Wigram feel strongly that the duck should be left alone.'[23] It took three months but by the end of March 1911, the duck shoot idea had been abandoned.

Then there was the matter of the Crown. The King's intention to crown himself raised objections from the Archbishop of Canterbury who felt that such a second coronation would require a religious service of consecration and this would be inappropriate before a vast concourse of mainly Hindus and Muslims. Moreover it was against the law to move the crown from England. A new crown had to be acquired. The King ordered one from Garrard (£4,000 to hire, £60,000 to buy) before even telling the Secretary of State. Bigge had to communicate hurriedly with the Viceroy, expressing the hope that the money could be raised — by subscription. They were now in difficulties, since only two weeks earlier the Viceroy had actively discouraged such a suggestion, and Morley — who was standing in for his successor, Crewe, away ill — had agreed with him on grounds of cost.

Back came Bigge, in a cable to the Viceroy: 'King is surprised . . . It

---

[22] CUL, Hardinge Papers, 104/No 3A, The King to Hardinge, 16 December 1910.

[23] *Ibid*, 79, Bigge to Hardinge, 22 December 1910.

was the first he knew of the negotiations. Morley has never mentioned to His Majesty. There are two indisputable facts, viz — crown must be available and none of the other regalia can be brought from England.' Therefore 'a crown is being made, and for present King proposes take no action on your telegram.' Another sting, and an unfair one, came in the tail: 'It is unfortunate that the idea, with so much to commend it from an India political point of view, was referred to official authority.'[24]

'It really is disastrous that Morley does not tell the King what is going on because this is a matter of all others which concerns His Majesty,' Bigge emphasised in a letter.[25] He followed that up a few days later with a Private and Secret cable: 'No communications have taken place between the King and Morley about the crown. Please therefore only correspond with me on the subject.'[26] Even the King was moved to complain: 'It is not so easy to work with Lord Morley as it was with Crewe . . . It is much better to let it stand over till Crewe [who was ill] returns to the India Office, which I hope he will by the end of May.'[27] The crown was duly made, and paid for.

The high point of George V's visit to India was the Delhi Durbar, and the King-Emperor's announcement of the dramatic decision to transfer the seat of government of the Indian Empire from Calcutta to the ancient capital of Delhi (a decision that was strongly opposed at home by the Conservatives). The idea had come from Hardinge, but the King came to feel, quite wrongly, that the announcement was in some special way a personal one of his, and so he regarded the Conservative criticisms of the plan — indeed any criticism or alteration (as proposed by Curzon in 1916) as almost amounting to *lèse-majesté*, and certainly as damaging to his dignity.

In Hardinge, the King had a close friend and collaborator as Viceroy. Hardinge had been one of his father's circle of advisers, when he was at the Foreign Office, and King George was even moved to write to him as 'My Dear Charlie' twice in Delhi, once when he escaped an assassination attempt, and once when his wife died.[28] In 1913 he encouraged Hardinge's suggestion that a separate political department should be created to save

---

[24] *Ibid*, 104/No 48, Bigge to Hardinge, tel, 30 March 1911.

[25] *Ibid*, 104/No 49, Bigge to Hardinge, 31 March 1911.

[26] *Ibid*, 104/51, Bigge to Hardinge, tel, 4 April 1911.

[27] *Ibid*, 104/51A, The King to Hardinge, 7 April 1911.

[28] *Ibid*, 105/34, The King to Hardinge, 26 December 1912.

the princely rulers from coming under the Foreign Department. 'I advocated it strongly to Morley when I returned from India seven years ago, but of course nothing was done. I will certainly speak to Crewe about it, and I trust he will accept your proposals.'[29] The King managed to prevail with his nominee for the post of Commander-in-Chief India, against the opposition of all the politicians and the War Office who were bent on sending Sir Ian Hamilton. 'It was everything getting Duff [Sir Beauchamp Duff] appointed Commander-in-Chief, and between ourselves, the King had a good deal to do in the matter . . . ,' Stamfordham told Willingdon, then Governor of Bombay.[30] The King, in his own words to Hardinge took the incident much further. 'I have had a hard fight to get him appointed. When the Prime Minister came to Balmoral, I found Seely had been at him, backed up by Haldane and the whole of the War Office and he had agreed to Ian Hamilton becoming the new Commander-in-Chief.' Asquith eventually consented to Duff, saying he was sorry for Ian Hamilton, the War Office candidate, who presumably thought the job was in the bag. Hamilton would, had he gone to India, have avoided the horrors of Gallipoli. 'The result has been most satisfactory, but I believe the War Office are rather sore,' was the King's last word on the matter.[31]

The King's involvement with India almost certainly sprang emotionally from the fact that much of the Indian Empire consisted of princely states whose rulers owed a particularly personal kind of allegiance to the Imperial crown. They were royal families in their own right. The King no doubt felt especially intent on responding to this esoteric kind of homage by looking after their interests as much as he could in the policy of democratisation which the British were unfolding in those areas which they controlled directly rather than as the protecting power. The latter was the basis of their treaty relationship with most of the Princes. Throughout the period of the Raj, it was the special relationship with the Princes which was to excite extra interest in India in the Royal mind.

One of the King's first interventions after 1910 — indeed at Asquith's

---

[29] *Ibid*, 105/51, The King to Hardinge, 31 July 1913.

[30] RA, GV/P543/4, Stamfordham to Willingdon, 10 November 1913.

[31] CUL, Hardinge Papers, 105/56, The King to Hardinge, 24 October 1913.

very first audience — using his office legitimately as a source of advice, encouragement and warning, was to suggest that Asquith hold a conference with the Opposition to discuss their differences both over reform of the House of Lords and Home Rule for Ireland. The conference, as we have seen, failed. As a result of the general election of December 1910, culminating by August 1911 in the abolition of a House of Lords veto, it became inevitable that Asquith would force through a Bill to provide some measure of Home Rule for Ireland. It was not just that this was a policy dear to the Liberals. Asquith's working majority in the Commons depended on the support of John Redmond and his eighty-two Irish Nationalists. The leader of the Irish Unionist Party, Sir Edward Carson, had already warned that he and his Ulster followers would refuse to submit to such a measure and would establish a separate government in Belfast. On 11 April 1912 the Bill was introduced, and went into its committee stage on 11 June. Later that summer the leader of the Conservative Party, Bonar Law, announced that he would give unqualified support to the Ulstermen in their resistance. By November the Ulster Covenanters, pledging their loyalty to the King, had attracted half a million signatories. As Nicolson observes in his biography of George V: 'Even in 1912 it was clear to many observers that the Home Rule controversy might threaten the realm with the abhorrent prospect of civil war: and that even at that early date there were some who sought to persuade the King that, should such a danger materialise, it was his right, and indeed his duty, to exercise his Prerogative and, when the Bill had finally been forced through both Houses of Parliament, to refuse the Royal Assent.'[32]

Clearly, in the minds of the King and his advisers, the main consequence of letting through the Parliament Bill with the threat of mass peerages had been not to save them from civil war, but to expose them to yet another risk of it, since the abolition of one recognised element in the system of parliamentary checks and balances only increased the likelihood that the King and his Prerogative would be drawn into disputes more quickly.

Esher gave expression to this thinking in his private journal in January 1912, ruminating on a speech by Bonar Law which had caused the King concern. Bonar Law had suggested that the King had the burden of

---

[32] Nicolson, *George V*, p 199.

deciding whether or not to give Royal Assent to the Home Rule Bill, regardless of the advice of his Minister. Esher thought that such a departure in constitutional doctrine was the direct result of the Parliament Act. Esher did not go as far as Bonar Law, though he invented an additional power to those of advice, encouragement, and admonition hallowed by Bagehot: the power of 'remonstrance'.[33] The King, if faced with an almost unpalatable piece of Ministerial advice was free to frame his objections in writing to the Cabinet, and insist upon a written reply. This he later did.

However, Bonar Law took the matter much further when he saw the King at a dinner party in Buckingham Palace on 3 May. Replying to the King's hope that the House of Commons would not witness any more scenes of violence he said:

> 'Our desire has been to keep the Crown out of our struggles, but the Government have brought it in. Your only chance is that they resign within two years. If they don't, you must either accept the Home Rule Bill or dismiss your ministers and choose others who will support you in vetoing it: and in either case, half your subjects will think you have acted against them.' The King turned red; and Law asked: 'Have you ever considered that, Sir?' 'No' said the King, 'it is the first time it has been suggested to me.' Law added: 'They may say that your Assent is a purely formal act and that the prerogative of veto is dead. That was true, as long as there was a buffer between you and the House of Commons, but they have destroyed this buffer and it is true no longer.'[34]

Bonar Law told Austen Chamberlain, who recounted this exchange in his *Politics from the Inside*, that he had thought he had given the King the best five minutes he had had for a long time. Eventually after more discussions with the King the following September, he wrote a memorandum for the King in which he suggested that George V, before giving Royal Assent, should ascertain the possibility of appointing another minister to advise him differently and allow the question to be put to an election; and failing that, or in any case, should put his difficulties so clearly to the Prime Minister that Asquith would feel it his duty to extricate the King from so terrible a dilemma.

---

[33] *Ibid*, p 200.
[34] As quoted in Nicolson, *George V*, pp 200-1.

During the autumn 1912 parliamentary session there were more scenes in the House of Commons, including a defeat for the government and other violent incidents. Asquith omitted to inform the King officially about these difficulties, and received a written rebuke from the King. He apologised, and went the next week with his wife to stay at Windsor.

Throughout 1913 the Home Rule Bill provided the ground on which political skirmishing took place with ever increasing intensity. The House of Lords threw out the Bill in January. It was resubmitted in March. The Conservatives tried to argue that it should be held over until the substantive reform of the House of Lords (promised by Asquith) had been achieved, since the Constitution, with only an interim second chamber, was in abeyance. Ulstermen mustered and trained. By the end of the summer the King could stand it no longer, and summoned Birrell, the Irish Secretary, to an audience in which he accused the government of drift, which was making his own position more and more difficult. Birrell admitted as much himself but said the Opposition had to make a move, rather than wait for the King, or some divine intervention, to save them. Throughout the summer the Palace was being inundated with letters and visits from anguished Ulstermen. Try as he might to preserve the King's susceptibilities from these appeals, Stamfordham had to concede that they affected him deeply.

'Things in Ulster are developing, and if the Home Rule Bill is passed there is bound to be fighting and the King's position will be a most painful one,' Stamfordham wrote to Hardinge in Delhi.[35] The King himself, in the same post wrote: 'I am absolutely convinced that there will be great bloodshed in Ulster if the Irish Home Rule Bill becomes law. I think that the Government at last are beginning to realise this but Mr Redmond is still holding a thick stick over them. I feel that I shall be placed in a most difficult and embarrassing position next spring unless the two parties are able to come to some arrangment by consent and can compromise.'[36]

Unsatisfied with Birrell's account of himself, the King summoned Asquith on 11 August 1913 and handed him a long memorandum setting out the situation with all its difficulties, and possible alternative sources of

---

[35] CUL, Hardinge Papers, 105/52, Stamfordham to Hardinge, 28 August 1913.

[36] *Ibid*, 105/53, The King to Hardinge, 28 August 1913.

action. Asquith replied with two documents, one dealing with the constitutional issues, the other with the purely Irish aspects. In his constitutional paper Asquith suggested that, though the King retained the right to dismiss his Ministers, even when they held a majority in the Commons, to do so now would be a constitutional catastrophe. In his Irish paper, he accepted the principle of a conference between the leaders of several parties, but feared that it would be hard for such a conference to succeed.

These two papers provoked a massive reply from the King, in which he took up several of Asquith's points and either made cogent observations on them, or else asked critical, indeed uncomfortable questions of the Prime Minister. He reminded Asquith that he could dissolve Parliament, even if the Prime Minister thought it would be 'inexpedient and dangerous' to dismiss his Ministers.[37] He went through Asquith's Home Rule policy piece by piece and concluded by saying he was glad that Asquith was ready to join in a multilateral conference. Asquith replied briefly the following month, and from then on it became clear that the avoidance of civil war would hinge on the capacity of all the disputing parties to agree on some minimum conditions for the exclusion of Ulster from the operation of the Home Rule Bill. That process, painful, unpredictable, and ultimately abortive, took the best part of the following year; and the King took the leading part in it.

As the months dragged on, and the apparent danger of civil war loomed larger, everybody seemed to act according to character. Balfour, as it were from exile, counselled compromise. Esher changed his mind, from originally thinking the King must act only on advice, to adopting the view that he must dismiss Asquith and find a caretaker Prime Minister to conduct a general election. Stamfordham redoubled his efforts to consult political leaders and warn everybody of the impossible position the King might soon face. Asquith remained bland and inscrutable, though always considerate to the King when a point arose. The King worried and warned. 'But I am not discouraged,' he wrote to Stamfordham in January 1914, 'and with your kind help, common sense, good judgement and advice I think I shall come out on top.' Of the Prime Minister he said: 'I shall keep on bothering him as much as possible.'[38]

---

[37] Nicolson, *George V*, pp 225-9
[38] *Ibid*, p 233.

In February he was warning Asquith that, if negotiations failed, many army officers would resign their commissions rather than fight the combatants in a civil war. He came close to suggesting another election, and left open the possibility that since 'he could not allow bloodshed among his loyal subjects . . .   without exerting every means in his power to avert it,' he might at some stage have to intervene.[39] Asquith was somewhat taken aback by this harder line and said he hoped that the King was not contemplating a refusal of Assent, something which had not been done since the reign of Queen Anne.

In March Asquith offered Ulster temporary exclusion from the Bill for six years, but the Opposition demanded it to be absolute. On the day, 19 March, that the Prime Minister saw the King for another anxious, but inconclusive Audience, the Curragh Incident blew up in their faces — vividly illustrating the King's warnings that the strain on the Army was of a much more serious nature than the Government had assessed.

The Government, anticipating the need to take measures against any uprising by the Ulster volunteers, had asked Sir Arthur Paget, the GOC in Ireland, to secure all military and naval depots and magazines in Northern Ireland. Sir Arthur, for reasons best known (or probably not known) to himself, bustled back to Dublin and announced to all his generals and brigadiers that they must present their officers with a two-hour ultimatum, to agree to take part in 'active operations' in Ulster or else resign their commissions, be dismissed the service and forfeit their pensions. General Hubert Gough returned to the Curragh Camp and told his officers in the Third Cavalry Brigade that he had personally decided to resign. Fifty-seven of his officers resolved to do the same. Paget hurried to the Curragh to implore the officers to reconsider their decision. He was asked by one whether or not the order was from the King — suggesting that the Army at least, in the heat of the moment, seemed to have forgotten their constitution, if they thought that the King still gave orders. Paget replied: 'Do you think for a moment that I would accept it unless I knew it had the sanction of the King? Of course it is his order.' Paget was so emphatic that his message was repeated again and again down the line of command. 'It was the King's order.' Gough's more colourful account of Paget's remark

---

[39] *Ibid*, pp 233-4.

was: 'Don't think officers that I take orders from those swines of politicians! No I only take orders — from the Sovereign.'[40]

As it happened, the unfortunate King, in whose name the 'mutiny' was being stifled, first heard about it from his newspaper on 21 March. He went swiftly into action, summoning Colonel Seely (the Secretary of State for War) Sir John French (the Chief of the Imperial General Staff), and Lord Roberts, and writing indignantly to the Prime Minister. He complained to Seely that he had not been told of the instructions to Paget, though he may have been told of the general plan in a Cabinet letter of 17 March — not that there was any constitutional need for him to be told, other than that everything connected with the Army and Ulster at that time was particularly sensitive. He warned French of the gravity of the situation, and the need for tact, otherwise there would be no Army left. A more cogent complaint of the King's was that he had not been told by Asquith on 19 March that the despatch of two battalions of troops from England and naval movements around Ulster had been set in hand that same day.

The King also busied himself with the military consequences. Seely, whose resignation had not been accepted by Asquith, was proposing to replace Gough with Chetwode. French told the King he would resign if Gough was not reinstated. He summoned Paget and asked him for an explanation. All the GOC could say was that all orders to the Army were the King's orders.

Charge and countercharge still seemed to fill the air, and the newspapers. The King left for a delayed tour of the North, while Stamfordham, in a letter read to the full Cabinet, formally remonstrated with the Prime Minister over the King's being unjustly accused of having taken the side of the officers. General Fergusson wanted to resign but was dissuaded from doing so by Stamfordham, in the King's name. Paget also wanted to resign but with regard to him the King declined to comment.

Gough was reinstated, but refused to go back until he had written assurances — initiated by Seely and French — that the Government had no intention of using the forces of the Crown to crush political opposition to the Home Rule Bill. He then returned in triumph, though the Cabinet

---

[40] Sir James Fergusson of Kilkerran, *The Curragh Incident* (Faber, London, 1964), p 115.

later repudiated these assurances, which in turn led to the resignation of Seely and French. The King had dissuaded Asquith from any further reaction — such as raising the matter with Gough — on the grounds that it would reopen the whole question.

Two major conclusions can be drawn from the Curragh Incident. The first is that it demonstrated both the untrammelled authority of the King over the armed forces, in contrast to the contempt in which politicians were held by the generals. As Fergusson later admitted in his address to rally his division, he 'had used the King's name freely; it was the most effective argument with those who were most stubborn. Loyalty to the King was in fact the determining factor in inducing many officers to withhold their resignations.'[41] It also showed how much the King accepted, indeed took for granted, his quasi-executive role as head of the armed forces. They belonged to him in a special way. They inhabited a pyramid of authority of which he was the apex. The world of rank and seniority was one he understood and had thrived in from his boyhood. It contained fewer of the uncertainties and subtleties of the world of politics.

The second point about the Curragh Incident is that it showed up the Army in a troubled, fractious mood, only five months before it was to be engaged in a major war on the European continent. Fergusson's nephew, who wrote an account of the Curragh Incident, maintains that its most serious result was 'its legacy of suspicion between military and political leaders. Both French and Haig . . . found it difficult when in command of the British Expeditionary Force in the years that followed to get on with those whom Kitchener termed "the frocks", and the brief growth of the Curragh incident may well have borne bitter fruit in that lack of frankness and of mutual confidence between Whitehall and the Army which hampered the conduct of operations during the First World War.'[42]

Certainly the effect of the Curragh Incident on the Palace was to induce much greater preoccupation with the morale of the senior ranks within the Army. This may have been even further emphasised as a result of the Army's suspicions of the political establishment; or, for that matter, it might have contributed to those suspicions, since the Palace seemed only too

---

[41] *Ibid*, p 110.
[42] *Ibid*, p 202.

happy to identify itself with these sentiments. Certainly, it led to the constant contacts between the Palace and individual officers which followed the accepted pattern of the involvement of the Sovereign with the armed forces.

Meanwhile the Curragh Incident certainly sharpened everybody's apprehension about the Home Rule Bill. The King continued his efforts to agitate the Prime Minister. He also approached the Speaker of the House of Commons, Lowther, to see if he would preside over a conference of the parties held 'at my own house' — Buckingham Palace. The Speaker said he would, but the Prime Minister continued to resist the King's urgings until 17 July when the conference was convened by the King at Buckingham Palace, where he welcomed the participants before withdrawing. After four meetings the Speaker informed the King that there was no point in continuing. George V then saw each representative privately and concluded afterwards that at least the conference had contributed to a better atmosphere, although he confided also to his diary that the political situation was turning very grave.

Graver, more momentous events were at hand. That very afternoon, 17 July, Austria delivered an ultimatum to Serbia, and eighteen days later Britain was at war with Germany and Austria. The Irish imbroglio was temporarily swept aside. On 30 July Asquith postponed discussion of the Amending Bill, which provided for the right of the six Ulster counties to opt out of Home Rule for six years. Instead the Home Rule Act was passed in September, although another Act specified that it would not come into operation until after the war to allow time for negotiations over Ulster. Asquith also pledged that no attempt would be made to coerce Ulster. Both the Conservatives and the King thought that Asquith by this action breached the agreed party truce on Home Rule for the duration of the war and it was with regret that the King gave his Assent to the Home Rule Bill. The King also made clear that he retained the prerogative to veto legislation.[43] Though the Irish question re-emerged after the war, it did so in terms which no longer threatened the very foundations of the British constitution. Nobody, however, can claim that the post-war terms contained a lasting cure for the Irish disease, which still saps the vitality of the British body politic.

---

[43] Bogdanor, *Monarchy and Constitution*, pp 130-1.

Although the Great War destroyed the old order, it may have saved George V his throne. The point reached in July 1914 had not got him much further away from the prospect he so dreaded, and against which his only perceived options were to dismiss his Ministers, refuse Royal Assent, or make so much trouble that the whole careful construction of the constitutional monarchy was turned into a scaffold. War was something with which he could cope. The day after war was declared he confessed ruefully, while walking with Lady Airlie, one of the Queen's Ladies-in-Waiting, that war had saved him from an Irish problem he could never understand.

When George V ascended the Throne he was related to the Emperors of Germany and Russia and to the Kings of Greece, Spain, Denmark and Norway. European diplomacy at the time could have assumed the hue of a family affair. His father had exhibited a taste and a flair for exploiting these relationships in the cause of foreign affairs. He would have been a hard man to follow down that path, and King George wisely decided — though given the fevered state of domestic politics he really had no other choice — to specialise in British and Empire affairs.

He did his best in foreign affairs, studying the telegrams and keeping close to Sir Edward Grey, the Foreign Secretary. He cultivated friendships with the ambassadors to the Court of St James's — all nine of them! He used his influence normally, therefore, over personal matters, though at the royal level in Europe personal matters almost always had political connotations, as in his decision to send the royal yacht for the exiled King of Portugal — over Grey's misgivings.

George V seemed to feel the inevitability of war with Germany: 'The King thinks the Emperor may be driven into war, whether he likes it or not . . . He won't like being called a "coward" by the Socialists,' Knollys told Esher in August 1911.[44] Presumably George V found the domestic and imperial challenges in front of him quite daunting enough, but at least circumscribed in some way by taking place within an area covered by his formal authority and his prerogatives. That would sufficiently explain his lack of engagement in European affairs.

In 1912 he decided to go and see for himself. He had set his mind on

---

[44] CCC, Esher Papers, 10/52, Knollys to Esher, 27 August 1911.

visiting Vienna, Berlin, St Petersburg and Paris in that order. The Cabinet, however, were troubled about his going to Berlin before Paris, since they feared that the Anglo-French Entente Cordiale might not survive such a sequence. The King wanted to do it his way; Queen Mary even more so. She was 'in favour of the K[ing]making a fight to pay the visits in the order he wishes to . . . Anyhow it can do no harm his making his wishes known to Sir E Grey, and if the Government after that think we ought to go to F[rance] then we must I suppose reluctantly acquiesce.'[45] Knollys concurred. He told Esher that 'if the Cabinet unanimously recommend to the King to pay his first visit to Paris would it not be rather unwise of him to act contrary to this recommendation . . ? Otherwise if matters did not go on smoothly between England and France, or if any misunderstandings arose between the two courtiers, I fear the King would be blamed for not having acted on the advice of the Cabinet and the responsibility would fall upon him. It is quite true that King Edward's visits were not looked upon as political and of course I don't see why King George's should be regarded differently, but apparently the Foreign Secretary thinks differently.'[46] In the end a compromise was reached, whereby the King and Queen went to Berlin to attend a family wedding — emphasising, by travelling without a Minister, that it was a purely family affair — and the President of France paid a state visit to London.

Because of the state of European politics the Berlin visit, though ostensibly a 'family affair', was beset with intrigues. George V later confided to Lady Wigram that the Kaiser was almost childish in his jealousy of the friendship of George V with the Tsar, who was also staying at Potsdam. The Kaiser never allowed them to be alone or to have any private talks together 'and on the few occasions that they did the King shrewdly suspected that the Kaiser's ear was glued to the keyhole'.[47]

This impression was not wholly corroborated by Sir Frederick Ponsonby, an Assistant Private Secretary. Reporting on the Berlin visit in a routine letter to Lord Hardinge, the Viceroy, Ponsonby observed that the Kaiser was not at all nervous or afraid of the King as he had been of Edward VII. In fact, he was quite at ease.

---

[45] *Ibid*, 10/52, Knollys to Esher, 27 September 1912, encl from Queen Mary.

[46] *Ibid*, 10/52, Knollys to Esher, 27 September 1912.

[47] Wigram Papers, Lady Wigram Diary, entry for 24 January 1927.

The Czar and the King being great friends and constantly having jokes together I thought he might be put out, but not at all . . . but when he sat next to Bigge at the luncheon, given by the officers, he let drive freely. He said that it hurt him very much to find we had agreed to send a hundred thousand men to help the French against him. "I don't care a fig for your hundred thousand. There you are making alliances with a decadent nation like France and a semi-barbarous nation like Russia and opposing us, the true upholders of progress and liberty" . . . On the whole, the visit was a great success but whether any real good was done, I have my doubts. The feeling in the two countries is too strong for a visit of this sort to alter.[48]

The shadow of war had also spurred the King in his efforts to influence the naval building programme. He was always on the side of a bigger naval budget, and was constantly nagging Esher and lobbying other members of the Committee of Imperial Defence (CID) to speak out against the First Lord of the Admiralty, Winston Churchill. The latter, for his part, complained to Knollys about 'the intrigues of Buckingham Palace against his scheme[for the abandonment of the Mediterranean and the concentration of the Fleet in the North Sea against Germany]'. But Knollys pretended not to understand what Churchill was talking about. He tried his best to mollify Churchill and 'I begged him not to come to loggerheads with the King as I said all his Ministers ought to support him just now' — a novel constitutional doctrine which Churchill let pass.[49]

Even Fisher, in retirement, re-entered the fray complaining to Esher that if he, Fisher, returned to use his influence in the right quarters, he would

lower the King's Prestige — I should have to — He has said things in his unguarded and loquacious way that he would have to take back — his sycophants are playing hell with him — a weather cock would be his crest if his character had to be represented — . . . He tried to bluff McKenna [a former First Lord of the Admiralty] into making Beresford an Admiral of the Fleet. McKenna told him he would see him d - d first! So the Prime Minister (*for political favours to come*!) lent himself to dirty tricks! and when the opportunity arose McKenna was shunted. Winston, alas! (as I have had to tell him) feared for his wife the social ostracism of the Court and

---

[48] CUL, Hardinge Papers, 105/48, Ponsonby to Hardinge, 3 June 1913.
[49] CCC, Esher Papers, 10/52, Knollys to Esher, 29 June 1912.

succumbed to the [naval] appointments of the two Court favourites recently
made — *a wicked wrong in both cases*! Winston has sacrificed the Country to
the Court — and gone back on his brave deeds . . . *So I've done with him!*[50]

His closeness to the proceedings of the Committee of Imperial Defence
had one fortunate result and gave rise to a lasting friendship from which
the King derived great comfort. Maurice Hankey, who was Secretary to
the CID, was received by the King in audience for the first time in May
1912. He became one of the King's most trusted advisers, particularly in
defence and scientific areas, though not limited to these. Stamfordham
did all he could to nourish the association. Hankey was an official who
worked at the very heart of the Government's strategic concerns. The
King could have no better contact. The first request Hankey received
from Stamfordham was for a summary of the CID's papers on the threat
of an invasion of Britain. Asquith, to his great credit, authorised Hankey
to give the King an account of all the discussions in the CID, although
there were obviously some dangerous, or at least unpredictable, aspects to
this diffusion of the Prime Minister's role as the Sovereign's adviser. Of all
people, Hankey was the man to cope with these difficulties, and he did so
with great tact and skill with four other Prime Ministers after Asquith.
The King, for the rest of his life had a source of information and advice,
other than the Prime Minister, at the very heart of government. It put him
in a very strong position. But he did not, as it were, sit back and allow
himself to be spoon-fed by Hankey.

On the contrary the King's involvement in the defence world both
before the war, and during it, was so intense, that he arguably betrayed the
trust Asquith put in him by placing Hankey at his disposal. Certainly the
existence of Hankey, and his privileged relationship with the King, did not
inhibit George V, or his courtiers, from an activist policy within the armed
forces which must have made the service ministers often wonder who was
in charge. It was as though the King felt that the Army and the Navy were
so particularly his own preserve that he was entitled to interfere as much
and as frequently as he wished. No minister really stood up to him. His
treatment of Seely during the Curragh Incident was peremptory to say
the least. But then Seely *was* only a Colonel and he *was* the King, the head

---

[50] CCC, Esher Papers, 10/43, Fisher to Esher, 24 April 1912.

of the armed forces, and all else besides.

Most of this work was carried out for him not by Stamfordham, who was charged with maintaining the King's relationship with Asquith and Grey, but by a young cavalry officer, Major Clive Wigram. Wigram had been recruited to look after the King during his visit to India in 1911, and he stayed on. He played an astonishing role in almost singlehandedly convincing the Imperial General Staff that the Palace was in charge or, if not in charge, that it should be.

One has to go back to George V's days in the Navy for some of the explanations about this preoccupation with the armed forces. Moreover, it was not just George V who displayed a particular passion for his connection with the forces of the Crown. It has affected the Royal Family as a whole generation after generation; and understandably so, since most of them have direct contact with officers and men through the honorary rank of colonelcies of regiments, and through the fact that officers are seconded to the Household as equerries and other functionaries. Perhaps, above all, it is because the Sovereign is head of the armed forces, and the object of a quite specific, pointed, almost obsessive loyalty, which is burnished by repeated ritual — daily ritual — in a way not evident among the civilian population, whose loyalty, though suspect, has to be taken for granted unless it is spontaneously expressed on great state occasions. As we have seen, the Curragh Incident revealed a gulf between the Army and the politicians which the King, and particularly Major Wigram, were to seek to fill during the First World War.

3

Embodiment of the Nation

After war was declared by Britain against Germany on 4 August 1914 there was an immediate clamour to strike the Kaiser and the Crown Prince from the list of honorary colonelcies of British regiments; to remove their Garter banners from St George's Chapel at Windsor; and to strip them of their honorary appointments to British orders of chivalry. To his surprise, George V was formally advised to yield to these measures by Asquith. Stamfordham's view was that the King would have quietly instructed that such action be taken in due course but resented having to do so in apparent response to public histrionics in newspapers and elsewhere.

George V was also greatly distressed by the anti-German clamour, which resulted in the quite unjustified removal of Prince Louis of Battenberg as First Sea Lord and Lord Haldane as Lord Chancellor. When Churchill proposed replacing Battenberg by recalling the seventy-four year old Fisher from his exile, the King strenuously opposed the appointment with all the stratagems and arguments at his disposal. Churchill, supported by Asquith, prevailed. But the King's warnings about Fisher were substantially borne out by events when the old Admiral resigned over the failure of the Navy to force the Dardanelles in May 1915 (an event which, ironically, led also to Churchill's removal from the Admiralty). Asquith later conceded that the King had been right about Fisher's appointment.

Following the outbreak of war the scene of activity for the King had shifted. No longer was the Royal Prerogative the stuff of constitutional argument and pressure. The main arm of government was now directed at mobilising the military strength of the nation. The King anyway saw himself as the embodiment of the nation: its successes were his successes, its reverses, his reverses, its moods, his moods. Moreover, his symbolic leadership of the country was essentially expressed by his command of the armed forces of the Crown. What more potent demonstration of that feeling could there have been than the massed crowds which immediately congregated outside the Palace on the declaration of war and cheered the King and Queen for three whole days. He turned his Palace into a service establishment. He donned uniform for the duration. Black stallions were ordered for the first wartime state opening of Parliament that November. Lord Sandhurst, the Lord Chamberlain, noted the fact that this was to save work, as the black horses needed less grooming (sixty of the Palace staff had enlisted).

The King had a special relationship with the generals and admirals which was denied to the Prime Minister, denied to the Cabinet. Through personal knowledge, tradition, friendships, his approach to the conduct of the war was one of a man who knows that his subordinates were operating in his chosen field, and he never let them entirely forget it. Wigram was the animator of this great exercise. Between 1915 and 1918 Wigram was writing sometimes daily, certainly weekly, to all the main general officers in the Army, and receiving their private letters in return. His overall intelligence, therefore, was probably as good as, maybe better than, that on which the Cabinet had to base its conduct of military affairs. It put the King in an enormously strong position in his discussions with the Prime Minister, the service ministers, the First Sea Lord and the Chief of the Imperial General Staff. The list of Wigram's correspondents reads like the opening pages of the leading page of the contemporary Army List. He was in close touch during all those years with Gough, Rawlinson, Robertson, Lambton, Monro, Pulteney, Birdwood, Godley, Allenby, Watson, Cavan, Shea, Howell, Hunter-Weston, Kentish, Nugent, Richardson, Bulfin, Kennedy, Ruggles-Brise, Ashburner, Wilson and Whigham. The King also received confidential reports from the Viceroy of India, the Governors of Madras and Bombay and the Governor-Generals of the Dominions, and ambassadors and ministers in foreign capitals. Moreover, the King's naval friends, such as Sir Rosslyn Wemyss, Sir David Beatty and Francis Hopwood, would write him long private letters in which they discussed their experiences and not infrequently voiced their anxieties or complaints. He would read all the correspondence with great care, registering all the details and instructing his private secretaries to keep in regular contact with his correspondents in order to elicit more information.

A week after war was declared, the King attended an Aldershot review. He remarked to Haig, who commanded the First Corps of the British Expeditionary Force (BEF) which was being sent to France, that he was delighted with the appointment of Sir John French as Commander-in-Chief of the BEF. Haig, who was destined to succeed French, demurred. He voiced his 'doubts' to the King as to whether French's

> temper was sufficiently even or his military knowledge sufficiently thorough to enable him to discharge properly the very difficult duties which will devolve upon him during the coming operations with Allies on the Continent. In my own heart I know that French is quite unfit for this great command at a time of crisis in our Nation's history . . . The King seemed anxious but he did not give me the impression that he fully realised the grave issues both for our country as well as for his own House, which were about to be put to the test; nor did he really comprehend the uncertainty of the result of all wars between great nations, no matter how well prepared one may think one is.[1]

When Haig dined with the King during the latter's visit to France in early December 1914, he found him also inclined to think that all soldiers were by their nature brave. He appeared to be ignorant, or oblivious of, the efforts necessary to keep up an Army's morale.

The King paid a visit to French's headquarters, where one of Wigram's sources, Brigadier-General the Hon William (Billy) Lambton (who was French's Military Secretary), was severely reprimanded by His Majesty for arriving late with the medals he was to present to some of the officers. French's headquarters never settled down. Lambton reported to Wigram in January 1915 that:

> It has always been my one object to keep relations between Sir J [French] and Lord K [Kitchener, Secretary of State for War] good; lately I have found the former much less easy to deal with . . . Like you I put this down to the evil influence of politicians of whom Winston Churchill is the chief, and my belief is that they are using him as a lever in their attempt to oust Lord K. His Majesty may rely on my efforts to keep the peace but there

---

[1]   Robert Blake (ed), *The Private Papers of Douglas Haig, 1914-1919* (Eyre and Spottiswoode, London, 1952), p 70.

are intriguers on his staff who make my task difficult and who for the moment seem to be rather in the ascendant . . . I have told you as fully as I can the difficulties here — of course you will keep to yourself except as regards His Majesty. These intrigues are most disturbing and I hate being mixed up in them.[2]

On 26 May 1915, Wigram asked Haig to help improve relations between Kitchener and French. But Haig was not sanguine given French's jealous disposition. The previous evening Asquith had revealed to the King the composition of his new coalition government, which had been forced on him in the wake of the Shells Scandal and the failure of the naval attack on the Dardanelles — which led to the resignation of Fisher and the demotion of Churchill. The King had been intimately involved in the formation of the new government and the protection of Lord Kitchener's position at the War Office by appointing his rival and chief critic, Lloyd George, to the new Ministry of Munitions.

Overwhelming evidence also suggests that the King, through Wigram, took a prominent part in senior appointments within the Army. In June 1915 a letter from Lambton at French's headquarters confirmed this trend.

> I don't quite know what to do about Army, Army Corps and Divisional Generals. Does His Majesty want my opinion or that of the C-in-C. I am sending him a list of the officers whom we have recommended as suitable to command Divisions and I always have a list ready of possible brigadiers. As regards the *Army Command*, by a process of elimination you come to two: Arthur Paget at the top, Pulteney at the bottom. There is also Allenby who would I believe do. I fancy Paget is to be the next choice.[3]

And this after the Curragh! A few days later Lambton wrote: 'It would be a good thing if HM saw Wilson as he can put the French case more clearly than anyone else.'[4] With this letter Lambton enclosed a personal missive for the King, prior to a visit home by French to confront Kitchener and the Cabinet. The King meanwhile had asked Hankey to give him a copy of his memorandum on general policy which was no doubt to form the basis of the Cabinet deliberations.

By July 1915 dissatisfaction with French's conduct of the war was

[2] RA, GV/GG6, Lambton to Wigram, 18 January 1915.
[3] RA, GV/GG6, Lambton to Wigram, 8 June 1915.
[4] RA, GV/GG6, Lambton to Wigram, 30 June 1915.

widespread in London, not least at Buckingham Palace. When Haig called on the King to receive his GCB on 14 July, he was treated to an amazing attack on French by the King. It was an extraordinary way to behave to one of French's subordinates, however senior a man, and however intimate he might have been with the King. George V started by referring to the friction between French and Kitchener, and said it was not like that in the Navy. He suggested that such friction would not occur if 'the officer at the head of the Army in the Field . . . was fit for his position'. He criticised French for his 'unsoldierlike' relations with Colonel Repington, the military correspondent of *The Times*, and the Northcliffe press. He said he 'had lost confidence in Field-Marshal French. And he had told Kitchener that he (K) could depend on his (the King's) support in whatever action he took in dealing with French. The King's one object was efficiency. He would approve of any action to ensure the Army being in as fit a state as possible to end the war.' He then asked Haig to write secret reports to Wigram, and also to Kitchener, which no-one else would be allowed to see. Later in the day Kitchener asked him to do the same. He said he 'would not reply, but I would see my proposals given effect to and must profess ignorance when that happened!' It is quite clear that both Kitchener and the King had agreed beforehand on the need to set up this secret channel of communication with Haig, bypassing French. The King, in fact, told Haig that 'he had said to Lord K with reference to it "If anyone acted like that, and told tales out of school, he would at school be called a sneak." K's reply was that we are beyond the schoolboy's age!'[5]

The disaffection with French soured strategic discussions for the rest of the year. The King now knew that Haig, one of French's Army Commanders, and Robertson, French's Chief of Staff, were firmly of the view that the Commander-in-Chief should be dismissed immediately. The King visited the Front in October 1915, where the message was the same. It was only because he was thrown by his horse, breaking his pelvis in two places, that it took another five weeks for him to move decisively on the question of the Commander-in-Chief, after the failure of an attempt by Esher to persuade French to go quietly. On 2 December, Stamfordham wrote to Asquith saying that he hoped the Prime Minister would now ask

---

[5]   Blake, *Haig*, pp 97-8.

French for his resignation: 'Moreover, the King feels that GHQ should not be left much longer without a C-in-C.'[6] In four days it was done. French became Viscount Ypres and was given command of the Home Forces. Haig, not surprisingly became C-in-C. French blamed the unfortunate Kitchener for his dismissal, though the latter was in the Mediterranean at the time.

It would not be an exaggeration to say that the dismissal of French had been orchestrated, coordinated and finally given its executive thrust at the highest level — the King himself. There were of course disclaimers, even in this confidential setting. In mid-November 1915, while the King was still convalescing, Haig had received a note from Stamfordham saying 'the King is quite sure of the two changes he ought to make in France, and at the War Office, but that *he* cannot make them.'[7]

In London, the King was having as difficult a time over Lord Kitchener. The Cabinet was by now almost all ranged against the Secretary of State for War. There was pressure to put his General Staff function more directly under the War Committee which would gravely diminish Kitchener's powers, and Wigram thought the old man could not stay on in those circumstances. But the King was still hoping Asquith would come up with a formula to retain Kitchener. The Palace was urging Robertson and Kitchener to agree a *modus operandi* which would convince the Cabinet. Then, much to Wigram's alarm, Kitchener impulsively offered his resignation to Asquith without first consulting Robertson.

The King told Hankey he wanted Kitchener to stay, and Kitchener stayed, although the agitation revealed a distinct unease in the Cabinet at the current direction of the war effort. It was not resolved by the time of Kitchener's sudden death at sea in June 1916. It was to take the resignation of Asquith and the formation of a new War Cabinet under Lloyd George in December 1916 to bring about a revitalisation of the war effort. The King was actively involved in all this.

The strain of the war effort had already exposed cracks in the Coalition Cabinet which Asquith had formed in May 1915. It was not just a general dissatisfaction with the course of the fighting in France, the bickering

---

[6] Nicolson, *George V*, p 268.

[7] David R Woodward, *Lloyd George and the Generals* (Associated Universities Presses, London, 1983), p 79.

between French and Kitchener, or French's attempts to stoke up press criticism of the government over the shells-shortage scare. Within the Cabinet there were individual Liberals for whom the brutality of war, and the unpleasant measures necessary, went against the grain of a lifetime's political philosophy. Things nearly came to a head in 1915-16 over the question of conscription. Ranged against the measure were the grandees of the Liberal Party — Sir John Simon, the Home Secretary, Reginald McKenna, the Chancellor of the Exchequer, Walter Runciman, the President of the Board of Trade, and even Sir Edward Grey, the Foreign Secretary. The King returned from his Christmas holiday at Sandringham in 1915 and threw his whole weight behind Asquith. The result was that Grey, McKenna and Runciman all stayed; only Simon resigned. However, it was only a half measure and did not completely quell opposition in the Cabinet.

The main threat was that Lloyd George and Bonar Law, although at opposite ends of the political spectrum, were both prepared to resign unless conscription was fully implemented. It took several meetings with Stamfordham, acting as honest broker, for the affair to be resolved in Lloyd George's favour. All the parties were doubtless chastened, and imbued with an extra spirit of urgency about the war, by the Dublin Easter Rising in 1916 which occurred in the middle of their argument. Yet, the lingering dissatisfaction with the conduct of the war could not, ultimately, avoid revolving around the question of Asquith's leadership. This had in the main, been exercised in much the same spirit, and at much the same pace, as he had always exercised it in peace or war. It was not only Lloyd George, with all his Celtic zest, who felt that wartime leadership required some extra fire in the belly of British politics. After Kitchener's death he took over the War Office and soon demanded that Asquith create a small War Council of Cabinet ministers with him as chairman. Asquith insisted that the authority of the Prime Minister must remain supreme. The struggle between them then intensified. It was not a struggle for the soul of the Liberal Party, because that remained safely with Asquith, and the Liberals subsequently formed the responsible opposition to the Lloyd George coalition. It was a struggle for the support of the Conservatives in the conduct of the war. Lloyd George was aided by Sir Max Aitken, who acted as mediator, and Carson, who was threatening to seize the Conservative leadership from Bonar Law unless matters improved. The existence of this alliance resulted in the elders of the Conservative Party informing Asquith on 5 December 1916 that they could no longer support him.

Asquith went to see the King and resigned. There followed two extraordinary days of political scrimmaging. The King first summoned Bonar Law to see if he could form a government; but the two men disagreed totally about the conduct of the war, as well as arguing about whether Bonar Law would be entitled to a dissolution. Bonar Law went away to see if he could persuade Asquith to serve under him, since in these circumstances he felt confident he could indeed form a government without the need for a dissolution. Asquith demurred on practical grounds, and the only suggestion of that morning to which all the parties agreed was one from Balfour that the King should convene a conference at Buckingham Palace that afternoon, attended by Asquith, Lloyd George, Bonar Law, Balfour and the Labour leader, Arthur Henderson. It was a remarkable encounter, during which all the main arguments were put on the table, while the proceedings themselves were opened and closed by the King. The result, in the words of Stamfordham's minute was 'an agreement that Mr Asquith should consider the proposals made to him, and let Mr Bonar Law know as soon as possible whether he would join the Government under him. If the answer was in the negative, Mr Bonar Law would not form a Government, but Mr Lloyd George would endeavour to do so.'[8]

Asquith hurried back to Downing Street to meet his Liberal colleagues. With one exception they decided not to remain in a government with Asquith in a subordinate capacity, but to form 'a sober and responsible opposition steadily supporting the Government in the conduct of the war.'[9] There were only two things left for the King to do. One was to receive Bonar Law and hear from him that he could not form a government. The other was to ask Lloyd George to do so.

Although the Liberal establishment held out against him Lloyd George was able to form a new coalition government dominated by Conservatives but with a War Cabinet consisting, under his chairmanship, of Lord Curzon, Lord Milner, Arthur Henderson and Bonar Law. The whole affair

---

[8] Nicolson, *George V*, p 291.
[9] *Ibid*, p 292.

seemed to take the Palace by surprise. Wigram wrote that 'I must confess I was completely surprised when Asquith resigned, and thought that it was a political coup to come back with a stronger hand, thinking that if he stood out with his party, no one else could form a government.'[10]

It was a shock to the King. Asquith, after all, was the only Prime Minister he had known. They had survived much together and the King had developed considerably in the previous six years, to a point where their relationship contained much mutual trust. It must have done, since a personality touchier or less secure than Asquith's, would have had good cause to complain about, or at least feel irritated by, the constant evidence of the King's meddling of which he was well aware. Indeed it is a measure of how urgently the King saw the need to take a grip on the government and the war that, during the Cabinet crisis, he sent Stamfordham to see Hankey to ask what he, the King, should do in the circumstances. Should he, for instance, take a more active share in the government? Hankey gave the wise advice that the war outlook and the financial and economic circumstances were so doubtful that the King should on no account take a hand, even though he wished to do so. He added that, though the King talked too much, he had admirable common sense.

The King now had a Prime Minister he had almost certainly not bargained for, and whom he cordially disliked. Six months earlier, when Kitchener died, he had asked Hankey to take over Kitchener's duty in keeping him up to date with the Cabinet's war plans. At the time the King had revealed the depths of his distaste for the little Welsh dynamo. He had asked Hankey who he thought should succeed Kitchener. Lloyd George's name, though only Hankey's second choice, provoked a furious royal diatribe against him. In vain Hankey tried to defend the Welshman; the King would not listen.

Now he was going to have to listen to the man himself. It was to be Hankey and Stamfordham who would have to act as the midwives to this new and uncomfortable relationship. As a consequence of the setting up of the War Cabinet Lloyd George created a proper secretariat, with Hankey at its head. The latter immediately asked the new Prime Minister for

---

[10] RA, GV/GG6.

instructions about sending War Cabinet minutes to the King. Hitherto the King had received a regular letter from the Prime Minister in long hand, describing the proceedings of each Cabinet meeting. After discussions with Stamfordham it was agreed that the King would be satisfied with full typed minutes of the War Committee meetings (in other words Hankey's minutes), but he would like the Prime Minister to adhere to the time-honoured custom of reporting Cabinet business by hand. Lloyd George detested writing and Hankey was sympathetic, adding that he personally hated time-honoured customs that wasted time, but that Stamfordham was very suspicious and moved quickly to the attack if he felt the King was not being properly informed.

The next two years of war witnessed a state of barely concealed hostility between the Palace and the Prime Minister, fuelled, it must be said, by Stamfordham and Wigram, rather than by the King. The King's dealings with Lloyd George, as one can imagine from the man's character, were always correct. There seemed less disposition on the part of the private secretaries, however, to overlook, or even informally iron out, those little wrinkles in the relationship which had happened often enough in Asquith's day without being put down to the congenital character defects or calculated anti-monarchism of the Prime Minister.

Indeed Lloyd George once remarked that he liked the King, and felt that the King liked him, but that their dealings were soured by the Household. Certainly there is an undercurrent of distrust in Stamfordham's and Wigram's approach to the Prime Minister, which had a personal edge to it quite different from the generalised contempt with which they referred to 'politicans' during Asquith's time. This distrust took unusual forms. They seemed to think that Lloyd George's motives were always personally suspect. This was not because he was no good at prosecuting the war. Indeed he was clearly better at it, from the political point of view, than Asquith had been. But they felt that his behaviour was politicised and geared to his own aggrandisement, at the expense not just of the military, those blood brothers of the royal private secretaries, but of the Monarchy itself. This pervasive suspicion of Lloyd George, as a man who was rightly assumed to be profoundly antipathetic to the military, only enhanced the Palace view that the King must exercise his leadership over the armed forces.

In January 1917 Wigram told Haig that the King had given 'direct orders' to the Quartermaster-General to see that the Australian troops had suitable winter clothing.[11] Wigram wrote also to GHQ in Cairo on the matter of promotions in general, which the latter had complained seemed to be scooped up by officers from the Western Front, while the claims of those in the Middle East were ignored. Wigram assured his confidante, Colonel Pollen, at GHQ, Cairo that: 'The only person who can keep the balance equal is the King, and HM is, I know, speaking to the Secretary of State for War on this subject to impress upon him that Generals out of sight are not to be kept out of mind.'[12]

There was a complete rapport with Haig. 'HM thinks the War Cabinet is afraid of you,' Wigram told him, while assuring him of the King's total support.[13] Apparently the last thing the War Cabinet wanted was that Haig should resign since, in Wigram's opinion, Lloyd George might then appeal to the country and come back as a dictator! The King himself, when subsequently meeting Haig, said almost the same thing, adding that his position would then be very difficult as he would then be blamed for causing the election.

The King at that time had his first big dispute with Lloyd George, who, at a conference with the French political and military leaders at Calais in February 1917, had agreed to place Haig and the British Army under the orders of the French C-in-C, General Nivelle, who was to plan an attack along the whole front. Haig and Robertson both felt that they had been hustled into such an agreement after Lloyd George had already settled everything behind their backs with the French. Certainly the agreement seemed to have been discussed by the War Cabinet some days earlier. Neither Robertson, the CIGS, nor Lord Derby, the Secretary of State for War, nor the King, was shown the minutes of that meeting. Haig complained to the King, who was furious about the whole episode. Apart from objecting that he had not been kept properly informed, leaving him in no position to veto the plan before it was adopted, the King could now only attempt through Stamfordham to discourage Haig from resigning and to encourage him to smooth the whole thing over with Nivelle. Most of the King's wrath, as it happened, fell on the long-suffering Hankey, who had subsequently to justify the procedure adopted by Lloyd George.

---

[11] RA, GV/GG6, Wigram to Haig, 3 January 1917.
[12] RA, GV/GG6, Wigram to Pollen, 18 January 1917.
[13] Blake, *Haig*, p 208.

Certainly the incident increased Wigram's suspicions of Lloyd George and encouraged him to be almost obsessively vigilant of the Prime Minister's every move from then on. Wigram told Lambton, à propos of an exchange of messages between President Wilson and the King, that: 'At one time we thought that LG was trying to usurp the position of His Majesty and telegraph direct to the President [Wilson] in the name of the Empire. This was rectified before the error was made, but we were done in the eye, as His Majesty's message did not reach the press until after the War Cabinet and Lloyd George's greetings to America. So long as we have a monarchy, the observances and rules of the constitution must be preserved and maintained.'[14]

Wigram pressed on with his campaign to keep the King in the Army's eye: 'I think that His Majesty stands well with his Navy and Army, and I hope that I am not taking a prejudiced view about this,' he wrote to 'Rawly' Rawlinson. 'As you know, my one object is to keep the King in touch with military opinion and to this end I am always trying to bring His Majesty into touch with distinguished officers in the higher ranks of the Army.' He appealed for ideas which would help to strengthen the King's position.[15]

After the Calais meeting the next bout between the Palace and the Premier, over the question of control of the military, concerned Lloyd George's pressure on the CIGS, Sir William Robertson, to resign in February 1918. Robertson objected to the Prime Minister's decision to subordinate Britain's strategic direction of the war to a joint Anglo-French Supreme War Council, sitting in Versailles, under the chairmanship of General Foch. As Churchill stated, it was undoubtedly Lloyd George's aim: 'to arm the Cabinet with an alternative set of military advisers whose opinions should be used to curb and correct the "Robertson-Haig" point of view.'[16] The Prime Minister had already revealed to Stamfordham the depths of his dissatisfaction with the War Office, and his desire to break away from its thrall.

Robertson objected to the Versailles plan despite, or maybe because of, Sir Henry Wilson's appointment to the Supreme War Council as

---

[14] RA, GV/GG6, Wigram to Lambton, 9 April 1917.

[15] RA, GV/GG6, Wigram to Rawlinson, 11 April 1917.

[16] Winston S Churchill, *The World Crisis, 1916-1918. Part II* (Thornton Butterworth Ltd, London, 1927), p 387.

Britain's military representative. Nor would he accept a switch between him and Wilson. He refused Stamfordham's request to reconsider his decision to resign. Stamfordham went on to advise the Prime Minister that the King took a dim view of Robertson's imminent resignation from the office of CIGS. The Prime Minister disagreed, and hinted darkly that if the King insisted on Robertson, he would have to find other Ministers. Lord Stamfordham quickly denied that the King was making any such insistence, so Robertson resigned, and Sir Henry Wilson took his place. The jockeying continued, both to protect Haig from what was seen now as a formidable London combination against him, with his old adversary Wilson as CIGS, and to find work for Robertson who, at such a stage in the war, seemed to be entirely wasted kicking his heels in disgrace. Wigram told his brother that the King was pressing the Prime Minister to send Robertson back to the Front in some capacity. 'Directly there is a lull in the proceedings, I am sure there will be another attempt to get rid of DH[Haig]. There is a very nasty combination against him with the PM, HW[Wilson], Winston and French, and Derby is too weak to resist.'[17]

Wigram was very critical of the new CIGS, Wilson, and his crew: 'too much of political sauce ... members of a mutual admiration society'. He predicted Haig might be the next victim of the 'cabal' and told one correspondent that 'Goughy [Sir John Hubert Gough] has already come under the guillotine'.[18] Sir Henry Wilson was not a man who would for long be unaware of this sniping. A smooth explanation to Wigram followed:

> There seems to be, from what I hear, some misapprehension about the inclination or wish on my part — or somebody's part — to make use of the services, in some capacity of Sir W Robertson. It is inferred that because Robertson is not employed in France the State is the poorer. This may, or may not be so, but his non-employment in France is due not to any fault at the WO. He was offered to the CinC for a Command, as his Chief of Staff, or as his QMG. Sir Douglas did not see his way to putting him in any of these posts. Robertson's seniority precludes his employment in anything but the higher appointments. I spoke to Sir Douglas about all this the day before yesterday and wrote again last night to ask him if he could think of anything else or if he would like Robertson to go out to talk

---

[17] RA, GV/GG6, Clive Wigram to Brigadier-General Kenneth Wigram, 12 April 1918.
[18] RA, GV/GG6, Wigram to Major-General J S Shea, 13 April 1918.

matters over as between old friends. I hope this is all clear . . . I gather . . .
that the King was nervous lest I should withdraw some of our Divns from
Italy if I sent down some of our skeleton Divns there. This was never in
my mind.[19]

Wigram replied in equally silken terms: 'You may rest assured that His
Majesty realises and appreciates all you have done to get Sir William
Robertson employment in France. His Majesty only longs to see harmony
amongst the higher commanders and a unified General Staff without any
sects, schisms or dissensions.'[20] The pressure to utilise Robertson continued
from the Palace, in the face of what could have been studied inertia by the
Prime Minister and the War Office. In May 1918 Stamfordham once
more wrote to Hankey, presumably at the instigation of the King. 'It is
really wicked that he [Robertson] should be performing ceremonies for
the Church Army at such a time of national crisis.'[21] Finally that month
Robertson was made C-in-C Home Forces after French became Lord
Lieutenant of Ireland. But he had to wait two more years to receive his
Field Marshal's baton.

It was not only Robertson's case which caused irritations between
Downing Street and the Palace. The King protested strongly about the
enforced retirement of Sir Hugh Trenchard, the Chief of the Air Staff and
virtual creator of the Royal Air Force. Once again he seemed not to have
received the War Cabinet minutes which had dealt with the matter at
length some days earlier. Stamfordham regretted the omission on the
grounds that if the King had known in time he might have arranged for
Trenchard's retirement to be more dignified and to have led to an
immediate reassignment in the field. Wigram wrote to Lord Cromer,
Assistant Private Secretary to the King, and later Lord Chamberlain,
'I believe Lord S[Stamfordham] and the PM had quite a stormy
discussion on the constitutional position of the King.'[22] He was right.
According to Hankey, the PM was angry and sent Stamfordham away
with a 'flea in his ear', saying the King was encouraging mutiny by

[19] RA, GV/GG6, Wilson to Wigram, 18 April 1918.

[20] Imperial War Museum (IWM), Sir Henry Wilson Papers, HHW, 2/31/2, Wigram to Wilson,
19 April 1918.

[21] Stephen Roskill, *Hankey Man of Secrets*, Vol 1, 1877-1918 (Collins, London, 1970) p 546.

[22] RA, GV/GG6, Wigram to Cromer, 16 April 1918.

taking up the cause of these officers.[23]

If Lloyd George had been able to see the kind of letters Wigram was writing to his military contacts, he might have felt his accusation was not far wide of the mark. 'The political strategy and tactics to oust the military party have been unfortunately well organised, and by dividing the general staff and higher commanders, have succeeded,' Wigram wrote to his brother. 'If the General Staff had stuck together and there had been no secession like that of HW[Wilson] and his crew, the military would now be running the war.'[24] Yet Wigram was against taking any remedial action. He told Rawlinson: 'Soldiers annoy me when they talk of the King turning out the Prime Minister and putting in soldiers and sailors to run the show. The people, the press, and Parliament would not for one moment stand such an unconstitutional act, and it is asking for disaster . . . The strategy of the politicans has been well organised and well carried out. They have defeated the military hierarchy in detail.'[25]

In a letter to *The Times* on 7 May 1918 General Sir Frederick Maurice, formerly Director of Military Operations, contradicted the Prime Minister's assertion, in response to the criticism that he was starving Haig of troops, that British forces in France were stronger in January 1918 than a year before. The letter led to a vote of censure in the House of Commons, which Lloyd George survived. Wigram concluded, sadly, that the House of Commons was prepared 'to support LG and his crew, and that any move to carry out the suggestions which you and others have put forward of the King attempting to take control would meet with the same fate [as Asquith].'[26]

Nevertheless Wigram had a grudging respect for Wilson. 'HW is, as you say, extraordinarily clever, and the combination of LG, Milner and him cannot be bettered, provided that their policy is sound.' Unfortunately, he confirmed, Wilson was not popular with commanders, the General Staff, or even the French, who seemed to regard Wilson as a kind of a hero, although as he had recently discovered, they also referred to him as

---

[23] Roskill, *Hankey*, Vol 1, p 519.

[24] RA, GV/GG6, Clive Wigram to Kenneth Wigram, 17 April 1918.

[25] National Army Museum (NAM), Rawlinson Papers, Vol 73, Wigram to Rawlinson, 18 April 1918.

[26] RA, GV/GG6, Clive Wigram to Kenneth Wigram, 13 May 1918.

'Le Tributeur'[27] (ie someone dependent on foreigners).

The Palace had not only to adjust to changes in the war leadership but also to the effects in Britain of the Russian Revolution. In March 1917 the Tsar, George's cousin and friend, abdicated. He was shunted around Russia for months in detention before finally being murdered with his family at Ekaterinburg in July 1918. There is no gainsaying regicide. It tolls the bell for any crowned head, however secure the foundations of the throne. It not only diminishes the numbers, it diminishes the idea of monarchy. Thus the rejoicing in London at the end of Tsardom cannot have sounded friendly, however muffled by censorship it was by the time it reached the ears of the royal couple through the Palace walls.

The King, as one would expect, responded to the Tsar's abdication with the warmth and spontaneity of a friend and kinsman — but not a fellow statesman. He sent a cable reminding the Tsar of his true and devoted friendship for him; and somehow imagined that such a cable could be passed off as a private act. It was intercepted by moderate elements in the Russian Provisional Government, who suggested to the British Ambassador in Petrograd, Sir George Buchanan, that it had better not be delivered, in case of misunderstanding. This message came back to Downing Street, which then asked the Palace for a copy of the original text. The King refused, on the grounds that it was private, and said, since the telegram had not been delivered to the Tsar, it should be cancelled. However, the King's close relationship to the Tsar caused his position to be widely misunderstood. On Stamfordham's advice, he decided firmly against any plan to offer the Tsar and his family asylum, and when he learnt that the government had done so he felt most aggrieved. The Prime Minister was urged by Stamfordham to withdraw the proposal in the light of the evident public hostility to the idea.

For George V the Russian Revolution was a godsend, though he may not have realised it. If the outbreak of war had saved his throne from imminent disaster, the Russian Revolution at the end of it ensured that the British monarchy had a future. At the time, though, it might have been felt to be a future which was very much on probation. Though Stamfordham

---

[27] RA, GV/GG6, Wigram to Shea, 13 June 1918.

and Wigram preserved a sense of calm before the outside world — calm tinged with a concern to be sensitive to all the new political and social currents at a time of particular volatility — inside the Palace a convulsive process of rethinking was going on. Wigram, as always, had been ahead of the field in detecting from where the threat might come. As early as 14 April 1917, after the Tsar had abdicated, he was in his sentry box. He wrote to Haig:

> Of course one has to remember the cleverness and the astuteness of the politician to divert this wave of popular feeling away into other channels. Hence, later on, when the people get more hungry in this country, there may be an attempt to have cock-shies at the Monarchy. I feel very strongly that the King should be up and as it were take the offensive before the enemy can contemplate any preparations. His Majesty should show himself more amongst the people . . . I am sure that he would soon rally moderate, or even wavering opinion on his side by showing the Royal Standard. Further, I think that His Majesty wants a better Press, and to get out of the habit of hiding his light under a bushel . . . [28]

As for the need for reform within the Palace, Wigram was emphatic:

> I sometimes nearly give it up in despair, and wish to send in my cap and jacket. The atmosphere here is too much that of the early Victorian period, and we do not move with the times . . . It is most important that Their Majesties and the Household should become, to use a hackneyed phrase, more democratic. Difficulties are always being seen ahead, when in reality there is no obstacle at all. Old Wal's [possibily Sir Edward Wallington, Private Secretary to Queen Mary] motto "Better Not" seems to pervade the whole place.[29]

His fears were not entirely groundless. Although Lloyd George later in his *War Memoirs* paid tribute to the King's role in inspiring the Home Front to maintain its effort, there must have been whole sections of working class society for whom the Monarchy was a distant, ceremonial affair, not closely connected with the rigours and austerities of war. In May 1917 the King and the Queen proposed to go on a tour of the cities in the North and the North West of England. The Mayor of Manchester sent a deputation to Wigram to say that under no circumstances could he recommend the

---

[28] RA, GV/GG6, Wigram to Haig, 14 April 1917.
[29] RA, GV/GG6, Wigram to Harry Verney, 19 April 1917.

Royal couple visiting his city, and that the whole tour should be put off because of strikes. The officer in command of the garrison at Barrow in Furness added his warning that the King should keep out of Barrow. Wigram sought advice from Arthur Henderson, who gave his full support to proceeding with the plans. The tour went ahead and was a great success. Even before the end of the war George V had started to come to terms with the British Labour party. He was no doubt by then discovering that the comfortable figure of Arthur Henderson, who had sat in on his council of war to find a successor to Asquith, was not many people's idea of a Bolshevik, and neither flashed red teeth at him, nor hammered red claws on the Palace furniture. By the end of the war, indeed, Stamfordham was sounding out Hankey about the best Labour man to have in the King's secretariat.

The King had already taken steps to meet the criticism that he, or any member of his family, was alien to the country. By naming his dynasty the House of Windsor (Stamfordham thought of the name) he made sure that, though it might still seem remote, at least it would be a British remoteness. Stamfordham took matters further:

> We must endeavour to induce the thinking working-classes, Socialists and others, to regard the Crown not as a mere figurehead and as an institution which, as they put it, "don't count" but as a living power for good with receptive faculties welcoming information affecting the interests and social well being of all classes, and ready, not only to sympathise with those questions but anxious to further their solution.[30]

He went on to suggest that the King show particular interest in industrial problems, without having to set himself up as an arbitrator.

His views were echoed by Cromer, shortly after the Tsar's family had been murdered in July 1918. 'The fact remains that the position of the monarchy is not so stable now, in 1918, as it was at the beginning of the war . . . No stone should be left unturned to consolidate the position of the Crown.'[31] These pious exhortations were all very well, coming from the courtiers. But the question was where should the process begin. The answer had to lie with the Court and the courtiers themselves, and nobody

---

[30] Nicolson, *George V*, p 308.

[31] John W Wheeler-Bennett, *King George VI: His Life and Reign* (Macmillan, London, 1958), p 159.

saw this more clearly than Wigram even though, as we shall see in the next chapter, some of his views carried too much of a flavour of war-gaming to be appropriate to an exercise for shaking up the Household.

The last great struggle of the war, between Buckingham Palace and Downing Street, grew out of the Palace's determination to see that Lloyd George did not collect all the laurels of victory. Wigram and Stamfordham felt that these should go to the Army, its commander and its soldiers equally, and that the King had a right and a duty to forestall and nullify any politician's attempt to extract advantage from the victory. There was an ulterior motive too, in the desire to inspire the returning masses with some feelings of patriotism and loyalty on the theme of not just a 'Country Fit for Heroes', but a King fit for them too. The Russian Revolution, as we have seen, was already casting a long and dark shadow of foreboding across Europe.

'The Boche is beat, but I fear a general revolution in Europe. Whether it will reach here, I know not,' Wigram wrote to his wife four days before the Armistice. Worried about returning soldiers who had been prisoners of war, he noted that 'the Government has done nothing to relieve their lot. After such abominable treatment they would come back very bitter: What can Their Majesties do to show their sympathy with them?' He suggested sending individual telegrams welcoming them home and encouraging them to wear their 'wound stripes' on their civilian clothes.[32]

There was some cause for concern. Haig's staff officers had reported that soldiers in hospitals were heard to ask: 'Why should we have a King . . . It's very costly . . . ', and so on.[33] Haig wanted to publish the King's telegram to him at the end of hostilities, along with Haig's reply which referred to the King's support for Haig and confidence in the Army. The King's private secretaries thought, however, that the reply had better remain unpublished as the Prime Minister might object that such a cable, sent by the King to the Commander-in-Chief in the Field, was unconstitutional. Certainly it had been sent off the King's own bat without any Ministerial involvement. If Lloyd George were to think that kind of cable unconstitutional, what indeed would he have made of the thicket of

---

[32] Wigram Papers, Wigram to Lady Wigram, 7 November 1918.
[33] Blake, *Haig*, p 344.

messages between the Palace and the British Army throughout the war? Stamfordham and Wigram must have been aware of these dangers, since they noted to Haig that the exchange of cables showed that the King supported Haig 'throughout the war', a phrase which might certainly have caused Lloyd George to prick up his pixie ears.[34]

The Armistice, when it came on 11 November 1918, was received in a touchingly mundane way inside the Palace. It was also marked by squabbling between the Palace and Whitehall. Wigram's account of that fateful day starts with the King feeling very deeply that the end of the war had come about in such a low-key way, without the Allies being able to bring to book the Kaiser and others 'who had by their behaviour proved to be the enemies of civilisation and humanity'. Wigram thought the King would have liked to try the Kaiser by court martial but, if this was his mood at the moment of the armistice, it changed later. At 9:30 on the morning of 11 November:

> The King was still murmuring about the Kaiser not being there to sign the armistice, and to have his guilt brought home to him. The Queen flew at me and shook both my hands . . . we had prepared four large placards with the news and were about to hang them on the railings outside when the Press Bureau said we were to stand fast as Mr L-G thought that the news should be kept for him to announce in the House of Commons in the afternoon. Did you ever hear anything so monstrous? This was soon rescinded and at 11 am flags went up, bombs exploded, bands played.

The Army Council and Lord Milner arrived to pay respects to the King — then the Board of Admiralty and the Air Council.

> The PM rolled up later on. We broke the pledge this evening and I had 2 glasses of Pop. It is curious that this day seven years ago Their Majesties left Portsmouth for India, how well I remember what a doleful departure it was. The whole of the Royal Family barring their Majesties got nerves and thought HM was going to be murdered in India, and that this was the last they would see of him . . . The King made 2 mistakes today due to too many cooks. He was not on the balcony at 11 am when hostilities ceased [but soon afterwards] and he should have attended St Pauls — the only 2 criticisms I have to make.[35]

---

[34] *Ibid.*

[35] Wigram Papers, Wigram to Lady Wigram, 11 November 1918.

The King immediately prepared to visit his troops in the field and the Navy at sea. First, however, in London there were jubilant crowds to satisfy, the service in St Pauls — *pace* Wigram — an address from the assembled Lords and Commons. 'During that jubilant week the King became for his people the hierophant of victory,' wrote Nicolson.[36] He left for Edinburgh to review the Fleet. But Wigram regretted that the Navy failed to arrange 'for the King to see the Fleet going out or coming in to claim 'their due' — the surrender of the German Grand Fleet.[37]

It was then the Army's turn. The King visited all the battlefields, and communed with his soldiers. About the chief soldier, Haig, however, and the honour he was to receive, there was some predictable trouble with Downing Street, both about the honour itself and the victory parade. Just before starting off for France on 27 November, the King and his party heard that Lloyd George was trying to arrange a victory reception for the Supreme Allied commander, Marshal Foch, the French Prime Minister, Clemenceau, and the Italian Prime Minister, Orlando, and Haig, in London during the King's absence. 'Nice people,' Wigram commented drily in a letter home, obviously convinced that it was a plot by Lloyd George to enhance his position and belittle the King's.[38] Haig duly received a telephone request from the CIGS, Wilson, speaking from No10, asking him to join the ceremonial drive through London. He heard that he, Haig, would be in the fifth carriage, with none other than Sir Henry Wilson. That was too much — 'more of an insult than I could put up with, even from the Prime Minister.'[39] Wigram's comment on this was: 'The skunks'.[40] Haig refused to participate unless ordered to by the Army Council. Stamfordham telephoned him to stiffen his resolve by saying he was sure the King would be much displeased at such a thing occurring in his absence.

The question of Haig's peerage was also proving troublesome. He was offered a Viscountcy by Lloyd George, which he declined until his soldiers got their rewards, though his real reason was pique since French had been rewarded with a Viscountcy after being brought home for incompetence.

---

[36] Nicolson, *George V*, p 326.

[37] Wigram Papers, Wigram to Lady Wigram, 20 November 1918.

[38] Wigram Papers, Wigram to Lady Wigram, 27 November 1918.

[39] Blake, *Haig*, p 346.

[40] Wigram Papers, Wigram to Haig, 30 November 1918.

Wigram was pressing for a Dukedom, 'so as to raise Haig and the British army to their right place in the estimation of the people, and thus prevent the politicians from continuing to make us play 2nd fiddle to the French.'[41] The King did not like the suggestion, believing that the democratic times would be against the creation of a Dukedom. Stamfordham had a word with Hankey, who confirmed that the Prime Minister would never agree to a Dukedom. They settled for an Earldom.

There was some other horsetrading to be done to satisfy some of the King's grumbles, and to calm the Prime Minister's fears. The King had suggested that Asquith be a delegate to the Versailles Peace Conference, though Lloyd George would not have it. He stonewalled until the question became irrelevant, Asquith having lost his seat in the snap general election called in December 1918. Another disagreement arose over the visit of President Wilson, whom the War Cabinet invited to London on Boxing Day. Stamfordham telephoned Hankey, with the King grumbling in the background about the ruination of his Sandringham holiday. His objections were put to the War Cabinet by Balfour, who reported back that the Cabinet's decision stood. It was a small point to lose to his Ministers especially as George V had, throughout the war, won so many points against them.

---

[41] Wigram Papers, Wigram to Lady Wigram, 1 December 1918.

4

Adjusting to a Changed Climate

King George V's reign divides clearly into two halves — before 1918, and afterwards. The whole climate in which he had to operate after 1918 had changed. As we have seen, Wigram was fully alive to this and the need for the Monarchy to make adjustments if it was to survive. There were, however, obstacles at Court. 'It is very hard to get a move on here,' Wigram wrote four days after the Armistice:

> Stamfordham produces the most excellent suggestions which he picks up dining out, but does not wait [ie persist] till the King says yes. I stand by like a Bookie's clerk. I had an hour with the Queen — very plain talking — and we discussed reorganisation here, a very necessary plan. I told HM the Household in these days could not hold one Dud, and that we had too many. I think Wal [Sir Edward Wallington became Treasurer to Queen Mary in 1919] is doomed — he is really a National Danger in the way he obstructs. As for Douglas Dawson [Comptroller of the Lord Chamberlain's Office], he grows more "gagga" daily. It is hard luck on Their Majesties to have such barnacles . . .[1]

The popular press had already waded in by referring to the 'Palace Troglodytes'. Wigram agreed: 'There are too many T's or Duds here, and I welcome these articles if only they will lead to drastic action.'[2]

Old Lord Esher was not to be left out of any symposium. He joined in with a solemn note to Stamfordham:

---

[1] Wigram Papers, Wigram to Lady Wigram, 15 November 1918.
[2] Wigram Papers, Wigram to Lady Wigram, 22 November 1918.

We stand at the parting of the ways. Some risks will have to be run. The Monarchy and its cost will have to be justified in the future in the eyes of a war-worn and hungry proletariat, endowed with a huge preponderance of voting power. I see a great future for the King in connection with the consolidation of "Imperial" control of our public affairs; but imagination and boldness will be required, necessitating the abandonment of many old theories of Constitutional Kingship. The King and Queen will have to take risks. The strength of Republicanism lies in the *personality* of Wilson [the US President], and the use he has made of his position . . . It is a lesson. He has made the "fashion" of a Republic. We can "go one better" if we try.[3]

There was, of course, opposition to this modernisation. When in 1919 the Prince of Wales asked Sir Frederick Ponsonby for his opinion on how he was getting on, Ponsonby replied that there was a risk in becoming too accessible. 'The Monarchy must always remain on a pedestal.'[4] The Prince disagreed. He replied that times had changed since the war and he felt that one of his tasks must be to bring the institution nearer the people.

His parents were of the same mind, but some of their courtiers less so. In January 1915 Wigram bewailed an incident in which Derek Keppel (Master of the King's Household) and Dawson had endeavoured to force a decision out of the King about future Court and State functions. They caught the King when he was very tired and, Wigram later reported: 'I am thankful to say that the Queen was summoned and knocked the monstrous ideas on the head. Of course a carefully selected committee is required to go into all these questions and to see how the various classes of the community can be accommodated. If Derek and Douglas Dawson try to rush the King we shall come a cropper . . . neither of them will move with the times, and are quite out of date . . .'[5]

Wigram was pressing for the complete revision of the old Court and State functions, opening them up to more than just the political establishment and the aristocracy. He felt that feathers and long trains at Court should be abolished. The next government could be a Labour one, and in these circumstances there was no place for stuffiness about the

---

[3] RA, PS/GV/Q724/110, Esher to Stamfordham, 4 November 1918.

[4] The Duke of Windsor, *A King's Story* (Cassele London, 1951), p 136.

[5] RA, GV/GG6, Wigram to Cromer, 2 January 1919.

Court. For instance there was no official retiring age for courtiers. 'There are many well over 70 who have no business to be there. The organisation and inner workings of some of the departments are puerile and pre-Victorian.'[6] The Palace troglodytes were, however, against Wigram. They opposed any modifications of the Court functions as lowering to the dignity and status of the Sovereign. 'They are hard nuts to deal with . . . We are up against them but the barriers have to be broken if the monarchy is to live.'[7]

Harry Verney, Groom-in-Waiting, was thinking along the same lines as Wigram. In a long memorandum, which he submitted to Wigram, he made a series of generalised suggestions for reforming the Court. Verney felt the King should be more exposed to the opinions of people other than his present advisers. The King should not abrogate any further prerogatives, and certainly not agree to award honours to people like Max Aitken (the first Lord Beaverbrook). 'Does the Labour man care a damn about these rich nonentities being created peers? Would he not more admire an attitude in the Sovereign of only rewarding men who have rendered distinguished service to the State — service which can be announced publicly — and not some dirty party work which can not even bear mention in the Press. These honours have done incalculable harm — but only to the King.'[8]

The Monarchy should be more studied and popularised, Verney thought. He recommended that all members of the Royal Family should be involved — the Princes and Princess Mary, whose governess, Mlle Dussau, should be pensioned off since 'she is now doing harm to Princess Mary's position and may become mischievous in the Household'. The Princess should be allowed out and about, visiting the great teaching colleges from where 'one of the greatest dangers to the Monarchy is to be feared — in the future — from their training and teaching'. The Princes should take steps

> to know personally almost every officer in the Brigade of Guards and through the officers get into some sort of touch with the thoughts and ideas of the rank and file. Revolution or no revolution — the King is safe if his Guards are all loyal to him. Is enough done to inculcate into young officers of the Navy and Army the fact that their loyalty is owed to

---

[6]   RA, GV/GG6, Wigram to Lang, 3 January 1919.

[7]   *Ibid.*

[8]   RA, GV/GG6, Verney to Wigram, 7 February 1918, enclosing memorandum.

the King?

Verney argued that the lower classes did not respect the King for being 'shabby in his "turn outs" because it is wartime'.[9] Nor was it sensible to try to make everybody tee-total in wartime. Moreover, the Royal Family should do more to give generously from their private purses to victims of special disasters, and such kindnesses should be made widely known. The National Anthem should be sung after every Anglican church service; the popular press should be read by the Palace as much as *The Times* and *The Morning Post* (Stamfordham saw that this was done); dinners and lunches at the Palace should be resumed and thrown open to a wider public (an innovation adopted by Elizabeth II some 40 years later!).

Wigram and Verney were merely two voices in a confusion of advice which must have swirled around the King and the Queen during those troubled postwar years, with the memory of the execution of their Russian cousins still lingering in their minds. It is a tribute to George V's innate common sense that he was susceptible to the changed climate and adjusted his procedures and perceptions accordingly. He did this without denting or changing his essential integrity, or remoulding the opinionated, authoritarian, profoundly conservative personality which he had brought to the Throne.

With the more far-seeing courtiers contributing to this reformulation of the role of the monarch, it is not surprising that things changed. But the opaqueness of the Monarchy, when you actually try to peer into its core, makes it difficult to discern how it changes, when it changes, and who decides that it should be changed. These things may be documented somewhere, but they do not often see the light of day, even in the official biographies. Yet change the Monarchy did.

Of course the King was fortunate in one sense, that the political situation did not for the rest of his reign expose him to quite such dangers as he had faced in the first four years. There was no talk of civil war; no talk of mutiny; no movement to restructure the constitution in a way which threatened the pillars of the Crown in Parliament. And yet something changed about his conduct of affairs. Interventions there continued to be, but somehow these were seldom reinforced with such an uncompromising

---

[9] *Ibid.*

assumption of his right to intervene as one detected during the war, and on many occasions before it. It was all very different in Russia; and after all there was no regicide when the central European monarchies were abolished. Somehow, though, the events of 1914-1918 had put all monarchies on probation. It was George V's achievement that his probation ended in triumph, in contrast with the fate of his cousin, the deposed German Emperor, William II.

The future of the Kaiser became rather a tangled one in the King's mind. Although Wigram seems to have formed the private view that the King wanted to see the Kaiser court-martialled, that was not at all the impression George V gave to his Ministers, or to Hankey, that repository of all Royal confidences, criticisms and perplexities where matters of official policy were concerned. In November 1918 Lord Curzon was keen for the Kaiser to stand trial. The King contacted him to show him a memorandum he had received from several German Princes warning him that such punishment might apply to a British King in future. Curzon prised the information out of Lloyd George, who said he had already heard all the arguments against the trial from the King — every one of them. The King did not like the idea of the Kaiser being tried by an 'international' tribunal, and agreed with Stamfordham who thought the best course was exile (eg the Falkland Islands) and no trial.

Again, when Lloyd George wished to announce to the House of Commons in June 1919 that the Kaiser would stand trial in England, Stamfordham pointed out, on behalf of the King, that President Wilson had said the trial should not take place in any big city. The King was against his cousin's being arraigned in his own capital city, and was doubly distressed to learn of such a decision — so affecting him personally — from the newspapers rather than through official channels. Hankey, as a consequence, received possibly the sharpest reprimand of his career. But the alarm was uncalled for, since the Dutch government refused the extradition of the Kaiser.

Whatever his disgust for the Kaiser's policies, however, the King cannot have felt at ease discussing the disposal of a man who had, after all, strutted, or jogged saddle to saddle with him, past so many guards of honour, had shared their royal caparisons, been united in pomp and heredity. The years and events in between served as a cruel reminder of how easily adversity could sever the connection between a crowned head and the body politic and people of his country.

The relationship between George V and Lloyd George, in spite of its inauspicious beginning and the more or less constant suspicion with which the King's courtiers regarded the Prime Minister's intrigues, prospered enormously during the peace. The King was not a suspicious man; sensitive yes — hypersensitive to criticism; meticulous; conventional, even obsessive about social, political and constitutional proprieties. But after the war he soon shed his doubts about Lloyd George's motives and the latter's hostility to the soldiers, although these suspicions were still harboured by the King's private secretaries. George V had always admired Lloyd George's courage and energy, and came no doubt to value the efforts he was making to cope with the difficulties of the peace. Somehow the pronounced conservatism of the pre-war King had been purged, or at least neutralised by years of coalition government — a natural and preferred state of things for most sovereigns, perhaps. Besides, Lloyd George was perched on top of a government which existed predominantly through Tory support, with the broken-backed Asquithian Liberals and the Labour Party acting as the Opposition. It was thus obviously easier to cope with Lloyd George in such a context. But the King's feelings for the little Welshman were much warmer than that.

When Bonar Law resigned for reasons of ill-health in 1921, Lloyd George discussed with Stamfordham whether or not the coalition government should be maintained. Stamfordham passed on these worries to the King, who wrote to his Private Secretary in the most fulsome terms about Lloyd George:

> I am sorry the Prime Minister is low on account of BL's resignation: but he must not be despondent as I firmly believe he is now more necessary to this country than he ever was and that the vast majority of the people are behind him . . . I should agree to any thing that would help him most . . . You can tell the PM that I have complete confidence in him and will do everything in my power to help him . . . I am very strong in maintaining a coalition government. I am sure it is the best plan at the present moment until these very difficult questions have been settled. Anyhow I am against a general election which would upset everything. There really ought to be two PMs! No man can do the work he, LG, has to do now. I quite understand his feeling lonely and almost lost without BL who did so much for him.[10]

---

[10] Lord Beaverbrook, *Men and Power, 1917-18* (Hutchinson, London, 1956), pp 337-8.

Lloyd George then stayed on as Prime Minister for another year, secure in the confidence of the King, if not of the Conservative Party, which eventually toppled him.

This mutual confidence grew, presumably, not so much because the King merely listened to Lloyd George at the weekly audience, and agreed with what he said (often he did not, and would never hesitate to speak out when he disagreed). Indeed the King was not on the whole one of nature's listeners. He was an inveterate talker. In his dealings with Lloyd George he made his presence felt all the time. Hankey or Grigg (the new Private Secretary at No 10 Downing Street) were constantly at the receiving end of instructions, complaints, queries, or suggestions. No doubt the weekly audience consisted of the same mixture. There is no sign that Lloyd George much resented it; perhaps he felt, with that professional paranoia so common to politicians, that it was worth putting up with any kind of schoolmasterly interference from someone who was clearly no political threat whatever, and actually seemed to be behind him on the big things, even if the little things gave rise to difficulties. And there were many little things about the governance of the country into which the King delved, almost every day. He saw it as his job to do so.

This often produced brushes between Stamfordham and Hankey about the King's being properly informed. It was not only Wigram who felt haunted by the spectre of no proper or regular flow of information. It was a recurring worry at the Palace, since without information how could the work of monitoring, prodding, advising and warning be done at all? Stamfordham still hankered for the personal Cabinet reports from the Prime Minister which were dropped when the War Cabinet and Cabinet secretariat was set up in 1916. He often complained on behalf of the King to Hankey about some failure to inform them of a decision taken by the Cabinet. Hankey would painstakingly turn up the relevant papers and prove that the Palace had been on the distribution list. In one case Stamfordham apologised. Another dispute concerned the Speech from the Throne. The King insisted on brevity, and on seeing a first draft, not the final one. It was the King, who after having misgivings shared by Hankey, saw to it that the Cabinet adopted the idea of the burial of the 'Unknown Soldier' at Westminster Abbey. On any matters covering ceremonial or the military the Cabinet would have thought twice before disagreeing with the King. Lord French received a direct and stinging rebuke for publishing his war memoirs.

It was not only the Prime Minister whose services the King had come to regard as indispensable. When Hardinge retired as Permanent Under-Secretary at the Foreign Office, Hankey was considered for the post. Esher wrote to Hankey saying that the King had flown into a fury at hearing the rumour and said that Hankey was the most important public servant in Whitehall, and the only possible link between government and any successive Sovereign. He added that Hankey was the guardian of the tradition of government and that he (the King) would die in the last ditch or go on hunger strike rather than allow him to accept the Foreign Office.

There was also much genuine concern at the Palace about unemployment, as attested by the volume of correspondence on the subject between Stamfordham and the Prime Minister's office. Stamfordham pressed both Lloyd George and then Hankey on the matter, urging that it be brought before the Cabinet. The King was hoping that the government's measures to alleviate it would involve work rather than simply the dole. During the threatened strike of coal, transport and rail workers in April 1921, the King was on hand to endorse emergency measures by Royal Proclamation. He was urgently summoned from Windsor to preside over the Privy Council, arriving just in time to catch Parliament before it rose for the weekend. After the Privy Council he apologised that, owing to the rush, he was attired in a frock coat and *brown boots*. Hardly a terrible solecism, but one he felt keenly about, since he had ticked off F E Smith (later, as Lord Chancellor, Lord Birkenhead) for wearing a brown bowler.

There were also the big questions, like Ireland. The Sinn Fein Party had captured 73 out of 105 Irish seats in the 1918 general election and declared Ireland an independent Republic. They were not given a proper hearing in Britain, so decided to resort to a campaign of terrorism and murder against British rule. This was met with counter-terror on the part of the British authorities, who reinforced the hard-pressed army and official constabulary with specially recruited ex-servicemen, called the 'Black and Tans' from their distinctive uniform. Violence flourished, for the 'Black and Tans' were loathed in Ireland and regarded with distrust by Westminster. The King, who increasingly came to see himself as the father of his people, was very unhappy at the persistent evidence that his Irish subjects were the victim of a wholly untenable policy of official reprisals. He badgered the government and officials in Dublin to give an account of themselves.

The King himself was due to go over to Belfast in June 1921 to open
the first session of the Ulster parliament, which had been established as a
separate entity under the Government of Ireland Act of the previous year.
Shortly before his departure from London he met Field Marshal Smuts,
the South African Prime Minister, and told him how much he deplored
the violence in the southern half of Ireland. Together they concocted a
plan whereby the King should use his speech from the Throne in Belfast
to appeal for reconciliation in Ireland. This raised an awkward
constitutional question, since it would have been unwise for the King to
suggest to his Ministers what the content of such an important speech
should be, though it was clear that the King's approach would certainly
be more conciliatory than that being drafted by Lloyd George. The King's
draft was therefore submitted with a letter from Smuts to Lloyd George.
Meanwhile Stamfordham went to Downing Street to complain that the
King was being kept in the dark about the speech he was due to make.
Lloyd George immediately scrapped the official draft prepared in the Irish
Office, and Grigg was commissioned to prepare a new one, which earned
the King's approval. The King's appeal at Belfast on 22 June 1921 for an
end to the feuding had a rapturous reception. Lloyd George himself came
to Euston station to welcome him home and was unusually effusive in his
congratulations. The King soon afterwards followed the speech up with a
note pressing Lloyd George to lose no time in starting to negotiate with
Eamon de Valera, the Sinn Fein leader. With Smuts acting as a valuable
intermediary, and incidentally advising de Valera from personal experience
that Dominion status was much to be preferred over Republicanism, De
Valera came to London. He was indeed offered Dominion status, albeit
with some qualifications connected with national defence. The offer was
unanimously rejected by the Irish Parliament (the Dáil) meeting in Dublin
on 16 August, and deadlock seemed to have set in. Only the tenuous truce
on terrorist acts remained; but for how long was uncertain.

Communications between the various parties continued, and it fell to
the King at Balmoral in September 1921 to make one final and decisive
intervention. The Cabinet was intending to send de Valera a stiff note —
by way of an ultimatum — but after the King had been through the draft
with Lloyd George, inserting substantial amendments in the process, which
considerably softened the British position, the Cabinet convened in
Inverness Town Hall and accepted the King's revisions almost verbatim.
The King, showing an almost uncharacteristic patience and understanding

of the moody volatile temperament of de Valera, which so exasperated the Cabinet, counselled an open mind to his Prime Minister. The parties finally came together, and the Irish Treaty setting up 'The Irish Free State' as a Dominion within the Commonwealth was signed on 6 December 1921 and narrowly passed through the Dáil by a majority of seven. The King, in his diary, generously credited Lloyd George with that patience and conciliatory spirit which the record shows to have been fundamentally inspired by himself.

George V also kept closely in touch with developments in India. In June 1916 Hardinge had returned to the Foreign Office and had been succeeded as Viceroy by Lord Chelmsford. The King hardly knew Chelmsford and seems to have been in favour of Lord Willingdon, the Governor of Bombay, as Viceroy. When Chelmsford was succeeded by Lord Reading, George V unsuccessfully pressed Willingdon's case again. The King was undeterred by these reverses. As we shall see in the next chapter, he finally secured Willingdon's appointment years later in circumstances of great confusion.

Chelmsford's first letter to the King as Viceroy was a long description of all he had been doing, ending with a request for guidance as 'to any special subjects on which Your Majesty would prefer me to write'.[11] It was Stamfordham who told him to carry on in the same vein, reassuring him that the King welcomed his informative letters. The Viceroy's quarterly letter to the King was a definite and regular benchmark in their relationship. It was similarly expected of all Governors-General, and the letters came within the hallowed limits of the Royal Prerogative — unmonitored by Ministers and undisturbed by historians. The writers were encouraged to be chatty, informal, indiscreet — in other words the eyes and ears of the Monarch. An essential guarantee against those qualities being held against them in the official world was that the confidentiality of the correspondence should be inviolate.

In 1920 there was a spat when Stamfordham lost one of Chelmsford's letters. 'It is very difficult for the Viceroy to continue his letters to His Majesty when they are not even acknowledged,' Chelmsford complained.[12] His letter

---

[11] IOLR, Chelmsford Papers, MSS EUR E264/1, Chelmsford to King, 16 April 1916.
[12] IOLR, MSS EUR E264/1, Stamfordham to Chelmsford, 22 August 1916.

of the previous August had not been acknowledged, so he had not yet written another one. Stamfordham was embarrassed, but could not find the missing letter. So he merely assured Chelmsford that the King had begged him to go on writing. A less inhibited view of the matter was taken by J L Maffey (later Lord Rugby), Chelmsford's former private secretary, who had returned to London from Delhi to help organise the Prince of Wales' forthcoming tour. After a visit to the Palace, he reported to Chelmsford that the loss of the letter had 'led to recriminations and a great hooroosh in the Holy of Holies. Apparently Lord Stamfordham frequently loses letters and had lost this. Cromer told me that they have great difficulty with the King in the matter of letters. He cannot be persuaded to write himself to anybody!'[13]

The King used to find himself becoming particularly involved in matters affecting the Princes or the Chiefs (as we have seen), even more than in other developments of which the Viceroy kept him informed. The broad thrust of British policy in India was one with which he went along, since he fundamentally accepted the premise that democratic and legislative institutions had to be introduced into areas where Britain was the administrative authority. He did not feel that policy applied to the princely states. On the contrary he believed that the Princes and Chiefs themselves should be brought much more into the structure of authority.

Stamfordham wrote to Chelmsford in 1916 that:

> It has come to his [the King's] notice very recently that the loyalty of the Rajput Princes has been questioned by Government officials in responsible places, or by members of their families, and disparaging remarks made in society, which have been repeated and needless to say have come back to the ears of those who — the King considers — have been so cruelly slandered . . . The King is indignant that aspersions of this character should be made upon Princes of whose loyalty he has no doubts. Ever since His Majesty first went to India, he has been impressed with the feeling that upon the loyalty of the Ruling Princes and Chiefs our rule must greatly depend, and that they would be our great stand-by in case of any formidable internal troubles in India. His Majesty begs that you will do everything in your power to stop this ill-natured and dangerous talk, especially in official circles.[14]

---

[13] IOLR, MSS EUR, E264/16, Maffey to Chelmsford, 27 April 1920.
[14] IOLR, MSS EUR E264/1, Stamfordham to Chelmsford, 22 August 1916.

On some matters George V's authority and even prejudice had a fairly important effect on British policy — for good or ill. After the troubles with the Amir of Afghanistan in 1919, the Viceroy and his Council felt it right to recognise the Amir as 'King', particularly at a time when he was about to establish friendly relations with the new Bolshevik regime in Moscow — something that could become inimical to British interests throughout South Asia. The King reacted angrily to the idea of 'His Majesty' of Afghanistan. The King gave Maffey a terrible time, as Maffey later reported to Chelmsford: 'The King, with his superficial knowledge of the subject . . . had evidently proved an easy prey to Curzon.'[15] The former Viceroy disapproved of this and other policies being pursued by Montagu, the Secretary of State for India.

Maffey had a forty minute audience with the King:

> I realise now what is is to have an "audience" of the King. A timid person would be an audience and nothing else. However, I interrupted bravely and frequently and got my views out on the Afghan question which he introduced. Unfortunately, he knew so little about it . . . [and] had succumbed at an earlier stage to prejudiced criticism that I do not suppose I influenced him much. Still, when I put my points they seemed to go home all right and to be a very new light to him. But the real difficulty is that he is ignorant of the elements of the situation. He began by exclaiming — "We ought to have made them independent! — Whatever that means." I pointed out that Afghanistan always had been outside British India. He was vehement on the title of His Majesty, but finally agreed that it would be a good thing to concede it when an agreement is reached. On that subject you will find it wise to be patient.[16]

The King then indulged in one of his regular pastimes — most frequently employed during the war — of savaging the reputation of ministers to their officials. 'He made it quite plain that Montagu was not in his favour. Montagu knows nothing about India at all, absolutely nothing.'[17] This of the joint author of the Montagu-Chelmsford reforms which the King had incidentally welcomed when Chelmsford had explained them to him at

---

[15] IOLR, MSS EUR, E264/16, Maffey to Chelmsford, 27 April 1920 and doc 555a, Maffey to Chelmsford, 17 May 1920.

[16] *Ibid.*

[17] *Ibid.*

length some two years before! Maffey found Montagu in a shaken state as a result of the King's agitation. 'He [the King] realises that he is about the only monarch left with a secure throne and hates the idea of creating a "Majesty" that may be toppled over at any minute and add to the scrapheap of royalty. There is room for sympathy with this personal point of view.'[18]

The King's almost feudal affinity for the subordinate Princes in his Empire did not always involve him in matters of high policy or protocol. There were sometimes more ticklish details that Stamfordham and the Viceroy had to deal with. At the height of the war, when one would imagine that Stamfordham had much more important matters jostling for his (let alone the King's) attention, he wrote to Chelmsford that:

> His Majesty has heard with very much concern that things are not going satisfactorily with regard to the young Maharaja of Jodhpur. It is feared that he is getting into trouble through the influence of his native entourage, including some of his own family, who are encouraging him to drink, and to associate with low female company. If this is not stopped in time it is probable that he will come to grief in the same way as did his father, which would be deplorable not only for himself but for the State and the whole of the Rathar family. As you know the boy was at Wellington College and the King has taken a personal interest in him and he showed every promise of being a really good fellow. One knows how difficult it is even with the best European surroundings to keep these young natives straight, and combat the evil influence of the Harem.[19]

He asked the Viceroy to take all necessary steps to 'arrest the evil' if what he reported was true. The Viceroy — long suffering official that he was — reported a month later that the young Maharaja had contracted venereal disease, and had been to a 'quack' instead of a properly qualified doctor. So, at least, the Maharaja of Jodhpur told the Resident. Now, he assured the latter, all was going well.

The King took his position as the 'Fountain of Honour' extremely seriously. Although in practice Ministers proposed honours and George V gave his consent, he exercised his prerogative as fully as possible, scrutinising the proposed Honours Lists with a critical eye. He repeatedly tried to restrain

---

[18] *Ibid.*

[19] IOLR, MSS EUR, E264/1, Stamfordham to Chelmsford, 1 August 1917.

Lloyd George from debasing the Honours system in order to secure the political support of the Press and to boost the contents of party coffers. Lloyd George had some fifty newspaper editors and owners made Privy Counsellors, peers, baronets and knights (including Beaverbrook, Rothermere, Northcliffe and Riddell). Industrialists and financiers received some twenty-six peerages, one hundred and fifty baronetcies and four hundred and eighty-one knighthoods. By the summer of 1922, when Lloyd George had proposed the elevation of various war profiteers and fraudsters to the peerage, the King, parliament and the people had had enough. George V expressed to him his

> profound concern at the very disagreeable situation which has arisen on the question of honours . . . I do appeal most strongly for the establishment of some efficient and trustworthy procedure in order to protect the Crown and the Government from the possibility of similar painful if not humiliating incidents, the recurrence of which must inevitably constitute an evil, dangerous to the social and political well being of the state.[20]

Lloyd George was forced to appoint a Royal Commission, the result of which was the establishment of the Political Honours Scrutiny Committee of three Privy Counsellors (who were not Ministers) to examine the credentials of all honours candidates before their names were submitted to the Sovereign. By the Honours (Prevention of Abuses) Act of 1925 penalties were imposed on both those who promised honours in return for cash and those who promised cash for honours. (There was to be only one prosecution under the Act, that of Maundy Gregory in 1933.)

There were overseas dramas as well, which did not escape the King's eye for detail. In 1922 the King noticed that the minutes of one Cabinet meeting recorded Lloyd George as saying that the Greek defeat at the hands of the Turks in Anatolia 'had been engineered by King Constantine, who finding himself in an impossible position, had removed two divisions and replaced his C-in-C by "a courtier reputed to be mentally defective"!' Stamfordham informed the Prime Minister's Private Secretary, Grigg, that the King was 'somewhat disturbed' by this suggestion. 'Can you tell me for HM's information if the PM had good grounds for forming this impression? It

---

[20] Kenneth Rose, *King George V* (Macmillan, London, 1983), p 252.

seems almost inconceivable that King C should have so utterly and completely "let down" his Army . . . '[21] The King never liked to see other monarchs letting the side down, but he was equally sharp with accusations he thought were unfair. His query provoked a long carefully worded explanation from Grigg why the Prime Minister had misgivings about King Constantine's behaviour. The King's reply indicated that he did not share Lloyd George's misgivings.

It was the Chanak crisis in October 1922, involving the possibility of war between Britain and the newly invigorated Turkish revolutionary government of Mustapha Kemal (Ataturk), which finally broke the Lloyd George coalition. The King and his Prime Minister were in direct and constant touch throughout the crisis. Lloyd George, for once, kept up a personal correspondence with the King, who was at Balmoral with his special train standing by in case he was needed. According to Stamfordham, the Royal Proclamation necessary to requisition ships to carry troops was permanently ready for signature sitting in the despatch box which went everywhere with the King. The war scare over Chanak abated, but it was enough for the Conservative party to decide to withdraw its support from Lloyd George and run its own candidates at the ensuing general election.

Lloyd George had already warned the King that he might have to ask for an immediate dissolution. The King hoped he would, making clear his wish that Lloyd George would remain his Prime Minister. His hopes were not met. Hankey had a very British encounter with the Prime Minister in the lavatory at No 10 Downing Street. 'You have written your last Minutes for me. I have asked the King to come to town, and this afternoon I shall resign,' said Lloyd George.[22] 'I am sorry he is going,' the King wrote in his diary, 'but some day he will be Prime Minister again.'[23] The King was wrong; an error caused no doubt by being too close to his subject.

After Lloyd George resigned in October 1922 the King sent for Bonar Law, although the latter had not yet formally been acclaimed as leader of the Conservatives. The post was still occupied by Austen Chamberlain,

---

[21] Bodleian Library, Altrincham Papers, MS Film 1000, Stamfordham to Grigg, 9 September 1922.

[22] Roskill, *Hankey*, Vol 2, p 296.

[23] Nicolson, *George V*, p 371.

who remained loyal to Lloyd George and opposed the Conservatives' decision to cut adrift from him. Bonar Law was told he had better look sharp, since the King needed a government to ratify the Irish Treaty before 6 December. Bonar Law duly complied. Then cancer of the throat struck the relatively 'unknown Prime Minister' and he went off on prolonged sick leave in April 1923, leaving Lord Curzon, the Foreign Secretary, in charge of the government. Bonar Law resigned the following month. He was to die in November.

As it was the Whitsun weekend, most senior politicians, including Curzon, the acting Prime Minister, were out of London. Significantly, Stanley Baldwin, Chancellor of the Exchequer and Leader of the House of Commons, was not. The King now had to choose between these two men. Harold Nicolson, the King's official biographer, has contended that Bonar Law was himself too ill to make any precise recommendation.[24] However, there were many Tory elders to hand, no doubt eager to advise the King. Lord Salisbury, it seems, was of the view that Curzon's claims should not lightly be ignored. Yet there is (in the archives at Hatfield) a letter to him from Stamfordham, written on the morning of 22 May before the issue was settled by the appointment of Baldwin that afternoon, which reads:

> all I have learnt directly or indirectly from Bonar's family is to the effect that, eliminating the *personal* factor and having regard to the larger issues involved he would, if asked to advise the King, have been in favour of the Prime Minister remaining in the House of Commons. With this knowledge & bearing in mind that before Bonar's operation the King was begged not to seek for his advice, I do not see that any advantage would be gained by now approaching the family in order to obtain from Bonar an opinion which they consider he has already expressed and which I have quoted above. The King will settle this afternoon upon whom he sends for — This may influence your plans.[25]

Stamfordham also reached for his pen to confide his thoughts to an old friend, Sir George Murray, who had been Rosebery's Private Secretary at No 10 Downing Street during Stamfordham's early years at the Palace:

> If ever a Sovereign had a difficult situation to handle George V has got one now . . . even if all ministers were here . . . I don't see much use in

---

[24] *Ibid*, p 377.
[25] Hatfield, Salisbury Papers, 4M/105/51.

consulting them excepting Curzon and he is the very one whose opinion at this period cannot be asked for, so I suggested to HM that I should have a talk with you and luckily you are at hand. Meanwhile I have asked Balfour to come to London to see *me*. He ought to be able to advise, always assuming he don't want to be PM himself. It seems to me to be either Curzon or Baldwin. The former has all the vast experience of both Houses, the intellect and ability, power of debate, knowledge of foreign affairs, *but* he is in the House of Lords. They say he is quite out of touch with the character both of the constitution and the debating part of the present House of Commons. He is the protagonist of thoroughgoing conservatism and is, I am afraid, personally unpopular. Baldwin is inexperienced as Leader of the House of Commons and absolutely ignorant of the special work of a PM but I am told he would be acceptable to the party. Another point against GNC [George Nathaniel Curzon] is that the House of Commons with Bonar as PM to lead was almost dangerously weak, but minus Bonar and with Baldwin only Curzon's lieutenant . . . it would from the government's point of view be perilously exposed to its enemies. BL's condition is such that he cannot be consulted. The *King must* settle and do what is best for the country — but I am afraid Curzon will consider that the reversion is his. The King is in that happy position that if he sends for anyone they will at once assume he is to be the man.[26]

Lord Balfour, the only surviving Conservative ex-Prime Minister, came up from Sheringham in secret to be consulted by Stamfordham. He recommended against the Premiership going to a member of the Lords. Stamfordham gave him to understand that the King held a very similar view, *viz* that the head of the government must be in the House of Commons where he could answer with authority the leader of the opposition Labour Party (which was not represented in the House of Lords). 'And will dear George get the premiership?' asked the ladies at Balfour's house party on his return. 'No,' said he with confidence, 'dear George will not'.[27] He was right; but 'dear George' thought otherwise. According to Leonard Mosley's biography of Curzon, Baldwin had been told by Bonar Law that, though he was not making a recommendation, Curzon would get the Premiership. Bonar Law's Personal Private Secretary, Colonel Ronald Waterhouse, who delivered the Prime Minister's resignation to Stamfordham, also submitted

---

[26] Blair Castle, Sir George Murray papers, Bundle 1681, Stamfordham to Murray, 20 May 1923.

[27] Winston S Churchill, *Great Contemporaries* (Thornton Butterworth, London, 1937), p 287.

a memorandum from J C C (later Lord) Davidson, Bonar Law's Parliamentary Private Secretary, which allegedly recommended Baldwin by improperly assuming that Bonar Law had endorsed him. This was subsequently held by the Curzon camp to have unduly influenced the King in Baldwin's favour, but the tone of Stamfordham's letter to Murray suggests that Davidson's memorandum could not have been decisive.

Stamfordham and Curzon have left memorable accounts of their meeting on 22 May at which Curzon was told that he was not to get the Premiership. The meeting occurred before, but only just before, the King appointed Baldwin. Curzon, apart from his personal disappointments, was quick to see that a principle might be at stake behind Stamfordham's explanation that the King wanted to find a Prime Minister in the Commons. Did this forever rule out a Prime Minister in the Lords? Stamfordham did not deny the point, though the King did when he met the disappointed Curzon later. Such a restoration would have been an unjustifiable infringement of his prerogative. There had been no Prime Minister in the Lords since Rosebery, but nothing then or since has explicitly ruled out the possibility.

Six months into his premiership the inexperienced Baldwin made one of the most spectacular miscalculations in British political history when he asked for a dissolution of Parliament in order to fight a general election over Tariff Reform. The King 'most reluctantly' granted the dissolution, saying that he had confidence in the Conservative government. A general election on such a divisive issue might plunge the country into the kind of chaos then being seen on the Continent and Baldwin might lose his majority. But Baldwin had committed himself too far to go back at this point. The results of the election on 8 December 1923 was not to his or the King's liking. The pro-Tariff Reform Conservatives lost ninety seats, together with their overall majority over the Free Trade parties. The final tally was Conservative, 258, Labour, 191, and Liberal, 158 (it was perhaps the only genuine three party election in the twentieth century).

Baldwin wanted to resign immediately. The King restrained him, quite properly advising him that, as leader of the largest party, and as the sitting Prime Minister, he should wait to face Parliament, and then only resign after defeat in the House of Commons. The King doubtless wanted to give him, and everybody else, time to adjust to the imminent prospect of the leader of the Labour Party, Ramsay MacDonald, becoming Prime Minister, meanwhile ensuring the continuance of government. There were many suggestions to Stamfordham about alternative courses of action, some doubtless attractive to the old courtier who was much more alarmed about the Labour Party than the King was. George V never seemed to waver from his view — the simple, common-sense view, so often his standby when there was confusion in the ranks of Tuscany — that after Baldwin was defeated in the House of Commons he should ask MacDonald to form a government (even though Labour had won just 30 per cent of the votes and held only 30 per cent of the seats in the House of Commons).

The day of decision eventually arrived when the King opened the new Parliament on 15 January 1924. Six days later at the end of the customary debate on the Address, Labour and the Liberals united to defeat the Conservatives by 72 votes on an amendment to the Address. Baldwin resigned on 22 January. The King, without in any way consulting his retiring Prime Minister, sent for MacDonald. The tension of the moment was no doubt relieved by the very complicated official procedure which was masterminded by the redoubtable Hankey.

Hankey had seen that the first complication was the fact that Ramsay MacDonald was not even a Privy Councillor. So Baldwin, before he resigned, had to recommend to the King to make him one. Hankey became ensnared in all sorts of constitutional wrangles with Stamfordham, the Speaker of the House of Commons, and even the King, over questions of timing, and the precedents for each and every stage of the change-over. Later he was to recount how Stamfordham kept telephoning him and he could hear the King's voice in the background, raising objections.

Hankey also related later how:

> I was sent for by the King who kept me for an hour talking over the arrangements for the next day's council to administer the oath of office to the next govt. I warned the King that hardly any were likely to possess frock coats. He didn't like it, but agreed to leave me to do my best. He gave me the list of new Ministers Ramsay MacDonald had just given to him and we gossiped and speculated about them.

Hankey was then called to the House of Commons, to meet MacDonald and his designated Cabinet and to explain exactly how they were to comport themselves at Buckingham Palace. He 'drilled them in the various formalities.'[28] He also cautioned them about dress. But, as he anticipated,

---

[28] Roskill, *Hankey*, Vol 2, p 356.

there were hardly any frock coats, and not too many available tail coats even!

In fact the King was as nervous of the impending meeting as they were, and was desperately keen to make it all work and to establish good relations with his new Ministers, especially with MacDonald. As soon as MacDonald had taken the oath as a Privy Councillor the King had an hour's talk with him. Both men spoke with some candour about their problems. It was an auspicious start. The King confided to his diary his initial opinion of MacDonald: 'He impressed me very much; he wishes to do the right thing. Today 23 years ago dear Grandmama died. I wonder what she would have thought of a Labour Government.'[29]

---

[29] Rose, *George V*, p 326.

5

In the Sunlight of His Days

The main domestic challenge which the King faced from 1924 was to achieve the absorption of the Labour party into the system of constitutional monarchy and to establish in the minds of Socialists that the Crown, whatever its class base, and whatever the cut of its cloth, was symbolically above the political battle. It was impartial as between party, constant as regards confidence, dedicated only to the preservation of moderate, humane government — in short, the King's charge. On the face of it, the King might not have appeared to be the most suitable person to achieve this new understanding. He was at heart a Victorian; by instinct, authoritarian; stylistically patrician in his pursuits, and socially olympian. But, as has been remarked, he was also, in spite of the trappings, the apotheosis of the ordinary man.[1] There was no vulgarity about his Court. Something more close to a temple to common sense and good manners would have been hard to find. While these qualities may not have combined naturally even with Fabian enthusiasms, they carried with them their own *bona fides*. They were certainly enough to convince leading members of the Labour Party, until the cleavage of 1931, that, in the King and his close advisers, they were not beholding the symbol of the 'class enemy'.

Of course the class-enemy bogey worked both ways, and the spectre of Socialist government had for some time haunted the imaginations of the King's courtiers, even though they adopted a stoical attitude to the inevitable. Two years before the advent of the first Labour government, in

---

[1] Robert Lacey, *Majesty: Elizabeth II and the House of Windsor* (Hutchenson London, 1977), p 30.

a discussion with Grigg on the merits of the Prime Minister 'keeping a grasp upon all the various Government Departments . . . ', Stamfordham had sounded a gloomy note about the coming Socialist Millenium:

> we are gradually but undoubtedly drifting towards a "One Man Government". If so, more than ever will it be necessary to have a strong Government and an equally strong Opposition — without an over-preponderating majority — otherwise the Government of the Country may develop into an autocracy of a very dangerous character, especially if we look ahead and contemplate the possibility of the Labour Party in Office.[2]

In fact the King and his advisers could not have wished for an easier Parliamentary setting in which they and the whole body politic were to adjust to the arrival of the first Socialist government. The Parliamentary arithmetic neutralised all Stamfordham's dark predictions, and made certain that no Labour administration would be formed with a full and unfettered Parliamentary majority until 1945. Nevertheless they handled the whole situation with great caution. As always, the King was averse to any change, but was quick to adjust to and almost welcome the consequence of such change once it was forced upon him.

The King was affability itself, and his new Labour ministers responded warmly. He made a point of indulging MacDonald's literary tastes and sense of history by conducting him round the library at Windsor. Later that summer the Labour ministers were in attendance at Balmoral and Queen Mary took them for drives in the Highlands. The King presented MacDonald with a memorandum, doubtless prepared by Stamfordham, summarising the procedure to be followed in their relationship. It is a keynote memorandum, reproduced in full in Harold Nicolson's official biography.[3] It provides the best possible insight into the special ingredients of the relationship between the Sovereign and the Prime Minister. The key to it is not policy; it is procedure. There is nothing about policy, but everything about procedure, and none of the procedures concerned could be held up by any self-respecting politician as restrictive or intolerable. Most of them are based on courtesy, and respect for the Throne. Yet they

---

[2]   Bod, Altrincham Papers, MS Film 1000, Stamfordham to Grigg, 27 January 1922.

[3]   Nicolson, *George V*, pp 388-9.

do, as a result, weave the two principals together in a way which means that the Prime Minister, whatever his policies, is bound by convention and procedure to associate the King — if only strictly on an information basis — with almost every act of government. Although nothing is said about the consequence of the King's approval *NOT* being obtained, it is clear from the note that it would be a positive breach of convention if it were not obtained. Such an omission would justify a complaint from the Palace which would have to be answered. If the answer was that the omission had been inadvertent, an apology would no doubt follow, thus establishing a procedure for the future. If, on the other hand, the procedure had been deliberately breached, the Prime Minister would have to explain himself. Otherwise there would clearly be political consequences. The King would, after all, then be at liberty himself to breach the convention by, for instance, withholding his approval from appointments or honours, which could make the day-to-day task of political administration very difficult for the Prime Minister. Sovereign and Prime Minister were thus bound to each other by chains of convention, precedent, respect, courtesy — qualities which in themselves might be considered secondary. But in aggregate they combined to create an everyday relationship which assumes considerable constitutional significance. It meant really that the King had to be informed. It adds the fourth 'right' — the right to know — to the others enshrined by Bagehot — to be consulted, to encourage, and to warn — which have been accepted doctrine ever since, but which could, if one considers it all closely, be almost meaningless, and certainly irrelevant, without the knowledge of the situation to give them weight.

One other sensible change occurred in the relationship between the Palace and Parliament as a result of MacDonald's premiership. This concerned the question of Household appointments, which hitherto had changed when the Ministry changed. MacDonald had no suitable or willing candidates to fill these posts at Court. After some discussion with the King and Stamfordham it was agreed that the Lord Chamberlain, Master of the Horse and Lord Steward would all cease to be political appointments, but would become permanent apolitical members of the Household, as would three of the six Lords-in-Waiting. The other three Lords-in-Waiting and three officers in the House of Commons (who acted as Whips) were to remain at the disposal of the Prime Minister. This compromise has survived until the present day.

The King did not have long to get to know Ramsay MacDonald before his government was defeated in the House of Commons on 8 October 1924 on a vote of censure over 'The Campbell Affair'. The latter case involved the withdrawal by the Attorney-General, Sir Patrick Hastings, of a prosecution for sedition against J L Campbell, the acting editor of a Communist publication, *The Workers Weekly*. MacDonald asked for a dissolution on 9 October which, in normal circumstances, he might not have received. The King only granted it with reluctance. He believed, rightly or wrongly, that the country shared his hatred of frequent general elections. Indeed, he felt strongly enough to send a note to MacDonald stating his view. He did not think the issue was vital enough for an election, though MacDonald had told the House of Commons that it was a matter of confidence on which he would resign if defeated. The King's fear was that an election, after only a year, might return the three main political parties to the House of Commons in roughly the same numbers as before, so that nothing would have been gained. The established doctrine about Prime Ministers and dissolutions was that they were normally entitled to them if they commanded a majority in the House of Commons, but not when they did not. What was to stop the King accepting MacDonald's resignation and asking Baldwin if he could form a government, since he led by far the largest party in the Commons? The King had in fact already satisfied himself on this question by ascertaining from the leaders of the two other parties that they were either unable or unwilling to form an administration. One other factor might have weighed heavily in the balance. A refusal of MacDonald's request was open to misunderstanding by the Labour Party, possibly with dire consequences for the future. So a dissolution was granted, a general election held, and Baldwin was returned with an impressive majority (413 seats). The outcome of the election had been influenced by the letter from Zinoviev, the President of the Comintern, instructing the British Communist Party to enlist Labour supporters for the armed struggle. This letter (recently proved to have been faked by a rogue MI 6 officer) was released by the Foreign Office to *The Daily Mail* four days before the vote. MacDonald felt that the Comintern and the Foreign Office had cost him the election.

After the fall of the first Labour government in 1924, George V was not called upon to face any unprecedented situation as he had so often in the past. The last twelve years of his reign were eventful, but the mixture of events was all in one way or another familiar. By 1924 he had faced civil war, constitutional crisis, mutiny, coalitions, hung parliaments, difficulties over the selection of Prime Ministers and even strikes. After 1924, with the exception of the Invergordon Mutiny in 1931, which was somehow less alarming than the episode at the Curragh, only coalition, of that daunting list of challenges, recurred. Moreover, his part in the formation and maintenance of the National Government was not really comparable to his involvement with the Cabinet during the Asquith-Lloyd George changeover in 1916, let alone the dramatic forays he had made into the quagmire of Irish policy both before and after the First World War.

With Baldwin back in the saddle between 1924 and 1929, there was something like a return to routine. The General Strike of 1926 caused momentary alarm. The King was uncertain whether it fell within ordinary politics or was more revolutionary, both in intent and in fact. He approached the subject with caution, in view of his natural distaste for conflict among his people. He was anxious that his sons should be kept out· of it. This was difficult to achieve, given the charged and militant response to the strike in London society. The Prince of Wales defied his ruling, and lent his car and chauffeur to transport the Government newspaper to Wales. Hankey's advice throughout was balanced, and not unsympathetic to the miners, which probably helped keep the Palace view in perspective. The King's advice to Ministers was persistently conciliatory.

The King, as usual, revealed a constant touchiness about procedure, particularly 'leaks' which breached his understanding that no Cabinet business should become public knowledge without his permission. This was a tall order and one which, on the whole, he only felt strongly about when the royal prerogative was concerned, such as appointments in the gift of the Crown. Hankey was normally the channel of complaint, and often managed to persuade the King not to pursue a matter once he had got it off his chest. When Stamfordham celebrated his eightieth birthday he wrote to Hankey to say their relations had been a 'joy'. Hankey in his quiet, punctilious way noted that this was an exaggeration as they had just had a tiff over summoning Royal Princes to Privy Council meetings, with Hankey having to apologise for his failure to follow precedent. Joy there may not have been, but Stamfordham was correct in his assessment of Hankey's importance. Later on, during the second Labour government from 1929 to 1931, the King was again badgering Hankey about an international proposal over the rights of belligerents at sea — something the King seemed to feel very strongly about, as he had some knowledge of the subject. According to Hankey he gave Philip Snowden, the Labour Chancellor of the Exchequer, 'a bit of his mind' on the subject, and when Hankey entered the Cabinet room the Prime Minister said: 'Here is Sir Maurice Hankey. As long as he remains in office there are two institutions which are quite safe. One is the Monarchy. The other our Maritime Belligerent Rights.'[4]

In December 1928 the King fell seriously ill, and six Councillors of State were appointed under the Regency Act. Any three of them could discharge his essential functions. The councillors were the Queen, the Prince of Wales, the Duke of York, the Archbishop of Canterbury, the Lord Chancellor and the Prime Minister. George V's convalescence took a long time; for six weeks he did not even see Stamfordham. Indeed, he was still recuperating at Windsor when the general election in May 1929 returned another hung parliament. Labour had 287 seats, the Conservatives 261, and the Liberals 59.

Stamfordham was immediately at pains to point out that the new situation was different from that of 1923. 'Then Baldwin came back with the largest number of his party in the House of Commons but not an overall majority; now Ramsay has the highest number though also not an overall majority. Personally I think Baldwin ought to resign,' he told Sir George Murray.[5] He expanded on this a few days later:

> Democracy is no longer a meaningless sort of shibboleth, and with the enormous increase of votes by the woman's franchise it is the actual voice, and for better or worse, the political voice of the state. Baldwin appeals to it. His last words, broadcast on the eve of the Poll were: "You trusted me in 1924, I ask you to trust me again." They have replied by turning him out. He has had his run: been beaten and like an Englishman taken his beating. The people will take their hats off to him, say he is a sportsman, and at the next general election will remember his behaviour and probably bring him back to power. Otherwise if he tries to hold on many of the electorate, who do not understand parliamentary finesse or appreciate the advisability of putting Lloyd George in a hole or obliging him to come out into the open and declare his colours, will merely say: "Here's Baldwin clinging to office and trying to arrange with LG [Lloyd George] to keep

---

[4] Roskill, *Hankey*, Vol 2, p 495.
[5] Blair Castle, Murray Papers, Bundle 1681, Stamfordham to Murray, 1 June 1929.

Labour out." I know the theory that the King should only be guided by the role of the Representatives of the People across the floor of the House of Commons, but there again I would take the vote of the people as interpreting what they want. The PM has asked to see HM tomorrow. For what I do not know. When Rosebery came here [to Windsor] in 1895 to "tender his resignation" to the Queen, we afterwards walked to Eton but he did not tell me what he had done at his audience.[6]

This was a salutary reminder of the almost confessional nature of the confidences which Prime Ministers exchanged with their Sovereigns, even at times excluding the Private Secretary from the privilege.

The King accepted Baldwin's resignation but was not yet physically strong enough to receive both the incoming and outgoing governments within twenty-four hours. For a day therefore, there was no official government. Baldwin gave up the seals of office — or very nearly so, since if the government was where the seals were, the government was Wigram's for twenty-four hours, since he had custody of the Great Seal for the night!

So MacDonald was once more in No 10 Downing Street, where he remained until his resignation in June 1935. According to John Gore, in his personal memoir of George V, the last years of the King's life were overcast by anxiety and over-work, imposing an extra load on to a man who had already been seriously ill once and might not anyway have ever entirely recovered physically from the accident when his horse fell on him in France in 1915. Certainly the King had been hard at work — very hard — for twenty years. He was rising seventy; his daily paperwork, described with characteristic modesty and brevity in his diary as 'Doing my boxes' was prodigious. He travelled much out of London, to be sure, but his boxes followed him. There was no genuine holiday for the occupant of the Throne. When he was out of London he had a holiday from ceremonial, and most functions, but never from State business, which, after all, is regarded as a full-time job in itself by senior civil servants and ministers. Wigram calculated in 1921 that the King actually spent two hundred nights of the year out of London — sixty-five at Sandringham, fifty-two at Balmoral, twenty-four at Windsor, nine at Ascot, seven at Aldershot, twelve

---

[6]   Blair Castle, Murray Papers, Bundle 1681, Stamfordham to Murray, 3 June 1929.

at Goodwood, seven at Bolton, four at Newmarket, four with the Fleet, four at Elveden, and five visiting the war graves in Flanders. The boxes came too.

Thus what Gore was describing was most probably a state of exhaustion. This is a more likely explanation than the one which concluded that the problems and anxieties of the 1930s were so very much more alarming than those of the 1920s. The view from the Throne, after all, was not an optimistic one. To a man nearing the end of his life, doggedly going about his duty without much hope that the work would, or could, attain any lasting success, it must have been a strain indeed.

The King was at Balmoral in August 1931 when crisis broke over Ramsay MacDonald's Labour government. The inability of the Cabinet to agree a programme of further taxation and swingeing cuts in public spending — particularly unemployment benefit — in order to balance the budget further undermined confidence in Britain's financial stability and accelerated a run on Britain's gold reserves which required an international loan to alleviate it. The New York banks were unwilling to agree to the loan without evidence that the Cabinet was prepared to carry through the cuts.

MacDonald had warned the King that his government might resign leaving it to Baldwin, whose Conservatives had only twenty seats fewer than Labour, to pass the measures through Parliament with Liberal support. Alternatively he might count on the latter's support to balance out defections from his own ranks. MacDonald was also faced with the absolute refusal of the TUC to countenance the programme of cuts in benefit. Their unwillingness to make even a gesture of co-operation may have hardened MacDonald's heart against his own party. Certainly when he went to the Palace to resign on 23 August and was invited by the King to consider forming a national government with the leaders of the other two parties, he appeared quite ready to do so. A meeting of the King, MacDonald, Baldwin and Sir Herbert Samuel (Lloyd George was ill) was arranged to take place at Buckingham Palace the next day.

The King's idea of a national government was supported by the leader of the opposition Liberal Party, Sir Herbert Samuel, whom the King had seen on 23 August. Samuel had suggested that the measures required to save the country would be much more credibly applied by MacDonald, either with a reconstituted Labour Cabinet or, failing that, at the head of a national government. The King had also seen Baldwin, who had concurred with Samuel's judgement, though Baldwin was also ready to carry on the government if he could be assured of the necessary Liberal support.

The next day the King welcomed the three party leaders to the Palace and at the end of two hours they had agreed all the essential details for the formation of a National Government to deal with the emergency. A general election would follow later. When MacDonald returned to inform his Cabinet of this agreement, all but three of its ministers deserted him and went into opposition. The surrender of their seals on this occasion was in stark contrast to the homely formality of 1924 when they had taken the oath of office. 'The atmosphere was solemn and funereal,' wrote J R Clynes. 'There was no talk. We entered His Majesty's study one by one carrying our seals in small red boxes. The King stood beside a table, one hand resting upon it. His face looked grey and lined. I placed my seal on the table, bowed, and silently took my leave.'[7]

The King was more robust in his dealings with MacDonald when the latter appeared at the Privy Council for the swearing in of the new Cabinet. MacDonald was looking mournful in black tie and frock coat. The King said laughingly to him: 'You look as if you were attending your own funeral. Put on a white tie and try to think it is your wedding.' Sir Samuel Hoare, who recounted this tale, added: 'From that day onwards the King never ceased to hold up the Prime Minister's hands.'[8]

When the King, who had in the meantime resumed his holiday at Balmoral, returned to London he found MacDonald in further difficulties over the proposed election. The Prime Minister told the King he felt he had failed and had better clear out. The King in his turn told him to brace himself up, and he should realise that he was the only person to tackle the crisis, and his resignation would not be accepted. The Prime Minister's principal difficulty lay in persuading all the party leaders to agree to a general election on a broad based policy — 'a Doctor's mandate' — to restore economic stability. After further meetings with MacDonald, as well as long interviews with Baldwin and — a 'very heated one' — with Samuel, the basis for an election, to be held on 27 October, was eventually agreed.

---

[7]   J R Clynes, *Memoirs, 1924-1937* (Hutchinson, London, 1937), p 198.

[8]   Viscount Templewood, *Nine Troubled Years* (Collins, London, 1954), p 22.

The day before polling day the King kept Hankey back after a Privy Council and said: "'Of course you are going to vote." "Well, Sire," Hankey replied, "as a matter of fact since the war I have rather made a point of not voting. I have my views of course but I like to keep a very detached point of view." "But this time it is different," said the King. "I want the National Government to get every vote possible." "Is that a command, Sire?" "Yes, you really ought to vote." "Very well, Sire," said Hankey, "You can claim to have canvassed one vote for the National Government."'⁹ The Coalition won an overwhelming victory at the polls, 558 seats to the Opposition's 56. Those who had opposed MacDonald had been truly put to the sword, something they never forgave him for. The King, as one can imagine, showed him every consideration and gave him all that concerned, rather than close-quartered, support, as was his custom, until MacDonald resigned four years later.

Wigram, in a letter to the Governor-General of Australia (Sir Isaac Isaacs), sounded the note of triumph which must have rung fairly freely throughout the Palace: 'The good old working class in this country . . . rose to the occasion when they thought the safety of their country was at stake. Thousands among the working class, including many unemployed and on the dole, voted for the National Party, but did not dare to wear the national colours on account of the tyranny of the Trades Unions.'¹⁰

The question has often arisen: did the King exceed his brief by assisting at the birth of the National Government? It has to be remembered that no party commanded a majority in Parliament. Two years had passed since the last election; and anyway, with the country facing a bankruptcy which could occur in a matter of hours if the banking system was deprived of confidence, the ponderous procedures of an election would have been irrelevant. There was thus a need for haste in finding an immediate political solution to the crisis. The King, if one looks at the record, did no more than use his influence by giving help and advice — trenchant advice perhaps — to politicians who needed definite and straightforward guidance on a matter about which they may have been indecisive if they had been left to act alone. MacDonald, in particular, was a man of doubts and

---

⁹ Roskill, *Hankey*, Vol 2, p 569.

¹⁰ RA, PS/GV/P284/320, Wigram to Isaacs, 29 October 1931.

dreams. He was never in more need of a counsellor who had the integrity, assurance and background that the King possessed. Constitutionally, George V acted — only on the advice of the Prime Minister. But he also advised, he encouraged — how he encouraged — and he warned the leaders of all three parties. The timing of his interventions was probably just as significant as the arguments that he used, since it was not in the King's nature to employ fine or complicated devices to express his hopes and fears for his country. Once the National Government had come into being, he could be accused of bias in its favour. The Parliamentary Labour Party, heavily depleted in numbers, certainly thought so. His injunction to Hankey to cast his vote for the National Government in the general election was clearly improper. But it was a touching quality since only to such an old and trusted friend could he have afforded to let his prejudice and indiscretion run so free.

Life under the National Government soon reverted to something like the routine of the late 1920s. With the resignation of Free Trade Liberals such as Snowden, following the establishment of the Ottawa system of tariffs, the National Government assumed an almost wholly Conservative complexion. But the situation overseas began to change with bewildering rapidity.

The growth of Dominion autonomy had received recognition in the 1926 Balfour formula which gave Canada, Australia, New Zealand and South Africa equality of status with Britain. This was followed by the 1931 Statute of Westminister which recognised the legislative independence of the Dominion Parliaments and stipulated that the British Parliament could not legislate for a Dominion without the latter's consent. The King disliked the new constitutional status of the former self-governing colonies. He also resented the fact that the Governor-Generals (who carried out the role of the Crown in the Dominions and were appointed by the King) were no longer responsible to the British government but to the Dominion governments. It was logical, therefore, that the Governor-General should be a native of the Dominion in question and appointed on the advice of that government. The Irish Free State had insisted on this since its first Governor-General, Tim Healy, was appointed in 1922. But this was regarded as the exception before 1930. When the King was obliged by the government of Australia in 1930 to accept an Australian, Sir Isaac Isaacs, whom he did not know, as Governor-General this set the trend for the future. It also led to a distinct cooling in the King's enthusiasm for his Dominions.

It was a different case with India, where the King retained his paternal interest in the welfare of both his ordinary and princely subjects despite their advance towards self-government. Considering how personally involved he was with India, and how directly he felt that the Viceroy's prime duty was to act on behalf of the Crown, it is remarkable what little success George V had in getting his choice of Viceroy appointed. It had been easier before 1930 to have his preferred representatives sent out to Canada, Australia, New Zealand and South Africa than it was to control appointments to the politically sensitive and significant post in New Delhi. The Viceroy was heavily involved in all the paraphernalia of the prerogative — honours, medals and precedence — in the obsessively formal world of British India. He was also a plenipotentiary of the Home government, operating in an area of high political exposure, where every development of policy came to be debated hotly on the floor of the House of Commons. In these circumstances, no government could afford to send out somebody just because he was close to the King.

The King failed to get Kitchener appointed in 1910. He failed in 1916 and 1921 to get Willingdon appointed. In 1925 he wanted Haig to go; but the Cabinet wanted a civilian. The King then suggested Edward Wood (who went to India as Lord Irwin, and later succeeded to his father's title of Viscount Halifax), though Birkenhead later claimed to have been the first to recommend him to Baldwin. However, it was the question of Irwin's successor, five years later during the second Labour government, which vividly illustrated the great negative power over appointments that the Sovereign possessed if he ever chose, or felt forced, to bring it into play.

Ramsay MacDonald and his Cabinet were anxious to show that they could field men of all talents for all the high offices of state — unlike the first Labour government which had had to borrow some peers to fill its ranks in the House of Lords. The Cabinet's first choice as successor to Irwin, was Lord Thomson, the Secretary of State for Air. He, however, was killed in the R101 airship disaster. The Cabinet then formed a sub-committee to find a Viceroy, and eventually identified Lord Gorell, a man without any obvious imperial background. There was nothing adverse in his record: he was a poet and army educationalist who had briefly served as Under-Secretary of State for Air in Lloyd George's government. He was first sounded out about the post by Arthur Henderson, the Foreign

Secretary, in an alcove at a party in the Soviet Embassy. Henderson made it clear that he, the Prime Minister and Wedgwood Benn, the Secretary of State for India, were all keen to show that the Labour Party had Viceroy material within its ranks. In due course Stamfordham got to hear of the matter (George Lansbury had mentioned that he was on a Cabinet Committee to choose a new Viceroy). The old courtier bridled at what appeared to him as a strange innovation to the hallowed procedure of informal 'soundings' by which all important Crown appointments were made. Then it emerged that the Cabinet had settled for Gorell and that Sankey, the Lord Chancellor, had even spoken of him informally to the King. 'What's his wife like?,' the King had asked, and on being told that the Queen knew her, he appeared to be satisfied.[11]

It was Queen Mary's accidental involvement in the saga which gave Stamfordham his opening. The likelihood of Gorell's being appointed had already been leaked to the press when Stamfordham discovered what he held to be a more serious breach of the prerogative, the appointment not having yet been formally submitted for the King's approval. It appears that Lady Brassey, who was involved in the John Murray publishing house where Gorell was a director, had written to Queen Mary's private secretary saying that if the Queen wished to see Lady Gorell before she went out to India she did not have much time because Lady Gorell was expecting a baby. Stamfordham seized on the letter as grounds for delay, and a review of the suitability of Gorell for Delhi.

The interval enabled Conservative, Liberal and Indian opinion to be stirred up against the proposed appointment. 'The question of your successor is giving the King some concern, and he wonders whether your views have been obtained on the subject by the PM,' Stamfordham wrote to Irwin. The latter replied expressing the hope that the King would feel at liberty to exercise his own discretion — which was, one assumes, a coded way of voicing objection to the Gorell appointment.

There is no evidence that Stamfordham personally was stirring up trouble, but he cannot have been too displeased with the furore which resulted — except in the breach of relations caused with MacDonald,

---

[11] Charles Douglas-Home Papers, from copy of George W Bergstrom, Jr, 'The Politics and Power of Lord Willingdon's Appointment as Viceroy of India' (2nd revised text, St Antony's College, Oxford), p 11.

which was probably not healed before the old courtier died. MacDonald reproached Stamfordham, 'I am a person of peaceful ways and do not court trouble . . . but I cannot help regarding the action you have taken on this letter[Lady Brassey's] as being very unfortunate. I wish to say nothing more than this — that I cannot help feeling it shows a surprising lack of confidence in me which arouses feelings of unhappy discomfort, and a grave injustice to Lord Gorell.' In fact, he did say more. He vowed, next time, not to give Stamfordham 'a chance' by putting the appointment straight to the King without a word to anyone first.[12] Hankey was on the Prime Minister's side, and exchanged sharp words with Stamfordham. In his turn he objected to the very notion of the Cabinet discussing the Viceregal appointment and tried to get the minutes of it expunged from the record. Hankey, of course, would have none of it.

The end result was that the formal submission of Gorrell's name for the King's approval never got past Stamfordham's desk. MacDonald then withdrew it and fell back on Willingdon as his second choice — thus fulfilling the wishes of the King and Stamfordham. The latter summed events up for Irwin:

> If the reports of Gorell's appointment "filled Indian opinion with anxiety" these feelings were more than shared by the King! His Majesty could only tell the Prime Minister that he hardly knew Gorell by sight and imagined that the world generally was ignorant of the man and his works! But he passed through some most anxious weeks during which however mercifully the Prime Minister was brought to realise, but not by His Majesty that the present momentous time in the history of India demanded the very best man available.[13]

In 1931 Gandhi came to London to attend the Round Table Conference on India. The question quickly arose, would he attend the garden party to be given by the King, and if so, would the King receive him? Hoare, Secretary of State for India, sought an audience for answers to these questions. 'What, have this rebel fakir in the Palace after he has been behind all these attacks on my loyal officers?' was the King's immediate reaction. 'Having let off steam,' recalled Hoare, 'he started to discuss

---

[12] RA, PS/GV/N2292/301, MacDonald to Stamfordham, 30 October 1930.
[13] IOLR, MSS EUR C152/1, Stamfordham to Irwin, 30 January 1931.

arrangements for the party, to which he at once assumed that Gandhi would be invited.'[14]

However, as was often the way with the King and his sons, these sudden bursts of temper could recur. He started again to protest at having 'the little man' in the Palace 'with no proper clothes on and bare knees'. The garden party duly occurred, and Gandhi was presented. It was a difficult moment. 'The King was obviously thinking of Gandhi's responsibility for civil disobedience. However, when they were once started, the King's simple sincerity and Gandhi's beautiful manners combined to smooth the course of the conversation' — though the King kept on looking resentfully at Gandhi's knees. At the end the King said 'Remember Mr Gandhi I won't have any attacks on my empire,' to which the Indian replied: 'I must not be drawn into a political argument in Your Majesty's Palace after receiving Your Majesty's hospitality.'[15]

On another occasion in 1933 it was the Princes who incurred the King's wrath when they appeared to pass a resolution in Bombay repudiating the proposal for an All-India Federation which the King certainly supported. He was incensed, and sent for Hoare, with whom he discussed Indian affairs in the evening and again at 8:30 the next morning, when his anger had increased. 'I won't see them when they come to London. Why should they come to London at all to spend a lot of money? Tell them to stay in their States and look after their own subjects.'[16]

The King knew many of the Princes personally, having shot tiger and bagged duck with them, which had given him vivid glimpses of local life. Hoare recalled later: 'His attitude to the Princes was that of a sympathetic but severe father who knew and understood his family's weaknesses and was determined to bring up his sons in the way that they should go.'[17] The Viceroy was instructed to notify them of the King-Emperor's displeasure, and they quickly retracted their offending resolutions.

In Europe the scene was beginning to darken under a Hitlerian twilight. Edward VII and, to a very much lesser extent, George V, had exercised some

---

[14] Templewood, *Nine Troubled Years*, pp 59-60.

[15] *Ibid.*

[16] Rose, *George V*, p 354.

[17] Templewood, *Nine Troubled Years*, p 87.

influence on the Continent before the First World War largely, but not wholly, because Europe was still then a concert of crowned heads, many of whom also had some executive powers of government in their countries. By the mid 1930s circumstances had greatly changed, and the Palace itself recognised that Europe had a new diplomatic map. Nevertheless, foreign governments and certainly foreign heads of state were still tempted to find short cuts into the heart of the British establishment through the King. The Palace, certainly under Wigram's stewardship as Private Secretary from 1931 (following Stamfordham's death), was obviously not averse to encouraging these contacts with the King through Britain's ambassadors overseas, whom the King anyway tended to regard as *his* representatives, with the embassy as a whole representing the British government.

The British Ambassador in Berlin during the early 1930s was Sir Eric Phipps. He wrote assiduously to the King, reporting on the flavour of Nazi Berlin, his conversations with the ex-Kaiser's son, the former Crown Prince, and so on. George V and Wigram were ready listeners when Phipps in June 1934 relayed a conversation he had had with the ex-Crown Prince who 'seems like the Bourbons, to have remembered nothing and to have forgotten nothing'.[18] Wigram found it astounding that the ex-Crown Prince could visualise a monarchical restoration in Germany and the 'King was amused at his hint that our Government might support such a movement against Hitler'.[19]

Wigram and George V harboured a residual suspicion of Germany which was not surprising after their experiences fifteen years before. 'I wish that we could all take for granted that Germany was not in any way possessed by a Military Spirit, and that all these marches, salutes and flag-flying was the German's idea of the sporting spirit. What by the way do they call the sport of Jew baiting?' Wigram asked Phipps ironically.[20] Phipps continued to register his growing concern with developments in Germany. According to Wigram, Phipps confirmed the King's own suspicions and led him to confine his personal message to Hitler to a New Year's greeting, ignoring the German leader's birthday.

---

[18] CCC, Phipps Papers, II, 3/1, Phipps to King, 7 June 1934.
[19] CCC, Phipps Papers, II, 3/1, Wigram to Phipps, 12 June 1934.
[20] *Ibid.*

In September 1934 Wigram asked Phipps to write to the King giving his views on a book which alleged that Germany was preparing for gas and germ warfare. The following January Wigram wrote that: 'The King felt that we must not be blinded by the apparent sweet reasonableness of the Germans, but he was wary and not taken unawares.' Phipps was fortified by the message — as was Vansittart, the Permanent Under-Secretary at the Foreign Office. Vansittart and Phipps, indeed, took advantage of their access to the King to argue against the appeasement policy of the government. After one audience, Vansittart was rebuked by the Foreign Secretary, Sir John Simon, and the Prime Minister, Ramsay MacDonald, for getting at the King and depressing him further after his illness.

The King dreaded another war. His failing energies in the diplomatic sphere were all directed to urging policies of peace and compromise on his Ministers. In his view, it did not imply disarmament, though he had once canvassed through Hankey the proposed abolition of the submarine through international agreement. When the Committee of Imperial Defence started to consider the abolition of naval air bombardment, however, the King was much less happy. He felt strongly that, as head of both the air force and the navy, he should have been consulted. He told Lord Londonderry, the Secretary of State for Air, to report to his ministerial colleagues that the King had decided views on the matter. The King and Hankey had heated arguments on the subject, but MacDonald finally reassured the King that there was no question of the abolition of naval air bombardment unless it was clear that other countries would do likewise.

In June 1935 MacDonald resigned the premiership, and the King appointed Baldwin — 'the Dormouse', as 'Chips' Channon called his leader.[21] There was no dissolution since it was assumed that the King would raise cogent, perhaps insurmountable objections, not least because the government had still such an overwhelming majority. In July 1935 Hoare as Foreign Secretary found the King a sick and worried man. The thought of another war — which seemed to be threatened by the Abyssinian crisis — haunted him. 'I am an old man. I have been through one world war.

---

[21] Robert Rhodes James (ed), *Chips: The Diaries of Sir Henry Channon* (Wiedenfeld and Nicolson, London, 1967) p 35.

How can I go through another? If I am to go on, you must keep us out of one,' was the gist of many of the talks Hoare had with him at that time.[22]

The King was to be spared the fate of leading his country through another world war. Early in December 1935 his sister Victoria died. The King, whose own health was deteriorating, cancelled his appearance at the State Opening of Parliament and instructed the Lord Chancellor to read the speech from the Throne. He then retired to Sandringham for Christmas. The last Privy Council was held at his bedside on 20 January 1936 to proclaim a Council of State to take over during his illness.

The question of holding the Council while the King was ill had troubled Hankey, Wigram and Lord Dawson, the King's doctor. If the King was not in a fit state to signify his Royal Approval of the Council's decision, it would not be regarded as valid. Hankey advised the Council that the King must give 'his full conscious assent'[23]. The form of signature could be settled according to the circumstances of the moment. Dawson said he thought the King might be able to pull himself together to make some semblance of a signature.

The Councillors met in the adjoining room, where they could see the King and hear him, without his being conscious that they were looking at him. Hankey, Wigram and MacDonald, three survivors of many confidences were there, and the King knew it. He apologised for taking so long to sign the warrant, but sign it he did, with great difficulty — dogged, and punctilious to the last.

He died at five minutes to midnight; but he left his Throne in the sunlight of his days.

---

[23] Roskill, *Hankey,* Vol 3, p 215.
[22] Templewood, *Nine Troubled Years*, p 159.

6

The Cap Did Not Fit

George V had set rigorous standards for the Monarchy and he doubted whether the Prince of Wales, who on his accession took the name of Edward VIII, could meet them. The old King had prophesised to the Prime Minister, Baldwin: 'After I am dead the boy will ruin himself within twelve months.'[1] This is, indeed, what happened. After less than a year on the Throne, Edward VIII abdicated. The interesting thing is that had he continued to be King he would have by virtue of his different conception of kingship from his father's, have wrought many changes in the Monarchy. As it was, his brother, and successor, George VI, in order to repair the damage done to the Monarchy by the Abdication, made a conscious effort to follow the example of his father, and was helped by the fact that he shared many of his father's qualities.

Yet to the public Edward VIII seemed to have the necessary talents to be a constitutional monarch. He had shown this through his boyish enthusiasm and informal manners which captivated audiences; his triumphant goodwill tours of the Empire-Commonwealth and North America, and his warm sympathy for wounded soldiers and impoverished workers, demonstrated that he had a flair for public sympathy which was so vital for the public duties of the Monarch. *The Times* wrote at his accession of the amazing spell he had cast 'upon the imagination of the many

---

[1] Keith Middlemass and John Barnes, *Baldwin* (Weidenfeld and Nicolson, London, 1969), p 976.

communities within what is henceforth his realm'.[2] His youthfulness (he was 41 at his accession) was seen by some as an asset for the Monarchy which, in a year (1936) that saw Germany's remilitarisation of the Rhineland, Italy's conquest of Abyssinia, and the start of the Spanish Civil War, might change the perception in Fascist countries of Britain as a tired and complacent country run by old men (Baldwin was 69 and Neville Chamberlain was 67). Some of Edward VIII's public remarks, such as that 'something must be done'[3] about the terrible conditions prevailing in the depressed mining areas of South Wales and his habit of making statements on foreign affairs without the prior approval of the Foreign Office, annoyed the politicians. But these comments enhanced his reputation with the public as a man of courage who was trying to galvanise his ministers into taking more decisive action both at home and abroad.

Although Edward VIII's accession was welcomed there was concern at his lack of a consort and of a family ensconced in domestic bliss in the royal palaces, and how this would affect the all-important role of the modern Monarch as representing the ideal of family life. It was also unclear whether Edward VIII would make the necessary transformation from playboy prince to dutiful king. The Court and the Government had even greater private doubts about the new King as a result of his character, social life and rejection of his father's legacy. This led to resentments, and then alarm. This had to be carefully concealed from the public, which did not become aware of the King's flaws until the news broke of his involvement with the American divorcée, Mrs Simpson.

A degree of tension between the new King and his Court was inevitable, given that they represented different generations and that they differed in their conceptions of Monarchy. But the tension was heightened by Edward VIII's insistence that his courtiers should condone, or at least not criticise, his liaison with Mrs Simpson. Shortly after his accession the King dismissed the Head of his Household, Admiral Sir Lionel Halsey, not only because he was regarded, at 63, as too old, but because he had told Edward, when he was Prince of Wales, that his affair with Mrs Simpson was damaging his reputation and that of the country. Wigram, who was the same age as Halsey, retired as Private Secretary after the traditional six month transition

---

[2] *The Times*, 22 January 1936.

[3] Philip Ziegler, *King Edward VIII* (Collins, London, 1990), p 301.

period from one reign to the next. His time was up, especially as he epitomised for Edward VIII the style of courtier he wanted to dispense with. The most obvious suitable man for the job was Godfrey Thomas, who had been the Private Secretary to Edward when he was Prince of Wales. But Thomas refused it, having had enough. He was prepared to be an assistant private secretary but wanted someone else to take the great strain of avoiding a constitutional crisis during Edward VIII's reign. On Thomas's recommendation, Alec Hardinge (son of the former Viceroy, Lord Hardinge), who was the same age as Edward VIII, succeeded to the vital post of Private Secretary. Alec Hardinge had been at the Palace for sixteen years, serving as an assistant private secretary to George V. He was intelligent, a stickler for hard work, and punctilious, pedantic almost, in his approach to the job. He was totally honourable but he and the King were temperamentally incompatible and therefore it was impossible for them to establish a proper working relationship. To his surprise, Alan Lascelles, who had resigned from the Prince of Wales' service eight years before and joined George V's Household, was appointed as an assistant private secretary. To the amusement of the courtiers, he managed to establish cautious but cordial relations with Mrs Simpson.

It was immediately obvious to courtiers such as Cromer, who felt it his duty to stay on as Lord Chamberlain, that the King was out of sympathy with the relics of his father's court. In his autobiography (published in 1951) Edward said that his father had looked to Queen Victoria as a model of the Sovereign's deportment — which was not entirely fair since George V had been his own model. 'His court retained a Victorian flavour to the end;' Edward remarked, 'and I had come to look upon it as at least sexagenarian in composition and outlook.'[4] Reflecting the restlessness of many of his generation, he rebelled against the old ways. Edward visualised his mission to be to modernise the Monarchy with its traditional strengths, to be a hard-working, hard-playing King on his terms; to reduce the formality and rigidity of the Court, and to make it more human and less distant.

Edward VIII had no plan for reforming the Monarchy but it was clear that he meant to impose his personality upon it. He was better equipped

---

[4] Windsor, *King's Story*, pp 278.

than his predecessors had been to mix on informal terms with his people,
having encountered all sorts at naval college, at Oxford, and on his travels.
In contrast to his father, he also understood and sympathised with modern
trends. Despite his father's admonition to him, 'Always remember your
position and who you are'[5], Edward's democratic education had the effect
of making him feel less royal and more like an ordinary man, which he
yearned to be. He became sceptical about his exalted status and
uncomfortable about the role he was expected to play. This was seen in his
adverse reaction to the ceremonial and regalia ('this preposterous rig'[6])
involved in his investiture as Prince of Wales at Caernarvon Castle in 1911.
Edward did not like the ritual and tradition which is such an elemental
part of the business of monarchy. 'What rot and waste of time, money and
energy' was his verdict in 1914 on the preparations for the State visit of
the King and Queen of Denmark.[7] It was clear that Edward as King would
reduce the pomp and pageantry which had been such a hallmark of the
Edwardian and Georgian monarchies.

Edward VIII certainly found the routine chores of kingship, the
paperwork and public ceremony uncongenial and tried to reduce them.
Thus, Court officials concluded that he disliked work and public ceremonies
and tried to dodge both. But Edward later sought to justify his behaviour
as part of his right to be King 'in terms of my own philosophy'.[8] He was
angered and mystified by the opposition of Court officials to his desire to
discard what he saw as outdated protocol. He did not share their fears that
by making the Monarchy more accessible he would, *pace* Bagehot, dissipate
that dignity and mystery which was the very essence of the institution. But
it was his attempt to make economies in the running of the Royal Household
in order to provide more money for himself and Mrs Simpson, that aroused
their full ire.

The King's first approach to the Household may not have been
calculated to startle them, but it naturally put every member on his guard.
He informed senior members of the Household that: 'I do not wish to give
the impression that I propose to make sweeping changes or reductions,

---

[5] *Ibid*, p 134.

[6] Ziegler, *Edward VIII*, p 27.

[7] *Ibid*, p 45.

[8] Windsor, *King's Story*, p 276.

but I am very definite in my opinion that reorganisation and coordination are necessary.'[9] He had asked Sir Lionel Halsey, before his enforced retirement, to investigate and report. The King's Financial Secretary, Sir Ralph Harwood, was able without much difficulty to cut the expenditure on food from £45,000 to £13,500. The running costs of the royal aeroplane and pilot were transferred to the Air Ministry, although the two were sometimes used to convey the King's friends across the Channel and to bring back goods for Mrs Simpson on which duty was not paid. This contrasted with the lowering of the drinks allowances, the abolition of livery compensation and, particularly, the reduction of the wages of the Household staff. Harwood protested at these unnecessary economies, given that the Privy Purse could well afford them, on the grounds that it would damage the morale of the Household staff.

'I can bring no enthusiasm to bear in either supporting or carrying out Your Majesty's wishes to cut down the emoluments of the existing servants. I fully admit that some of the allowances are excessive and that some of the wages are possibly over-liberal,'[10] he pointed out, but the usual practice was to apply reductions only to the rate at which new entrants were paid (ie even if lower wages were paid to new recruits, it would be unjust to slash the salaries of those who were already in royal employ). Furthermore, the new Civil List allowed for an increase in wages and it would be a breach of faith to reduce them and then utilise the surplus for private purposes. There was no need for these economies, since there was a large surplus, simply in order to make a huge income greater still. In the vain expectation of increasing a large income by a few thousand pounds through cuts in every allowance Harwood went on:

> Your Majesty will exchange a contented and willing staff for one which will be unhappy and seething with discontent. Inevitably Your Majesty's popularity in the Household will suffer severely . . . Your Majesty has several times mentioned to me that Your Majesty does not wish to be regarded as a "pincher" but . . . this very term accompanied by even more objectionable suggestions is being freely used with reference to Your Majesty.[11]

---

[9] RA, GV/GG6, King Edward VIII to Wigram, 16 April 1936.
[10] RA, GV/GG6, Harwood to King Edward VIII, 20 June 1936.
[11] *Ibid*.

Edward VIII took note of the last point, underscoring it in red ink, but he was not to change his mind. Edward VIII's position in the Household was a source of great dissatisfaction. It was unlikely, in these circumstances, that he would command the kind of unquestioning loyalty and devotion which he was going to need in any crisis. For his part, Edward VIII resented the opposition and criticism coming from his courtiers and did not therefore take them into his confidence. It was a recipe for disaster.

Edward VIII's relationship with his Government was also fraught with difficulties. Baldwin, the Prime Minister, had seen Edward on 19 January 1936 as his father lay dying, and had impressed on him the magnitude of his task. It was, in its way, not unlike the Prime Minister's own, and they would have to work together. Baldwin told Chamberlain, the Chancellor of the Exchequer, that he had been encouraged by Edward's response and his apparent 'sense of his responsibilities'.[12] But the Prime Minister also had his doubts, which he confided to Tom Jones: 'You know what a scrimshanker I am. I had rather hoped to escape the responsibility of having to take charge of the Prince as King. It is a tragedy that he is not married.'[13] The subject of Mrs Simpson, whom the Prince had just visited in her London flat, was never mentioned between them.

Although Baldwin was lavish in his praise of the qualities and qualifications of the new King, he reflected the opinion of the Court officials to whom he had spoken when he confided to Clement Attlee, the leader of the opposition Labour Party, that he had doubts whether the King would 'stay the course'.[14] Moreover, Baldwin and his ministerial colleagues were not pleased by Edward VIII's anti-authoritarian, rebellious and impatient attitude, his tactless manner, and his intentionally indiscreet public statements, which so contrasted with the behaviour of his father. George V knew to a nicety (and from the start of his reign) what he might and might not do in exerting influence with his ministers or in the exercise of a Sovereign's prerogative. Edward VIII 'knew little and interfered much'[15].

---

[12] Ziegler, *Edward VIII*, p 240.

[13] Thomas Jones, *A Diary with Letters* (Oxford University Press, London 1954), p 63.

[14] C R Attlee, *As It Happened* (Heinemann, London, 1954), p 85.

[15] Dennis Barden, *Portrait of a Statesman* (Hutcheson, London, 1956), p 146.

His wilful behaviour meant that he failed to establish any real rapport with his ministers, let alone gain their respect and trust, and he could therefore exercise no real influence on the Government.

Ministers, Court officials and civil servants were also unhappy with the King's work habits. He started off by initialling every State paper he read. The practice soon stopped, revealing how little he was actually reading. He lacked his father's sense of duty and punctual habits and begrudged any time spent on his duties that might be better spent with Mrs Simpson. He reported to Baldwin: 'Before her, the affairs of State sank into insignificance.'[16] As the Simpson crisis deepened the King stopped reading papers altogether. His red boxes remained unopened, which meant that their return was delayed and no action was possible by his Private Secretary. In March 1936 Lady Hardinge recorded in her diary: 'Nothing but a ghastly conversation with — and — two old members of the Household about how awful the new King is.'[17] Confusion in his affairs was beginning to grow. In May Lady Hardinge noted that Cromer, the Lord Chamberlain, had had a row with the King (over his need to see him from time to time to do his job properly) and had threatened to resign. Alec Hardinge had become depressed by the King's irresponsibility. Most Court officials were fretting at the fact that they could not despatch their business properly as he was always at Fort Belvedere. The courtiers could only go to the 'Get-Away-from-People house'[18] near Windsor by invitation, and even when invited they were kept hanging about for hours. Eventually, Baldwin and Hardinge restricted the documents going to Fort Belvedere to those which required the Royal signature only, so the King was effectively deprived of any official information. He seemed also increasingly reluctant to help ministers and officials by carrying out State duties, refusing, for example, to see King Carol of Romania or to invite the Regent of Yugoslavia, Prince Paul, to any functions during their visits to Britain.

This disruption of the accustomed routine of His Majesty's business was by then becoming an open secret in the higher reaches of the political establishment. 'I do not believe he [the King] has the constitutional spirit

---

[16] Middlemass and Barnes, *Baldwin*, p 979.

[17] Helen Hardinge, *Loyal to Three Kings* (William Kimber, London, 1967), p 89.

[18] Duchess of Windsor, *The Heart has its Reasons* (Michael Joseph, London, 1956), p 192.

within him so as to work with any government,' Ramsay MacDonald wrote to Lord Tweedsmuir (the writer John Buchan who was then Governor-General of Canada). 'That of course may be youth and high spirits and will pass. It does not influence our policy regarding him today. His very active enmity to all the old servants of his father is, however, a disquieting factor in his relations with us.'[19] Hardinge later remarked: 'He appeared to be entirely ignorant of the powers of a constitutional sovereign and of the lines on which a King's business should be carried on.'[20]

In fact, Edward VIII's determination to intervene in the affairs of State, in particular on unemployment and Anglo-German relations, was to pose problems for Ministers. His outbursts about unemployment and housing problems, especially his remark that 'something must be done' during a tour of the depressed mining areas of South Wales, implied a censure of his Ministers which was picked up by the Press. It may have made him popular with the man in the street, but Ministers and even opposition politicians like Herbert Morrison deplored the King's intervention in such politically controversial matters.

The way in which the strongly pro-German Edward pressed his views on Anglo-German relations upon the Baldwin government also showed that he did not understand the limits of his position as a constitutional monarch. There was an early indication of this in June 1935 when, as Prince of Wales, he crossed swords with his father and the Cabinet over a speech that he gave to the British Legion, in which he recommended that a group of members should visit Germany, thereby extending the hand of friendship to the Germans. The speech was welcomed by the Legion but not by the French government or the British Foreign Office. The latter thought that the speech had complicated the then current Anglo-German negotiations for a naval-disarmament treaty. At the Cabinet's suggestion, George V had pointed out to Edward that his proposal for a visit to Germany by the Legion ran contrary to the policy of the Foreign Office and that he must not speak on controversial matters without consulting the government. The Prince was unrepentant and told the German

---

[19] Queen's University, Kingston, Ontario (QU), Tweedsmuir Papers, MacDonald to Tweedsmuir, undated [but 1936].

[20] Ziegler, *Edward VIII*, p 275.

Ambassador in London, Leopold von Hoesch, that 'he was not retracting and was convinced that he had said the right thing'[21]. Hoesch had already in April 1935 reported back to Berlin that the Prince of Wales had criticised the 'too one sided attitude of the Foreign Office' on German affairs and how he had again showed 'complete understanding of Germany's position and aspirations'.[22] The Prince's proposal was welcomed by the Nazi leadership who turned the subsequent visit of the British Legion party to Germany into a great propaganda event.

When Edward acceded to the Throne the anti-appeasement elements in the Foreign Office and the Palace had to adjust to a new emphasis towards Germany on the part of the Sovereign. George V, it is true, had been desperate for his Ministers to avoid another European war at almost any cost, but that did not delude him as to the nasty things which were going on in Germany. Phipps and Vansittart knew where he stood. The Phipps correspondence with the Palace then more or less petered out except for one flurry when the ambassador had to use his best offices to dissuade the ex-German Crown Prince, 'Little Willy', from coming to Britain, let alone calling on his cousin the King.

On the day of the Accession, the German Ambassador in London, von Hoesch, reported to Berlin that: 'King Edward will naturally have to impose restrictions on himself at first, especially in questions of foreign policy, which are so very delicate. But I am convinced that his friendly attitude towards Germany, might in time, come to exercise a certain amount of influence on the shaping of British foreign policy.'[23] If that sober, and perfectly proper, assessment did not excite Hitler, the next message about the new King certainly must have done so. It was a report of a conversation that Edward VIII had had at George V's funeral with another cousin, the Duke of Saxe-Coburg, a Nazi sympathiser. The Duke reported that the new King regarded a German-British alliance as 'an urgent necessity and a guiding principle for British foreign policy . . . To my question whether a discussion between Baldwin and Hitler would be desirable he replied in the following words: "Who is King here? Baldwin or I? I myself wish to

---

[21] *Documents on German Foreign Policy, Series C, Vol IV* (HMSO, London, 1962), pp 330-1.

[22] *Ibid*, pp 1016-17.

[23] *Ibid*, p 1023.

talk to Hitler, and will do so here or in Germany. Tell him that please."
The King is resolved to concentrate the business of government on himself.
For England, not too easy.'[24] One must make allowance for the fact that
this conversation apparently took place within a week or so of the old
King's death, and for the fact that the Duke was a rather pathetic relic of
Imperial Germany, currying favour with Hitler by trading on his family
associations. He was also a notoriously unreliable witness and one wonders
whether the King really spoke like that, even in a mood of braggadoccio
to a poor relation. Whether he did so or not is not greatly relevant. Once
the conversation was reported to the Nazi leadership it became part of the
received view of Edward's role and his intentions with regard to British
policy towards Germany. In particular, Ribbentrop (whom Hitler sent to
London to replace Von Hoesch in the mistaken belief that he had a special
relationship with the King and Mrs Simpson) became convinced that
Edward VIII was 'a kind of English National Socialist', who was thwarted
in his desire for an agreement with Germany by anti-German forces in
the British government. In fact, Edward was too concerned with personal
matters in the last months of his reign to give any close attention to this
matter. Ribbentrop and other Nazi dignitaries paid assiduous attention to
Mrs Simpson, who shared Edward's views on the merits of National
Socialism and the decadence of the French, in an attempt to influence the
King. She was a regular guest at receptions at the German Embassy in
London but there is no evidence that she, or anybody else in the King's
pro-German clique, passed on information gleaned from secret papers in
the King's possession, as was feared by Court and government officials at
the time.

'But if suspicions against Mrs Simpson seem to have been based on
very little,' wrote Frances Donaldson in her biography of Edward VIII,

> there is no lack of evidence of the King's indiscretions. First there is the
> direct evidence of the captured German Foreign Office documents, and
> the memoirs of German agents in London. These often show a naive
> understanding of where power resides in England, and it is easy to dismiss
> each individually as the unimportant vapourings of a German agent who

---

[24] *Ibid*, pp 1062-4.

wished to ingratiate himself with the Nazi regime. Together they add up to a considerable body of evidence that the King differed from his Ministers in many aspects of their foreign Policy and allowed himself a freedom of expression which was completely unconstitutional, creating in Germany an impression of warm sympathy and an exaggerated idea of his power and influence.[25]

When the demilitarised zone of the Rhineland was reoccupied by Germany in March 1936 Edward VIII told Baldwin, so the German Embassy in London believed, that he would be opposed to any British intervention. Given that Baldwin and Chamberlain were determined to avoid war over what they regarded as a secondary issue, it is unlikely that Edward VIII actually issued such a directive to the PM, that 'old so-and-so'.[26] But the King's relation of this episode to German Embassy officials was certainly an unconstitutional action.

During the Abyssinian Crisis Edward told the Italian Ambassador in London, Count Dino Grandi, and the German Foreign Minister, von Neurath, that peace in Europe required the full satisfaction of Italian and German needs for colonial markets. He opposed the imposition of sanctions by the 'will-o-the-wisp' League of Nations for Italy's invasion of Abyssinia. He deplored the resignation of the British Foreign Secretary, Sir Samuel Hoare, following a secret accord he reached with the French Foreign Minister, Laval, which would have given Italy most of what it wanted in Abyssinia. He also refused to accede to the advice of his new Foreign Secretary, Anthony Eden, to grant an audience to the exiled Abyssinian Emperor, Haile Selassie, on the grounds that it would offend the Italians.

Edward VIII's abdication was to be seen in Germany not as a constitutional question but as a manifestation of the anti-German movement in Britain which wanted to get rid of a singular and influential friend of the Reich. Edward VIII had to abdicate, Ribbentrop was wont to say, because Baldwin realised that Britain would have to fight a paramount Germany, under Nazi leadership, and was not certain that the King, because of his views, would cooperate in an anti-German policy. Ribbentrop was due to lunch with Lord Davidson on the day after the

---

[25] Frances Donaldson, *Edward VIII* (Weidenfeld and Nicolson, London, 1974), p 193.
[26] Quoted in Brian Inglis, *Abdication* (Hodder and Stoughton, London, 1966), pp 70-1.

Abdication, and was so out of touch with the realities of the crisis — and the absence of any real support for the King — that he telephoned to suggest cancelling the lunch in case there was shooting in the streets. He had already that morning been on the telephone to Hitler, suggesting the possibility of revolution with Beaverbrook and Churchill leading the King's party! For him, the abdication finally sealed his hopes of an understanding with the British government, or, perhaps it just gave him an excuse for the failure of a mission which had never had a hope of succeeding. Hitler was also said to be upset by the abdication of Edward VIII: he had even instructed Ribbentrop to try to prevent it since it would weaken the Crown and undermine the British Empire. He saw the ex-King as an adherent of the 'Führer-prinzip' who sought to introduce it to Britain.

Although Edward was pro-German, he was no admirer of Hitler or a Fascist sympathiser. But his subsequent behaviour towards Germany (his October 1937 visit and his indirect contacts with the Nazis in 1939-40) certainly lent credence to the rumours and confirmed the suspicions of many that he would have been unreliable as a bulwark against Nazi aggression had he remained on the Throne. It was later rumoured that Hitler had planned to restore Edward to the Throne if the Germans had occupied Britain in 1940. The rumours may have been unsubstantiated but the very fact of their existence demonstrated Edward's lack of political judgement during his short reign. They also illustrated the dangers for the Monarchy of intervening so publicly in foreign and domestic politics. It was the wrong model for the modern British constitutional monarchy.

Although Edward VIII refused to follow the rules for a modern monarch established by his father, there is no evidence that Baldwin, the Cabinet or Hardinge sought to depose him, as has been alleged (at the time by Warre Bradley in *Why Edward Went*, and after his death by Lord Beaverbrook in *The Abdication of King Edward VIII* and more recently in 'The Traitor King' television documentaries). As we shall see, Edward VIII abdicated of his own free will, not on the official advice of his ministers but (and this is an important distinction) because of their opposition to his marrying the twice-divorced Mrs Wallis Simpson. Although there was no law preventing the King from marrying whom he pleased, as long as she was not a Catholic (prohibited under the Act of Settlement), he did not in practice have the same freedom of choice as his subjects. This was because his wife would become Queen and therefore, like him, a representative of the nation.

Consequently the view of the nation, as expressed through its elected representatives (Baldwin and the Cabinet), on his choice of wife had to be respected since an inappropriate Queen would damage the Monarchy. Edward eventually realised this, as well as the constitutional implications of proceeding with a marriage which was disapproved of by the Baldwin government, especially as the latter might resign, thereby involving the Crown in politics and causing a full-blown constitutional crisis.

Edward VIII had not anticipated the widespread opposition to his marrying Mrs Simpson. Nor had he realised how public the life of the Sovereign had become, in part due to the modern monarchy's own emphasis on its dignified functions (and the representation of the royal family as a domestic ideal), but also because of the relentless scrutiny of every detail of royal life by the Press. The growing public appetite for royal news presented the Monarchy with the opportunity to exert great moral influence as long as it conformed to the ideal of family life. By continuing to lead a cosmopolitan private life which was so at odds with the example of domestic simplicity set by his father, Edward VIII largely forfeited his chance to be a constitutional monarch. He later ruefully admitted that if a King was a contented family man this counted for much in a constitutional monarchy.

Although the sophisticated Mrs Wallis Simpson was a singularly inappropriate choice to follow Queen Mary, Edward came to the Throne secretly determined that she should become his consort. He made it clear from the start that he meant Mrs Simpson to be part of his life. Nobody was more observant of this resolve than Chips Channon. At the official proclamation of Edward VIII's accession at St James's Palace, Channon noticed that a huge black car (the King's) was one of the first to drive away with the blinds half down — and Mrs Simpson inside. Again, as George V's funeral procession passed St James Palace, Channon saw the King look up to the part of the Palace which had been commandeered by Mrs Simpson and her party. The Simpsons attended the King's first official dinner (it was the last time Ernest Simpson was to accompany his wife to a Court function) so that Ernest Simpson could introduce his wife to the Prime Minister. If Baldwin was unaware of the significance of the meeting, Lady Astor was not. She thought Lady Cunard (also there) and Chips Channon were bad influences. In her view the announcement in the Court Circular that the Simpsons and Lady Cunard had attended the dinner was the worse news that *The Times* had carried for years.

It was the events of the summer which lent credibility to society rumours of an impending marriage. In August and early September 1936 Edward VIII and Mrs Simpson went on a yachting holiday aboard *The Nahlin* in the Adriatic and the Aegean. It was an enjoyable, if somewhat indecorous, cruise. It had the benefit, however, of raising Britain's stock in Yugoslavia, Greece, Turkey, Bulgaria and Austria. While the American and European papers seethed with the subject of the King and 'his girlfriend', an olympian silence, as can only be achieved by self-censorship, had settled on the gossip-domes of Fleet Street. At Balmoral that September there was the usual house party, but not the usual official guests. The Court circular announced on 24 September that Mrs Simpson was there. Some guests noticed that the King seemed preoccupied and there were signs of the mounting stress he was under as he sensed the growing difficulties in the way of his marrying Mrs Simpson. Queen Mary was receiving letters from many troubled people, including the Duchess of York.

After the summer holidays the pace quickened. Mrs Simpson's divorce was soon to come through and she would then, technically, be free to marry the King. He was, though less free, at least in a position to admit that he wanted to marry her. On 20 October, after members of the Cabinet had warned him that he had to intervene to stop the divorce, Baldwin at last took the plunge and raised the matter with the King. The Prime Minister opened the conversation by saying that he was getting more and more letters of complaint about the King's relationship with Mrs Simpson. At this stage, of course, all he could legitimately discuss were matters of taste and behaviour, since the King had not done or suggested anything which overtly affected his official duties, let alone the constitution. Baldwin asked the King to persuade Mrs Simpson not to divorce her husband (which meant that she would not be able to marry the King and cause a constitutional crisis). But the King declined to intervene in 'the lady's private business'.[27] The Archbishop of Canterbury, Cosmo Lang, offered to intervene only to withdraw his offer when he realised that Baldwin was advocating that the King should keep Mrs Simpson as a mistress in the background. Lang hoped to have a quiet word with the King when they discussed the Coronation service. Lang, however, in his caution, formality

---

[27] Ziegler, *Edward VIII*, p 293.

and slight unctuousness, represented everything Edward VIII hated about his father's reign. He was, as Lang admitted in October 1936, 'very emphatic that on the subject of his relations with Mrs Simpson he would listen to nobody but Mr Baldwin, who had the right to speak to him and advise him'.[28]

On 27 October 1936 the divorce petition was heard at the Assizes in Ipswich, and Mrs Simpson was granted a decree nisi. The decree absolute was to follow six months later. The King and Mrs Simpson, therefore, had a vested interest in spreading the falsehood that they had no thought of marriage. This not only reassured the Cabinet but was the basis on which the King persuaded Lord Beaverbrook to muzzle the British and some European newspaper magnates about the affair. The Canadian newspapers were similarly silenced, but shocked Canadians were soon regaled with news from generally sympathetic American papers of the Simpson divorce and Mrs Simpson's intimate relationship with the King. Lord Tweedsmuir reported to Hardinge from Ottawa on 27 October (in response to an enquiry from Hardinge about the Canadian reaction) that Canadian opinion was anxious and disquieted. Hardinge showed his letter to Baldwin. It was not until 10 November that Mrs Simpson's name was first mentioned in public in Britain. During questions in the House of Commons about the forthcoming Coronation, an Independent Labour Party MP, John McGovern, jumped up and shouted: 'Why bother, in view of the gambling of Lloyds [Coronation insurance risks had gone up from 4% to 21% in three months] that there will not be one?' Amid roars of: 'Shame!', he called out: 'Yes — Mrs Simpson'.[29]

It was at this point that Hardinge learnt that two affidavits alleging collusion over the Simpson divorce were about to be filed. If they held up to scrutiny the King's Proctor would have to reopen the case and the King's alleged misconduct with Mrs Simpson could be cited as a reason for annulling the divorce. Although Hardinge said nothing about this to the King, he sat down and wrote to him at Fort Belvedere to warn him that the Press was about to burst out on the subject of Mrs Simpson, and that the Prime Minister and his senior colleagues were meeting to consider the

---

[28] J G Lockhart, *Gordon Cosmo Lang* (Hodder and Stoughton, London, 1949), p 399.

[29] Ziegler, *Edward VIII*, p 296.

situation — with the possibility of their resigning. If no alternative administration could be found a calamitous general election would follow, in which the King's personal affairs would be the chief issue. Hardinge's urgent recommendation was that Mrs Simpson should go abroad 'without further delay'.[30] He showed a draft of this letter to Geoffrey Dawson, the editor of *The Times*, and to Baldwin's private secretary at No 10 Downing Street. It is a measure of the gulf which must have already opened up between Hardinge and his Sovereign that this letter was the first time that the subject had been broached between them (imagine Knollys and Edward VII keeping silent for so long on an important subject). Shortly after sending the letter Hardinge left London to go shooting. Not surprisingly, the immediate reaction of the King was to think of dismissing Hardinge, with whom he was out of sympathy anyway. He was dissuaded from this by his old barrister friend Walter Monckton (who had become Attorney-General to the Duchy of Cornwall). Even Monckton thought Edward VIII's temporary separation from Mrs Simpson was the most prudent course. The King asked Monckton to act for him as an intermediary with Baldwin. Hardinge's role, therefore, as the principal link between Monarch and Prime Minister, was effectively performed by somebody else during these crucial days. Hardinge informed Tweedsmuir on 16 November:

> things are moving. From what I hear by the time you get this the Press may be in full swing and the government may have intervened. The harm that is being done, in spite of the little that people know, is tremendous. The subversive elements are being given a splendid opportunity and the state of affairs cannot be allowed to continue. It is all very tragic — and at the moment it is difficult to see the way out. The repercussions, too, are incalculable. A year ago would one have thought such degradation of the British throne possible?[31]

Hardinge's letter to the King did, however, have the effect of galvanising Edward VIII into action. On 16 November he called Baldwin to Buckingham Palace. The Prime Minister would, in any case, have requested an interview. Three days earlier he and senior Cabinet ministers had decided that it was time to end the scandal. Baldwin rejected the proposal

---

[30] Hardinge, *Three Kings*, p 133.

[31] QU, Tweedsmuir Papers, Hardinge to Tweedsmuir, 16 November 1936.

of the Chancellor of the Exchequer, Neville Chamberlain, that the government should formally advise the King to sever his connection with Mrs Simpson since, if this became known, it would arouse public support for the King. This would obscure the constitutional issues and cause a division of opinion. Baldwin and the Cabinet were anxious that the King should remain on the Throne. But if he did decide to abdicate rather than give up his desire to marry Mrs Simpson, then the damage to the Monarchy should be limited and the succession carried out smoothly. Baldwin, therefore, made it known informally to Edward VIII on 16 November that his intended marriage to Mrs Simpson, who would become Queen, would not be approved by the country and was therefore unacceptable to the government. The King countered by saying that he intended to marry Mrs Simpson and that, if necessary, and if there were no alternative, he would abdicate in order to do so.

The King's complaint was that he only wished, in marrying Mrs Simpson, to do what any of his subjects was free to do. There were two flaws in this argument. The first was that, as Sovereign and Supreme Governor of the Church of England, he could hardly contemplate taking the Coronation oath as Defender of the Faith (ie Anglicanism) if he was also contemplating marriage to a twice-divorced woman. In 1936 the Established Church did not remarry a person whose former spouse or spouses were still alive. The second drawback was that, although there might be no statute law against his marrying Mrs Simpson — it lay outside the Royal Marriages Act — it was a convention of the Constitution that, while the Sovereign did not explicitly need the advice of ministers before marrying, if his choice of woman as Queen was somebody whom ministers could regard as unsuitable, it would in fact become a constitutional matter. Baldwin said that in the choice of a Queen the voice of the people must be heard. The King felt this was dogmatic. Public opinion *would* tolerate Mrs Simpson, given the opportunity. 'I believe I know what the people would tolerate and what they would not', said Baldwin.[32] There is little doubt that in the social and political climate of 1936, Baldwin, rather than the King, was right.

The King asked the Prime Minister for permission to see the only two

---

[32] Windsor, *King's Story*, pp 331-2.

ministers in the Cabinet whom he regarded as friends — Sir Samuel Hoare and Duff Cooper. The request was granted by Baldwin, although the very fact that the King wanted to see these ministers suggests that at the back of his mind lay the possibility either that Baldwin was not faithfully representing the views of the Cabinet as a whole, or else that he might have been able to detect different attitudes among ministers, which could be exploited to his advantage. It was an odd request — almost unconstitutional — and it is a credit to Baldwin's patience and tireless efforts to provide the King with as much time and help as he needed, that he consented to it. Nothing came of the meeting. Hoare would not be drawn except to say that the country would support Baldwin in his opposition to the marriage. Duff Cooper was more forthright, counselling delay until after the Coronation, when Edward VIII would be in a stronger position to try again. It was bad advice and cynically given, since either Duff Cooper meant the King to ignore the weight of his Coronation Oath, or he thought that any delay might help cure the King of his infatuation, even one which risked this all recurring after the Coronation. The King honourably declined to consider the advice on the grounds of his Oath as Defender of the Faith.

There was one last lifeline: the proposal for a morganatic marriage. This was possibly inspired by Winston Churchill and was put to Mrs Simpson by the press baron Esmond Harmsworth (later the Second Viscount Rothermere), who owned *The Daily Mail*. It appealed to the King who on 25 November asked Baldwin for formal advice as to whether it would be possible. Morganatic marriage was known in European royal families because their members were obliged to choose from a severely circumscribed circle of royal dynasties. There was no such restriction on the British Sovereign so morganatic marriage was unknown in British law. It would require in turn legislation, for which the King would need government approval. A morganatic marriage meant that Mrs Simpson would not become Queen, and that no child issuing from the marriage could succeed to the Throne. The Prime Minister rejected morganatic marriage on the grounds that the British people would not accept it. He also told Duff Cooper that the Dominions would not agree to it, and Parliament would therefore not pass the necessary legislation. Baldwin was supported by the Cabinet and by the leaders of the Liberal Party, the Labour Party and the TUC, all of whom expressed opposition to the marriage. Baldwin was irritated both by Harmsworth's intrigues, and by the antics of a so-called 'King's Party' revolving around the rotund figure of the Conservative backbencher Winston Churchill, who was sitting it out below the gangway in the House of Commons. If there was a confrontation and Baldwin resigned, Churchill might replace him. Since Churchill could not survive in the House of Commons he could demand a dissolution, and at the ensuing general election the country would be dangerously divided into two camps, for and against the King. Moreover, if Britain and the Dominions remained divided over morganatic marriage, it could split the Empire, which was symbolically kept together by the Monarchy.

So the Dominions were officially consulted. But the telegrams were phrased in such a way by the Dominions Office as to emphasise the opposition of the British government and people to either the King marrying Mrs Simpson and her becoming Queen, or a morganatic marriage. Abdication and the succession of the Duke of York seemed the only alternative. Only the Irish Free State favoured morganatic marriage. When the Irish government later decided to back abdication, the Prime Minister, Eamon de Valera, stipulated that Edward VIII could not remain King of Eire. In New Zealand, where the King was very popular, Prime Minister Michael Savage thought morganatic marriage might work, but he was soon dissuaded of this by the Governor-General. Australia and South Africa, and to a lesser extent Canada, were forthright in their opinion that abdication was preferable to Mrs Simpson's becoming Queen or a morganatic consort.

Meanwhile the pace of events in London suddenly accelerated. Following a sermon by the Bishop of Bradford, A W F Blunt, criticising the King for his neglect of his duties as head of the Church of England, the press broke the story about Edward and Mrs Simpson. *The Daily Mail* and *The Daily Express* supported the King, while *The Times* backed the government. Fearing that *The Times* would launch a fierce attack on Mrs Simpson, the King asked Baldwin to stop it, only to be reassured by the editor, Geoffrey Dawson, that its intended editorial was harmless. The King showed how far he had trespassed into a political minefield by devising a plan to broadcast to the nation, stating his intention to marry Mrs Simpson but not insisting that she should become Queen. He would then leave England for a while (he planned to go to Switzerland) so that the country could reflect calmly on the matter. If the people wanted him back he would continue to rule with Mrs Simpson as his consort. If not, he would abdicate.

The King put his plan to Baldwin on 3 December, apparently oblivious of the fact that he was proposing to make his desire to marry Mrs Simpson and stay on the Throne a wider political issue than the privileged discussions between the King and his Prime Minister. He was calling on an extra constituency to attend those audiences. He was invoking a referee to arbitrate between himself and his Prime Minister. Baldwin, ever patient, agreed to put it to the Cabinet but made it clear to the King that he thought his proposal was unconstitutional since it would place him in opposition to his ministers. When the King baldly stated: 'You want me to go, don't you?', Baldwin was forced to admit that he could see no alternative.[33] On 4 December the Cabinet backed Baldwin and rejected the King's proposal as an attempt, in Ramsay MacDonald's words, to get the nation and the Empire 'to throw over his ministers'.[34]

Only Churchill, whom Baldwin made the mistake of allowing the King to consult, now still sought to make mischief with the royal prerogatives. He went to Fort Belvedere on 4 December and tried to galvanise the King into fighting against his ministers, to barricade himself in, to buy time 'for the big battalions to mass'.[35] When it was put like that, with all the colour and vigour that Churchill could command, the King saw at last what was being suggested and cried off. Under no circumstances, he said, would he be party to a constitutional crisis, betraying once again his inability to see how his actions would *automatically* achieve that result.

Public opinion, as it manifested itself to MPs during their visits to their constituencies during the weekend of 5-6 December, backed the government. Given this fact, there was no possibility that ministers, let alone the King, would back Churchill's compromise that the King should not marry without ministerial consent but that the matter should be left pending. Leo Amery set out his opinion of Churchill's real motives in a letter to Tweedsmuir on 7 December:

> Winston has seen in it a wonderful opportunity for attacking Baldwin.
> The line he is taking is that a ruthless and dictatorial Government, wishing

---

[33] Ziegler, *Edward VIII*, p 316.

[34] *Ibid.*

[35] Donaldson, *Edward VIII*, p 279.

for a thoroughly tame monarch, have suddenly put the King into an impossible choice between his inclinations and his Throne and are prepared to 'bump him off' without giving him time to look around and reflect on the situation. With a public that knows nothing . . . the danger of his succeeding in getting up a really formidable agitation is a real one . . . Winston has got a certain number of younger Conservatives to back him. There is also latent a tremendous fund of the kind of royalism which is for the King right or wrong. It is significant that not only Winston but Oswald Mosley has rushed into the breach as the King's champion. Winston has flopped badly — the House of Commons was dead against him today.[36]

Shortly afterwards, the King's party almost entirely disappeared. With regard to MPs gauging public opinion, Baldwin later told his biographer, G M Young, that: 'I have always believed in the weekend. But how they do it, I don't know. I suppose they talk to the station master.'[37]

Baldwin tried once more, on a visit to Fort Belvedere on 8 December, to persuade the King to reconsider his position. The King said that his decision to abdicate if he could not marry Mrs Simpson stood. Baldwin again pressed him on the grounds that he would have to give Royal Assent to his own Act of Abdication. The next day Baldwin reported to the Cabinet that it was useless to try any further. His ministers, however, made one last plea to the King to reconsider. The King replied immediately that he could not reconsider his decision. His abdication was now an accepted fact and only the details remained to be worked out.

The sensitive matters of Edward VIII's financial settlement and his future status had to be resolved, in both of which the Royal Family (especially the Duke of York, who was to succeed to the Throne) were closely involved. Edward had excluded the rest of his family from the constitutional discussions. It was only after he had informed Baldwin on 16 November of his intention to marry Mrs Simpson that he broke the news to his mother. Queen Mary greeted her son's decision with anger and pain. She was adamant in her opinion that it was his duty to give up Mrs Simpson. He had no intention of doing so and refused to discuss the matter further with either his family or his advisers. Sir Godfrey Thomas complained about

---

[36] QU, Tweedsmuir Papers, Amery to Tweedsmuir, 7 December 1936.
[37] GM Young, *Baldwin* (Rupert Hart-Davis, London, 1952), p 242.

this to the Duke of York, who had been similarly excluded from the King's counsels. The Duke of York pledged that: 'If the worst happens and I have to take over, you can be assured that I will do my best to clear up the inevitable mess, if the whole fabric does not crumble under the shock and strain of it all.'[38]

It was the discussion of the financial settlement, and in particular Edward VIII's lie to both the Duke of York and Churchill that he was poor (in fact he was a millionaire) and needed to be subsidised by the government or the new King, that did more than anything else to sow discord between Edward and George VI, the Royal Family and the Prime Minister. Edward insisted that the terms of his father's will should be strictly carried out. George V had left Sandringham and Balmoral to his eldest son, expressing the forlorn hope that Edward VIII would live in those estates for some of the time and cherish them. To his younger sons, the Duke of Gloucester and the Duke of Kent, he left trusts amounting to over three million pounds, all in the control of Sir Edward Peacock of Baring Brothers. After some highly ticklish negotiations, it was agreed at a meeting at Fort Belvedere that Edward should sell his life interest in Sandringham, and if necessary Balmoral, for a sum to be determined. He should also drop any claim to the royal heirlooms. He would not receive the proceeds as a lump sum. Instead the new King would make him an annual allowance of £25,000, if Parliament did not make such a provision in the Civil List, although Edward would forfeit this if he behaved badly after his abdication. The new King would also assume responsibility for his brother's share of the royal pensions. It was not until 1938 that a full agreement was to be hammered out in an atmosphere of bitter acrimony.

On 10 December 1936 Edward VIII signed the Instrument of Abdication in the presence of his brothers at Fort Belvedere. Since the succession to the Throne had been defined by the Act of Settlement, the King's declaration had to be confirmed by Parliament. The latter gave legal effect to the Instrument of Abdication in 'His Majesty's Declaration of Abdication Act', which excluded Edward VIII, or any of his descendants, from the Throne. The Act also provided for the Duke of York to succeed him as King. During the passing of the Bill, Baldwin, with utter simplicity

---

[38] Wheeler-Bennett, *George VI*, p 283.

told the full story to a mesmerised House of Commons: 'I have never known in any assemblage such accumulation of pity and terror', wrote Harold Nicolson. When it was over, the members filed out 'broken in body and soul, conscious that we have heard the best speech that we shall ever hear in our lives. There was no question of applause. It was the silence of Gettysburg.'[39]

'People who have been licking Mrs Simpson's boots should be shot,' Nancy Astor sang out to Chips Channon, as they left the Commons chamber.[40] She need not have bothered, because the people in question did not for long draw attention to themselves — their hurried apostacy being encapsulated in Osbert Sitwell's privately circulated poem 'Rat Week'. Publicly, the Archbishop of Canterbury referred to them as alien to all that is best in the English instinct and tradition.

Lord Salisbury in the House of Lords, struck a different note from the simple humanity of Baldwin. But it was a valid point to make at a moment of unparalleled drama in the long saga of kingship: 'An abdication of a Sovereign is a momentous, almost desperate act. He has a mandate from nobody to whom he can return his trust. He sits there by an authority which is outside the ordinary human methods of appointment, and his abdication is a wound in the body politic which is a disaster.'[41]

For his part, Edward was furious at Baldwin for not mentioning in his speech, as requested, that Mrs Simpson had tried to dissuade the King from abdicating. His determination to put the record straight in an abdication broadcast to the nation now raised the question of what he should be called. The Director of the BBC, Sir John Reith, proposed to introduce him as 'Mr Edward Windsor', but the new King thought: 'That is quite wrong . . . He cannot be E W as he was born the son of a Duke. That makes him Ld E W anyhow. If he ever comes back to this country, he can stand and be elected to the H of C. Would you like that? No. As D of W he can sit and vote in the H of L. Would you like that? S replied No. Well if he becomes a Royal Duke he cannot speak or vote in the H of L

---

[39] Harold Nicolson, *Diaries* (Collins, London, 1966), pp 285-6.

[40] Robert Rhodes James, *Chips: The Diaries of Sir Henry Channon* (Weidenfeld and Nicolson, London, 1967), p 99.

[41] *Hansard*, 103 HL Deb, 5s, col 734.

and he is is not being deprived of his rank in the Navy, Army or Royal Air Force. This gave Schuster a new lease of life and he went off quite happy.'[42] Edward liked his new title and Reith was told to introduce him as 'His Royal Highness, Prince Edward'.

The courtier Eric Mieville related how Edward's:

> Last Act prior to Broadcasting his message and then leaving the Country, was to sit in his Bedroom with a whiskey and soda having his toe-nails seen to! His three brothers being in the Room with him! There is no doubt that he is a little mad. He is certainly not normal and the danger is what is going to happen to him. He is *not* drinking — least he wasn't doing so before he left. But what is he going to do for the next four months — to say nothing of afterwards — is impossible to foretell'.[43]

Edward's broadcast speech was generally well-received. It is best remembered for the line that he 'had found it impossible to carry the heavy burden of responsibility and to discharge my duty as King as I would wish to do, without the help and support of the woman I love'[44]. After a moment of tearful reflection, however, the nation turned its attention away from Edward, Duke of Windsor, towards the new King. Before departing for Europe and a life of exile, Edward bade his family farewell. When he was gone, those he left behind, socially, politically and dynastically, had now to pick up the pieces.

The Abdication Crisis had lasted a mere six weeks, from Mrs Simpson's divorce on 27 October to the Abdication of 10 December. Speed of action by the principal protagonists was probably an essential element in protecting the institution of Monarchy, that careful house of cards made up of precedent, courtesy, convention and mutual trust which had been built up between the Palace and key institutions in the body politic. Speed, moreover, in the resolution of the crisis, was facilitated by the fact that there was, in reality, very little to discuss. The issue was relatively simple — it was not one in which Edward VIII was in danger of aligning himself with one movement or another within British politics (in fact he had

---

[42] Wheeler-Bennett, *George V*, p 295.

[43] IOLR, MSS EUR F97/1, Brabourne Papers, Mieville to Brabourne, 27 December 1936.

[44] Ziegler, *Edward VIII*, p 331.

explicitly rejected the idea that his supporters should form a 'King's Party'). There was not a range of issues to be thrashed out in debate. He was not seeking to make a general political point, only a personal one — indeed too personal a one. This was to invite the body politic to change or modify the constitution, not for a principle, or to recognise and adjust to some shift in the correlation of constitutional forces, but to suit the personal convenience and passion of the man who then happened to be on the Throne.

The crisis thus always came back to the question of Edward's personal behaviour, and in this he was always at a disadvantage. His conduct since his accession had earned disrespect — nowhere more so than in the office of his Private Secretary. It was Alec Hardinge who really had to mastermind the Abdication and preserve what he could of the King's business in the process. 'For six months Alec *was* king,' his widow observed to me with understandable hyperbole forty years after the event.[45] In her book she cited a newspaper article to the effect that his basic task was to guard the Royal Prerogative, to maintain the happy relations of Buckingham Palace with Downing Street and Whitehall, as well as with Ottawa, Capetown, Canberra and Wellington, to keep the wheels of the Constitution working always smoothly, and to act as the first link between the Sovereign and his people.[46] She maintained that her husband contributed a fundamental stability that the King lacked. 'Those few who were able to see that King Edward, because of his emotional state, eventually became incapable of transacting the simplest official business, were surprised to note that the Sovereign's work went on almost as before. Alec did nearly all of it for him.'[47]

Alec Hardinge, exhausted, indeed broken by the drama, was sent on three months leave by the new King (Wigram was recalled as a stand-in). Before Hardinge left for India, he wrote to Lord Brabourne in Bombay: 'The events of this year have left me rather played out . . .'[48] They had indeed; but he was to live and fight another day. Indeed his finest contribution to the Monarchy was yet to come.

Behind the high drama of the constitutional crisis, the statements in Parliament, the leading articles in the newspapers, there were more sordid

---

[45] Charles Douglas-Home interview with Lady Helen Hardinge, 1976.
[46] Hardinge, *Three Kings*, p 14.
[47] Douglas-Home interview with Helen Hardinge.
[48] IOLR, Brabourne Papers, MSS EUR F97/1, Hardinge to Brabourne, 20 December 1936.

details about sex and money. And, since it was a King's affair, these sordid details had to be discussed in the Cabinet. It is this aspect of the affair which in the end goes to the heart of the Abdication saga — and which was never entirely understood by what Eric Mieville called 'The Chief Conspirator'.[49] Edward's business as King was the nation's business. The Monarchy was then, still is, and will always be if there is to be a Monarchy, a symbol of something more than an individual wearing a crown. The individual has to accept this partial sublimation of his personality, suffer it, and reconcile it to the act of consecration and dedication which is made at the Coronation service. When the curtain is lifted on these entrails of the Abdication it becomes unquestionably clear why it was fortunate Edward VIII never had to go through with his Coronation. If the cap did not fit, no more would the crown have done.

The crucial point about the Abdication Crisis, certainly in terms of historical analysis about the Monarchy, is that it showed the totality of the institution, its wholeness. It would be impossible to separate all the different aspects of the Monarchy and to weigh them up after the Abdication in separate balance sheets. The crisis of 1936 was not just a matter of the King wanting to marry a divorcée, and society and the Church being unready for such an occasion. It was a crisis because Edward VIII was the sort of man he was. If it had not been a divorcée who brought him face to face with the difficulties of life on the Throne, it would have been something else. He had bridled at the restrictions put on his role as a constitutional monarch and had grudgingly carried out some of his duties. If he had remained on the Throne, he would have tried to reduce the pomp and the pageantry which were so essential to the social and psychological success of the Georgian monarchy. If he had succeeded in this, and he would have been firmly resisted by the Court officials, the popularity of the Monarchy would have probably been diminished. This situation never materialised. But the success of the new King, George VI, who consciously modelled himself on his father, would seem to indicate that the people, the politicians and the courtiers wanted a family man as Sovereign, a king who performed his duties in a constitutional way and with plenty of splendour and ceremony. The Abdication Crisis confirmed this.

---

[49] *Ibid*, Mieville to Brabourne, 27 December 1936.

7

His Own Man

The new King, George VI, faced a situation, as he declared at his Accession Council on 12 December 1936, which was 'without parallel in the history of our Country'[1]. No previous British sovereign had voluntarily abdicated. It was an act that struck at the very heart of the institution of monarchy, which functioned on the hereditary principle. Moreover, the former King was still alive, in exile, presenting a rival centre of attention and comparison, and a potential source of embarrassment. It was 'the heavy task' of the new King not only to overcome this difficulty but to restore the image of monarchy, which his elder brother had so tarnished.[2] George VI hoped, as he told Baldwin, 'that time will be allowed me to make amends for what has happened'[3]. During his short reign, from 1936 to 1952, he was to earn the respect of the nation and the Commonwealth by his determined and conscientious performance of his duties during the troubled years of appeasement, war and reconstruction. In doing so he helped to restore the reputation and role of the monarchy to its former place in the life of the nation and the Commonwealth.

At the start of his reign doubts were voiced in the newspapers, the City of London and Society about whether George VI's history of ill-health and his stammer would allow him to carry out the heavy duties of kingship. His delicate appearance, however, masked his stamina and courage, which

---

[1] Wheeler-Bennett, *George VI*, p 288.
[2] *Ibid*.
[3] *Ibid*, p 297.

had enabled him to control his speech impediment. Although he had none of his elder brother's easy charm and crowd-pleasing skills, he shared his father's qualities of decency, sense of duty, commonsense, sympathy, as well as a capacity for hard work. Like his father, he was also prone to fits of temper, known to his family as his 'gnashes'. Above all, he had a supportive wife, Queen Elizabeth, and a happy and secure family life with his two daughters, the Princesses Elizabeth and Margaret. After 'the strange interlude', when Edward VIII resided mainly at his weekend retreat of Fort Belvedere, the Royal Family returned to their traditional residences at Buckingham Palace, Windsor, Sandringham and Balmoral, progressing from one to the other on a seasonal basis. Court life became more serious and formal and George VI reappointed his father's old advisers. The new King, who had chosen his title deliberately, was keen to stress the continuity of tradition and values between his reign and that of his father, and thus to restore the image of his father. It was symbolised by his Coronation on 12 May 1937, the day that his brother had been due to be crowned.

George VI had one advantage over his elder brother and his father, in that he had a thorough knowledge of the conditions under which the industrial working class laboured. In the sixteen years before becoming King, he had studiously visited factories and small businesses in over a hundred different areas, and his annual visits to the Duke of York's Boys Camp familiarised him with a whole generation of young men who were to become the soldiers of the Second World War. In the 1926 General Strike — the last great social upheaval on the British domestic political scene, if one excludes the nagging though pervasive issue of unemployment, the young Duke of York had attended the daily debates in the House of Commons and listened, in the words of his official biographer, Sir John Wheeler-Bennett, 'to the cold logic with which Sir John Simon pronounced the Strike to be unconstitutional and he bore away his impressions for future contemplation'.[4] His knowledge of his acquaintance with the main British trade union leaders was to prove valuable in enabling him to understand the aims and actions of the Attlee governments after the war. George VI may have been a conservative by political instinct, like his father, but he learned to be politically neutral, again like his father, and to

---

[4] *Ibid*, p 209.

gain and to keep the confidence of his Labour ministers.

George VI was to a large extent ill-prepared for his constitutional duties. He complained to his cousin, Lord Louis Mountbatten, 'I've never seen a state paper.'[5] He was 'appalled at the volume and nature of the business which emerged day by day from their leather-clad despatch boxes . . .'[6] His official biographer, Sir John Wheeler-Bennett, bemoaned the fact that George V had refused to allow his second son, or the Prince of Wales for that matter, to be initiated into the ordinary everyday workings of government. After the Duke of York completed his Empire tour in 1928, he and Stamfordham had considered that it would be desirable for him to be more closely informed by the Dominions Office and the Foreign Office about developments in the Empire and in international affairs in general. George V objected to this. He felt that it was no part of either of his sons' duties to receive such confidential information. He overlooked the fact that when they went on these tours abroad they were naturally expected to be conversant with imperial and international matters. The Prince of Wales, then in his thirties, had not been allowed to be present at George V's audiences with ministers, or to see the contents of his father's official despatch boxes. According to Wheeler-Bennett, George V 'discouraged his [Edward's] association with political leaders'.[7] The Prince of Wales and the Duke of York, both of them destined to be King in 1936, were allowed to see only a limited selection of Foreign Office and Dominions Office cables — 'and this only with the greatest misgivings and after considerable resistance'.[8]

It is true that the exercise of influence, which is within a Sovereign's rights — to advise, encourage, and warn — is not something given to his sons, even to the heir presumptive. To that extent access to official knowledge which is necessary for the Sovereign to discharge his functions is not necessary for his sons. Nor is it advisable, since the essence of the Sovereign's position, and any weight which might be given to his influence, rests in great part on the confidentiality of his relations with ministers.

---

[5] *Ibid*, p 294.
[6] *Ibid*, p 293.
[7] *Ibid*, p 233.
[8] *Ibid*.

That confidentiality would inevitably suffer under a system where the confidences were diffused to a wider circle, even if it only included the Sovereign's children. The ability to exert influence from the Throne is something which can really only be learnt on the job, since it entails so many ingredients of timing, personality and modulation, that cannot be assessed at second hand. Having said all that, there still must have been a good case for seeing that George V's eldest sons were better equipped to be Kings, and more familiar with the business of Monarchy — the rights, the duties, and the crushing work load — than they were. At times of sudden transition, such as occurred at the Abdication, the unpreparedness of the new Monarch for the esoteric political tasks that await him can become glaringly obvious.

The problem was compounded by the fact that George VI did not have any political friends he could confide in. Nor did he know his Private Secretary, Hardinge, or any of his assistants, such as Lascelles, well enough to place implicit confidence in their judgement. Moreover, as soon became clear after Hardinge returned from his well-earned rest following the Abdication Crisis, there was a fundamental incompatibility of temperament between the King and his Private Secretary. Thwarted by what he saw as Hardinge's excessive caution and negativity, George VI should have moved him to another post immediately. That he did not do so was due to the fact that he valued Hardinge's loyalty during the Abdication Crisis. Instead, the King sought his political and constitutional advice elsewhere, from his friends Lord Halifax and Lord Cranborne, and from Lord Hankey (the Cabinet Secretary and Chairman of the Committee of Imperial Defence). When the time came for the latter to retire, in 1938, the King expressed a desire for General 'Pug' Ismay to be his successor. In the event, Hankey's job was split, the Cabinet side going to Sir Edward Bridges and the Defence side to Ismay. Sir Alexander Cadogan, the Permanent Under-Secretary at the Foreign Office, was also ready with advice and information whenever the King summoned him. But this process of consultation was to cause problems. Hardinge seems to have been unaware that the King sought the counsel of Halifax and Cranborne. Hardinge was also frustrated by the King's determination to work in his own way: not recording conversations with Ministers, faithfully studying his papers and not being content merely with submissions from his Private Secretary.

At the time when George VI was assuming his heavy duties and preparing for his Coronation, he had also to deal with the problem of his elder brother, the ex-King. George VI must have been overwhelmed by the emotional, rather than the constitutional, trauma of the Abdication. It was then, and perhaps it remained so for him and his Queen until the end of their days, more poignantly a family crisis than a political one. Of course, they saw the dangers to which his elder brother had exposed the Monarchy, which was the intimate business of all of them. But George VI's account of the comings and goings of the Abdication shows how confused a crisis it was, charged with family turmoil and lack of communication. It was a hand-to-mouth affair at the family level, shorn of any of the majesty or convention of the machinery of state which gave the formal procedures of the Abdication some dignity. Within the Royal circle, when all the constitutional trappings were torn away, it was just a family at war with itself, with its members scurrying about not knowing what to do, with the Duke of York, soon to be King, sometimes sobbing like a child when he confronted the shame his brother had brought upon the House of Windsor.

Consequently the early preoccupations of George VI were still predominantly family ones. He was now head of the family, yet the succession, as he was to complain, had not been a smooth one occasioned by the death of the last King. The ex-King, Edward, was still very much alive, and near at hand, demanding money, title, precedence, and telephoning his brother every day to tell him how to do the job. He had to be expunged from the family circle and the body politic before the new King and Queen — who discerned this urgency even more vividly than her husband — could feel psychologically secure on the Throne.

George VI started by requesting his elder brother to stop telephoning, much to the anger of the Duke and Duchess of Windsor. Relations between them and the King and Queen deteriorated rapidly, and were never to be restored. This was especially the case after George VI discovered that his elder brother had lied to him about his considerable personal wealth; something which David (as Edward, Duke of Windsor, was known to his family) would not admit. After protracted, complicated and increasingly embittered negotiations, a financial settlement was reached in 1938 which essentially followed the lines of the Fort Belvedere agreement (mentioned in the previous chapter). The King refused to allow a member of the Royal Family to attend the wedding of the Duke and Duchess of Windsor, since the Church of England would not recognise the legality of Mrs Simpson's first American divorce. Moreover, he would not agree to admit her into the family by conferring on her the style of 'Her Royal Highness' (HRH). It was these two matters which led to the estrangement between the two brothers and their wives.

The new King and Queen cannot have felt happy at the fact that the scars of the Abdication — to them at least — would not heal so long as the elder brother was on the scene, if only in the form of querulous noises-off from the wings. In October 1937 the Windsors visited Germany in circumstances which were, to say the least, undignified. They were being manipulated by Nazi supporters ostensibly to study labour conditions, but more realistically to make mischief for the British. The British government certainly took this view, and saw to it that the Windsors were only greeted at Berlin station by the Third Secretary at the British Embassy — the Ambassador, Sir Nevile Henderson, having unexpectedly left the German capital. The tour caused irritation in Britain, and embarrassment and distress at the Palace. It also aroused such criticism in the United States that the second leg of the Duke's tour, a 'study of housing and labour' conditions in the United States, was prudently cancelled. On both sides of the Atlantic, any residual respect for the Windsors was swiftly dissipated. Their conduct also increased the determination of both the King and his government to prevent the Duke of Windsor from returning to Britain lest he become a focus of discontent for extremist groups, such as Oswald Mosley's Blackshirts, and a threat to the Throne. The decision of the King, supported by his government, to distance himself and the institution of monarchy from the unseemly behaviour of his elder brother was the first real political act of his reign.

George VI, unlike Edward VIII, acknowledged his political inexperience and the need for good advice. The two men who, alternating the premiership, had advised his father since 1923 — Ramsay MacDonald and Stanley Baldwin — retired from active politics following the Coronation in May 1937. The new Prime Minister, Neville Chamberlain, had been the obvious successor to Baldwin. The unanimous backing for him to become the leader of the Conservative Party meant that there had been no need for George VI to take soundings or to seek advice from the Tory grandees. The cold and austere Chamberlain had, as Chancellor of the Exchequer, already helped the King over the Civil List and the financial settlement with the Duke of Windsor. After becoming Prime Minister, he made a real and successful effort to befriend and win the trust of the King and the Royal Family. A cordial relationship developed, though this was somewhat marred by Chamberlain's failure to keep George VI always informed on important matters of State. The King sympathised at least initially, as did most of the nation, with the Prime Minister's strategy of appeasement for dealing with the ominous international outlook. This was much regretted by Hardinge, who was from the first a fervent anti-appeaser.

It is often forgotten that one of Chamberlain's earliest exercises in appeasement concerned Commonwealth affairs. In December 1936 the de Valera government had taken advantage of the Abdication to persuade the Dáil to pass the External Relations Act, under which the Irish Free State dropped its allegiance to the King. However, as long as other Commonwealth states owed allegiance, the Dáil was prepared to recognise the King as head of the Commonwealth and to allow him to accredit diplomats and to sign treaties on its behalf. After the Irish Free State (henceforth known as Eire) adopted in 1937 a republican constitution in form, if not in name, the King was no longer head of state in Southern Ireland. He was merely 'an organ or instrument' or, in a phrase to which he took exception, a 'method of procedure' which was authorised by the President of Eire (the new head of state), to perform a certain role in foreign affairs.

Although the External Relations Act and the Irish Constitution were not really compatible with continuing allegiance to the Crown, the other members of the Commonwealth were prepared to overlook this in order to keep Eire within the Commonwealth (a precedent for India's republican membership of the Commonwealth in 1949). To help attain this objective, the Chamberlain government tried to resolve the outstanding points from the Anglo-Irish Treaty of 1921. The opposition of the Government of Northern Ireland prevented the British government from issuing a declaration that it favoured the modification of the Partition of Ireland; which was intended to go some way towards meeting de Valera's call for the reunion of Ireland. A financial and economic settlement, however, was reached. More controversially, Britain returned the Irish Treaty ports to Eire under the Anglo-Irish Agreement of 1938.

George VI, who had been kept informed of the progress of the negotiations by Malcolm MacDonald, the Secretary of State for Dominion Affairs, congratulated Chamberlain on his success and expressed the somewhat optimistic hope that it would inaugurate a new era of friendly relations between Britain and Ireland. The hope was never realised. While de Valera continued to govern Ireland, it was always deemed 'inopportune' for George VI to fulfil his wish of meeting the former rebel against the Crown. In February 1938 the Foreign Secretary, Anthony Eden, and his Parliamentary Under-Secretary, Lord ('Bobbity') Cranborne, decided to resign in protest at Chamberlain's increasing interference in foreign policy in pursuit of his appeasement of Hitler and Mussolini. The King only learnt about this from the press and radio and he complained to Chamberlain (through Hardinge) that he had been caught unawares, with no warning that a major Cabinet disagreement was in the air. As a result he was effectively prevented from intervening to help resolve ministerial differences. Hardinge and Hankey, still the Cabinet Secretary, subsequently argued that such surprises should not be sprung on the King in future. They would be avoided by his being sent a draft copy of the Cabinet minutes, and by the Cabinet Secretary's prompting the Prime Minister to inform the King of any crisis, as had happened in Lord Stamfordham's day. It was not until November 1938, however, that the King actually received the draft minutes of the Cabinet on a regular basis.

When Eden came to surrender his Seals of Office on 22 February, he was pleased to find that the King sympathised with his point of view and expected to see him as a Cabinet Minister again soon. These were not mere words on the King's part. Although he had found the Foreign Secretary difficult to talk to, because the latter stuck to his Foreign Office brief, he respected his intellect and distinguished record of public service. He was also angered by Chamberlain's treatment of him, and was prepared to listen to the anti-appeasement views of Eden and Cranborne after the Nazi annexation of Austria in March 1938 and the threatening moves against Czechoslovakia. George VI also expressed concern to Chamberlain about the dismissal of Lord Swinton, who more than any other man was responsible for preparing the RAF for war.

If George VI regretted the departure of Eden and Swinton, he welcomed the appointment of Lord Halifax as Foreign Secretary. Halifax and the King found that they shared sporting and country interests. Lady Halifax was also a Lady-in-Waiting to the Queen. The Halifaxes often dined *à quatre* with George VI and Queen Elizabeth. The King enjoyed Lord Halifax's company and, most importantly, came to trust his judgement. He gave Halifax a key to Buckingham Palace Gardens in order that he might enjoy them on his walk to and from the Foreign Office.

Since Halifax supported Chamberlain's policy of appeasement at this juncture (he was to change his mind after the Munich Agreement in September 1938), he acted as a counterweight to the anti-appeasement views being offered to the King by Cranborne and Hardinge in the months leading up to the Munich Crisis.

The King's support for his Prime Minister during the convulsive events of September 1938, when Europe seemed on the brink of war, was fulsome and spontaneous in its warmth and persistence. Chamberlain spent four days (31 August-3 September) at Balmoral briefing George VI on the threatening condition of Europe. The King tried hard to persuade his Prime Minister to fit in an extra day's shooting by arranging for him to fly down to London. Chamberlain declined, saying he had never flown and hoped he would never have to as he was terrified of being in the air. By a stroke of fate, he soon found himself in an aircraft flying to Germany in order to meet Hitler in an effort to settle the Czechoslovak question and reach an Anglo-German understanding before the crisis became critical.

Through every step of the Munich Crisis Chamberlain kept the King closely informed, and the King, for his part, gave the Prime Minister all the encouragement he felt he needed. His first impression of Hitler, he confided to Lady Wigram was: 'Never have I ever seen such an appalling cad.'[9] The King several times offered to make a personal appeal to Hitler, but Chamberlain and Halifax, without ruling it out completely, were not satisfied that the time was right to risk the King being humiliated by Hitler's reply. George VI then gave up the idea and on the morning of 28 September, 'Black Wednesday', he presided over a Privy Council meeting which confirmed by Royal Proclamation the preparations for war which had already been taken (such as the mobilisation of the Fleet) and the declaration of a state of emergency. After the Privy Council meeting Duff Cooper, the First Lord of the Admiralty, stayed behind and found the King cheerful, envisaging the outbreak of war with great equanimity. The emergency preparations, the Privy Council meeting, and the drama of great events, gave the King new confidence in himself. This was perhaps born of a recognition that he was a necessary and therefore useful cog in the whole machinery of government.

---

[9] Wigram Papers, Lady Wigram's reminiscences, 1939.

However, it was with great relief that the King and his subjects greeted the news from Berlin that Hitler had invited Chamberlain to a Four Power Conference in Munich. Chamberlain returned from Munich to Heston Aerodrome in West London on 30 September with his 'piece of paper', the Anglo-German Friendship Agreement — 'the Peace with Honour' — which saved Europe from the immediate threat of war at the expense of the territorial integrity and independence of Czechoslovakia. George VI had wanted to meet Chamberlain on his arrival at Heston, in order to express his and the nation's gratitude for the successful diplomatic efforts of the Prime Minister. But he was dissuaded from doing so by Hardinge. Instead, the King commanded the Prime Minister to come to Buckingham Palace so that he might express his 'heartfelt congratulations' on the Prime Minister's triumph. The two men, together with the Queen and Mrs Chamberlain, stood on the Palace balcony and shared the plaudits of the crowd who felt that war had once more been averted. George VI's seeming endorsement of Chamberlain's policy aroused strong, if muted, criticism among those prominent Conservative, Labour and Liberal politicians who opposed it. Although the King was informed of this by Hardinge and Lascelles, he tended to dismiss the importance of the anti-Munich sentiment. When Duff Cooper resigned from the Cabinet over Munich on 2 October, the King was quite relaxed, saying that he 'respected those who had the courage of their convictions', even though he disagreed with them.[10]

Hardinge was 'horrified at the whole course of events, and the government's defeatist attitude'.[11] If the German Army marched into Czechoslovakia in a few days, Hardinge felt it would in the long run be the best solution 'because it would force us to fight'. The British diplomat, Oliver Harvey, noted that Hardinge 'is absolutely disgusted at our attitude'.[12] Hardinge observed to the King that this had to be the last time that Britain tried to appease Hitler. He went further and drew up a long memorandum entitled 'Why Chamberlain has failed', which chronicled

---

[10] Andrew Roberts, *Eminent Churchillians* (Weidenfeld and Nicolson, London, 1994), p 22.
[11] John Harvey (ed), *The Diplomatic Diaries of Oliver Harvey, 1937-40* (Collins, London, 1970), p 187.
[12] *Ibid*, p 189.

the Prime Minister's failures in foreign policy. Vansittart, who had been replaced as Permanent Under-Secretary at the Foreign Office by Sir Alexander Cadogan, was evidently in league with Hardinge. This is borne out by the frequency with which the Private Secretary refers, in criticism, to the way Chamberlain acts without consulting the Foreign Office. It was an extraordinary campaign, on the part of the Private Secretary, to distance the King from his chief minister. Hardinge obviously thought it was necessary in view of the King's inexperience, but it is inconceivable that he, or any of his predecessors, would have dared to be so persistently hostile to any of George V's Prime Ministers. Hardinge also felt keenly that the Queen's influence on the King was not healthy at this time. She was very anti-French, in his view, pointing out France's weaknesses and repeatedly predicting that Britain would be left in the lurch. It should not set too much store by the French. These sentiments were not altered by a successful State Visit (their first) to Paris in July. Possibly Chamberlain was made aware of the fact that he had such a critic at Court, for through the King, he offered Hardinge an Indian governorship, to get him out of the way. But Hardinge, after much deliberation weighing up the pros and cons, concluded that the biggest con would be leaving the King entirely at the mercy of Chamberlain. He stayed on.

George VI soon began to appreciate the strength of opposition to the Munich Agreement, not so much because of Hardinge's influence but as a result of the doubts voiced to him by Cranborne and Halifax. The Foreign Secretary had spared the King a great deal of embarrassment by advising against the immediate offer of an honour to the Prime Minister, which Chamberlain would have refused, in view of the strong criticism of the Munich settlement which was sure to arise in Parliament. Halifax had, in fact, undergone 'an almost Damascene conversion from appeaser to resister as a result of what he saw as Chamberlain's craven acceptance of Hitler's bullying tactics at Munich.'[13]

Halifax was now convinced that Hitler could only be stopped if Britain used the brief respite bought at Munich to rearm quickly and to pursue a

---

[13] Robert Rhodes James, *A Spirit Undaunted: The Political Role of George VI* (Little Brown, London, 1998), p 146.

more forceful foreign policy. Chamberlain rejected this as too expensive and anyway unnecessary. Halifax began to distance himself from Chamberlain, something which the Prime Minister was slow to understand, but came to resent. In particular, Chamberlain rejected Halifax's advice that he should form a coalition government, including the leading Labour and Liberal figures as well as the prominent Tory rebels. Halifax was the ideal broker for such a coalition, having retained contacts with Eden, Cranborne, Amery and Churchill and having good relations with the leaders of the Labour Party and the Liberal Party.

Halifax's change of view had a marked impact on the King who, in audience with the Prime Minister on 19 October, urged the importance of rapid rearmament as a vital aid to diplomacy, and the need for the establishment of a Ministry of National Service or Supply and the formation of a national government. But Chamberlain's only concession to the King and Halifax was to invite Lord Samuel, a pro-Munich Liberal, to join the government as Lord Privy Seal; an offer which Samuel rejected. It was not until April 1939 that Chamberlain announced the appointment of a Minister of Supply, who was the National Liberal MP Leslie Burgin rather than the more dynamic Churchill. The King volunteered to lend his personal authority to the government's actions by broadcasting an appeal for nationwide voluntary service as a preparation for war. The offer was not, however, accepted by the government in case it scared people into thinking that war was imminent and led to a collapse of the Stock Exchange.

It was clear from the autumn of 1938 that the King felt it was his duty to warn Chamberlain in a subtle way about the consequences of his policy of appeasement while encouraging and supporting him in the carrying out of his heavy responsibilities. It was a delicate and complicated task which depended on the anaylses of the domestic political and foreign scenes provided by Halifax, Hardinge and Cadogan.

Chamberlain also did not share the concerns of King Carol of Romania about Hitler's aggressive aims in the Balkans in the wake of Munich. George VI brought these to the attention of the Prime Minister after the State visit of the King and Crown Prince of Romania to Britain in November 1938. That same month Parliament ratified the Anglo-Italian Agreement, concluded the previous April, which aimed to ease the friction between Britain and Italy in the Mediterranean and the Middle East. The King then offered to write to the King of Italy, Victor Emmanuel, expressing satisfaction at the good state of relations between the two countries. But the Chamberlain government thought such a message would be premature and, embarrassed by Italian transgressions, wished to postpone it.

After Chamberlain and Halifax paid a visit to Rome in January 1939, the King expressed the hope that: 'Although nothing concrete has come out of it, in the way of pacts etc, I am sure that your visit has done good in the way of personal contact with Mussolini and Ciano.' In fact Halifax was beginning to realise that Mussolini was second-rate and useless as a possible conduit to Hitler. He considered that, despite the outward show of cordial relations, Britain and Italy were worlds apart. Much of the British Establishment thought that Mussolini was now firmly in the German camp.

George VI's faith in his Prime Minister's policy of appeasement was severely shaken by Chamberlain's prediction, shortly before German troops marched into Prague in March 1939, that the international situation had seldom looked better. Unlike Chamberlain, George VI became convinced, as did Queen Elizabeth, Hardinge and Lascelles, that war was now inevitable. He intimated as much in a letter to Chamberlain, in which he said that the world would be in no doubt that Britain had tried its utmost to find a peaceful solution to Anglo-German differences.

George VI welcomed Chamberlain's surprise denunciation of Hitler in a speech in Birmingham on 17 March and the issuing of Britain's guarantee to Poland on 31 March. Despite formal and tense relations with Hardinge, George VI now paid more attention to his Private Secretary's views on the foreign and domestic political situations, especially as they were confirmed by Halifax and Cadogan. Hardinge called for a national government to include Labour, Liberals and rebel Conservatives like Churchill and Eden (but not Hoare and Simon) which could effectively pursue the new foreign policy. Although the King had his doubts about Churchill and Eden he was rapidly being won round to their view of the international situation. He was steadily moving away from Chamberlain's belief that war could be averted, a belief which made the Prime Minister a lukewarm supporter of the new vigorous foreign policy. Although George VI was constitutionally bound to continue to show loyalty to Chamberlain as Prime Minister, he did so with less and less conviction.

George VI's growing confidence in his own judgement and ability to assess men and their conflicting views was given a considerable boost in May 1939 when the King and Queen (accompanied by Lascelles but not Hardinge) visited North America. It was the first time that a British

Sovereign had ever set foot in Canada or, for that matter, the United States. George VI and Queen Elizabeth were nervous about how they would be received in both countries. This was especially the case after unflattering comparisons had been made between the new King and his elder brother, who chose this moment to broadcast an appeal for world peace from the Verdun battlefield. In fact the Canadian tour proved a great success not only for George VI but for the Monarchy (by reinforcing Canadian loyalty to the Crown which had been shaken by the Abdication). It also bolstered British interests and the fortunes of the Canadian Prime Minister, W L Mackenzie King. Ably advised by the Governor-General, Lord Tweedsmuir, the King and Queen deftly handled the vain, insecure and egotistical Canadian Prime Minister. This was to prove of inestimable value on the outbreak of war.

The US visit was kept intentionally apolitical, so as not to offend isolationist opinion, by the decision that Halifax should not accompany the King as Minister-in-Attendance. But its underlying purpose for both sides was to create links which might be needed in time of war. Everywhere the Royal visitors won friends and influenced people, none more so than in the White House. The First Lady, Eleanor Roosevelt, was impressed by the King's knowledge (the result of detailed preparation) of the names and occupations of important figures in the government and industry, and by his familiarity with the aims of the New Deal programmes. Harry Hopkins, President Roosevelt's assistant, also found himself converted from a lifelong Anglophobia by a simple gesture by the Queen. She had heard that Hopkins' small daughter had been disappointed to see her in ordinary clothes since she longed to meet a real 'Fairy Queen'. So, before the banquet at the White House, the Queen had gone upstairs to the girl's bedroom clothed in a magnificent ballgown and wearing her tiara and Garter ribbon. The gesture not only thrilled Miss Hopkins, but had the most remarkable effect on Harry Hopkins' own attitude towards Great Britain, which might have been worth a destroyer or two in the long struggle ahead.

While in the United States the King and Queen had stayed with the Roosevelts on their family estate at Hyde Park, on the Hudson River, eighty miles north of New York. George VI had two long working sessions with President Roosevelt (Mackenzie King, who had insisted on accompanying the King south of the border, was present at only one of these sessions, much to his chagrin). Roosevelt was at his most expansive, throwing out ideas about US naval patrols in the Western Atlantic and the use of British bases in Canada and the West Indies in the event of Britain going to war with Germany. The King made extensive notes and was able to communicate the substance of his talks to ministers on his return to London. Although Roosevelt later modified his talk of aiding Britain in the event of war, in deference to American public opinion, this does not detract from the fact that the US President had demonstrated his willingness to support Britain in its stand against Nazi Germany.

George VI felt, justifiably, that he had won his spurs in the 'efficient' business of Monarchy as, with the Coronation behind him, he had already done with the 'dignified' part. It might have been a telling decision not to take Hardinge with him on his North American trip. Certainly his confidence grew apace as a result of it. As Wheeler-Bennett noted: 'The North American tour was indeed a climacteric in the King's life. It had taken him out of himself, had opened up for him wider horizons and introduced to him new ideas.'[14] Now at last he felt he could trust in his own judgement, and define a style of kingship which truly reflected his own tastes, and his new maturity. He told one of his advisers during the North American trip that 'there must be no more high-hat business, the sort of things that my father and those of his day regarded as essential as the correct attitude — the feeling that certain things could not be done'.[15]

The British public were impressed by the success of the tour and gave the King and the Queen a tumultuous welcome on their return to Britain on 22 June. The next day, in a speech at the Guildhall in which he fulfilled his role as head of the nation and the Empire-Commonwealth, the King articulated the emotion felt by him, and his people, that the principles of liberty, justice and peace which they held so dear, were under threat and that they must be defended at all costs. George VI was now ready for the war, and the special fusion of identity between him and his people which he was later to feel, was forged in that bloody crucible. He was his own man.

---

[14] Wheeler-Bennett, *George VI*, p 392.

[15] Sarah Bradford, *The Reluctant King* (St Martin's Press, New York, 1989), p 299.

8

Looking the East End in the Face

Europe was in a state of ominous calm in the summer of 1939, while the Allies and the Germans bid for the favours of the Soviet Union. The newly-confident King suggested to the Prime Minister and Foreign Secretary that they use his cousin, Prince Philip of Hesse (who had acted as a personal liaison officer between Mussolini and Hitler) to convey a warning to the German leader that Britain would stand no more Munichs. Chamberlain and Halifax turned down the idea. Following the conclusion of the Nazi-Soviet Pact on 22 August, and the abandonment of the Anti-Comintern Pact which so astonished the Japanese, George VI was quick to propose that he should write to the Japanese Emperor, Hirohito. Halifax thought this unwise as the gesture could be rejected and Britain would lose face. Under pressure from President Roosevelt and other leaders, the King then proposed that he make a direct appeal to Hitler, though he had little confidence that it would work. Chamberlain thought the moment inopportune. The time for appeals soon vanished. On 1 September the Nazi blitzkrieg hit Poland.

The King, Parliament and the people expected Britain to declare war on Germany immediately, and feared a repeat of Munich while Chamberlain prevaricated. It took considerable pressure from the Cabinet, and the threat of a revolt in Parliament, to force the Prime Minister to issue an ultimatum to the Nazi government that if it did not agree to withdraw from Poland by 11am on 3 September Britain would consider itself at war with Germany. This duly occurred and the King broadcast to the country and the Empire, declaring his belief that the right of Britain's cause would triumph over the might of Nazi Germany. It struck the right note and gave encouragement to the British Empire in its time of peril.

The King was immediately faced with a constitutional problem in South Africa. Australia, New Zealand and Canada had followed Britain in declaring war on Germany. In contrast, South Africa was divided between those Boer nationalists, led by the Prime Minister, Hertzog, who favoured neutrality, and the moderate Afrikaners and English-speakers, led by the deputy Prime Minister, Smuts, who supported going to war. After the South African Parliament voted to declare war on Germany, on condition that South African forces did not serve outside Africa, Hertzog requested a dissolution from the Governor-General, Sir Patrick Duncan. In the exceptional circumstances of the time, when a general election could be so divisive, Duncan refused a dissolution on the grounds that Hertzog had only minority support in both his Cabinet and Parliament. Consequently, Hertzog resigned and Smuts, whom Duncan knew could command a majority in Parliament, became Prime Minister. His government declared war on Germany on 6 September.

Although the exceptional circumstances may have justified Duncan's actions, there was some nervousness among the King's advisers over the fact that no modern British monarch had refused a Prime Minister's request for a dissolution. When the Governor-General of Canada, Field Marshal Lord Byng, had refused a dissolution to the Liberal leader, Mackenzie King, in 1926 and then granted one to the Conservative leader, Arthur Meighen, he caused considerable resentment. Duncan's action raised even more controversy in South Africa. Hertzog was to join with the Nationalists in January 1940 to try and get Parliament to pass a motion calling for the end of the war. The motion was narrowly defeated in the lower house. But many South Africans continued to oppose involvement in what they saw as Britain's war.

The outbreak of war heralded a new routine for the King and involved him more closely in the conduct of official business. This was partly because the pace of government obviously quickened — at least that part of it which was concerned with the war effort. Partly it was because the King was a natural bridge between the political and military worlds, as no one else was. He was in a privileged position in both communities — the touchstone of the Prime Minister on the one hand, and the focus of all seniority and loyalty on the other. Like his father, he wore uniform every day until the war was over. He performed an extraordinary role and it took its toll on his health. Hardinge wrote after the war that: 'the King was in the unenviable position of receiving all the unfavourable reports of a highly secret nature, without the power of taking any action which seemed to him necessary to remedy the misfortunes. The strain of enforced inaction in time of crisis is exceptionally great, and there is little doubt that it told heavily on King George during those terrible years.'[1]

Following the outbreak of war Chamberlain had been forced by Parliament and public opinion to bring Churchill back to the Admiralty, and to appoint Eden to the Dominions Office. The King had his doubts about Eden and found Churchill difficult to converse with, but he hoped to remedy this. The King had been disappointed that Chamberlain had not brought in Labour and Liberal politicians to form a truly national government so as to reflect the nation's unified determination to fight the war. But the fact was that Chamberlain and Attlee hated each other and Attlee had peremptorily dismissed Chamberlain's half-hearted approach to him.

George VI was also appalled by the defeatist and narrow-minded attitude of the US Ambassador in London, Joseph Kennedy, towards the Allied cause. He took the opportunity of a tea-time chat to stiffen Kennedy's backbone, and then followed it up with a sharp letter, which had to be toned down by Chamberlain and Halifax. The King was responsible, with ministerial approval, for bolstering the confidence of another representative of a neutral country, King Boris II of Bulgaria, in his attempts to stay out of the Axis orbit. George VI contributed to the conclusion of the Anglo-French alliance with Turkey in September 1939 by convincing the head of the Turkish Military Mission to London that this was desirable despite the fact that Britain and France would not be able to spare much military equipment for Turkey.

The outbreak of war required the King to confront the problem of what to do with his elder brother. The Duke and Duchess of Windsor were living in the south of France and, as if the King and the government did not have enough on their minds, the Duke started to play up. He said he would refuse to board a special aeroplane sent to take the Windsors back to England unless he and his wife were asked to Windsor Castle. The

---

[1] Hardinge, *Loyal to Three Kings*, p 188.

aeroplane was not sent. The question of a job then arose, and Chamberlain told Walter Monckton, who was acting as intermediary, that the Duke of Windsor could either be Deputy Regional Commissioner for Wales or Liaison Officer in the British Military Mission to General Gamelin, the French Commander-in-Chief. The Windsors eventually motored to Cherbourg, whence they were taken across the Channel in HMS *Kelly*, whose captain was Lord Louis Mountbatten.

Their sojourn in England was a disaster. The Palace refused to send a car for them; there was no official greeting; and the Wales regional commissionership, which the Duke of Windsor tentatively accepted, was effectively dropped. He had one meeting with the King, another with Chamberlain, Churchill, Halifax and Hore-Belisha, the Secretary of State for War. He was invited to the War Office, where the Chief of the Imperial General Staff, Field Marshal Lord Ironside, told him he was to be assigned to the British Military Mission at the French Army headquarters at Vincennes, outside Paris, as a Major-General (he was still, of course, technically a Field Marshal). He was to leave as soon as possible. The Duke did not want to surrender his Field Marshal's baton, and he also wanted to spend some time first in the Home Commands of the UK, getting to know troops and, incidentally, taking his Duchess with him.

This was too much for George VI, who sent for Hore-Belisha. 'He was in a distressed state,' Hore-Belisha recalled in his diary.[2] The King thought that if the Duchess of Windsor went to the Commands she might have a hostile reception, particularly in Scotland. He did not want the Duke to go to the Commands in England. The King seemed very disturbed and walked up and down the room as he spoke. Later that day, in another interview, the King remarked that all his ancestors had succeeded to the Throne after their predecessors had died. 'Mine is not only alive, but very much so.'[3] He wanted the Duke to go to Paris at once. There were other wrangles about rank, pay — or rather no pay — and whether or not the Duke could retrieve his honorary colonelcy of the Welsh Guards.

Eventually the Duke of Windsor went off to Vincennes. Although he may have engaged in his liaison duties with some enthusiasm and allegedly

---

[2] R J Minney, *The Private Papers of Hore-Belisha* (Collins, London, 1960), p 238.
[3] *Ibid*.

did some good work, it cannot really be denied that his experiences in England, and the generally dismissive way he was treated, left him disgruntled — ripe for the kind of manipulative flattery to which he was soon to be exposed by emissaries of the Nazi regime.

He clearly had not yet learnt how to behave, or how to come to terms with his new status. His habit of visiting the troops of the British Expeditionary Force (BEF) in France as if he was still a King and a Field Marshal caused problems. When London restricted these activities, however, he reacted badly. In November 1939 he sent a message to Monckton to say that he intended to fly over to London on a private plane to contact the King. George VI refused to see him unless the CIGS, Ironside, was present. In the event, the latter dissuaded the Duke from journeying to England, but the whole episode further embittered the Duke's attitude to the war. He and Beaverbrook even discussed the near treasonable possibility of the Duke returning to England to agitate for a peace settlement with Germany. He was dissuaded from this by Monckton, who pointed out to him that his return would make him liable to pay British income tax, something he was always loath to do.

The King fretted, as did many of his people, at the frustration and inactivity of the protracted stalemate on most fronts in the war. It was a period which an American journalist dubbed 'the Phoney War'. He was somewhat reluctant, a reluctance only increased by his tendency to stutter when under pressure, to resume his father's habit of broadcasting a Christmas message to Britain and the Empire on Christmas Day. Yet his first Christmas broadcast struck the right note due to the King's poetical allusion to the Almighty guiding the British Empire through the dark days of war, and his homely and halting delivery. He was a much better broadcaster than he gave himself credit for, and his Christmas broadcasts were to give great comfort to an embattled people.

The King also had to bolster a Prime Minister who was suffering from ill-health and a collapse of confidence following the failure of his policy of appeasement. Chamberlain's weakening grip on the situation and his reliance on the King's support was again demonstrated during the great 'Pill-Box Row', which led to the resignation of the flamboyant, reforming Secretary of State for War, Hore-Belisha, in January 1940. It was the King who, after a visit to the BEF in France in early December, first alerted the Prime Minister to the great resentment felt by the Commander-in-Chief of the BEF, Lord Gort, and his generals at Hore-Belisha's criticism of their defensive preparations along the Franco-Belgian border (in particular, the provision of adequate pill-boxes).[4]

The need to resolve a potentially dangerous dispute which might weaken the war effort led the King, along with two powerful civil servants, Sir Horace Wilson and Sir Edward Bridges, the Cabinet Secretary, to press Chamberlain to replace Hore-Belisha.[5] Although the Prime Minister learnt at first hand of the dissension between the BEF and the War Office when he visited France in mid-December 1939, he refused to remove Hore-Belisha. By the New Year, however, Chamberlain had decided to offer 'H-B' the Ministry of Information. But he withdrew his offer at the last minute on the advice of Halifax and Cadogan, who objected to the allegedly negative effect that a Jewish propagandist might have on neutral opinion. An indignant Hore-Belisha rejected Chamberlain's substitute offer of the Board of Trade, a post which was outside the Cabinet. Worried by the prospect of 'H-B' making trouble and a hostile press coverage the Prime Minister wrote to the King requesting him to assuage Hore-Belisha's wounded pride when the Secretary of State for War surrendered his seal of office. The King's sympathetic handling of Hore-Belisha at an audience on 9 January helped to defuse a potentially explosive situation.

Hardinge thought that the government would survive the critical debate in the House of Commons on 7-8 May 1940 on the Norwegian campaign, but that it would fall after the next disaster, perhaps opening up the way for Churchill to become head of a national government. In order to avoid these undesirable events, Hardinge believed it vital for Chamberlain to bring the Opposition into his government. The great obstacle to such a move continued to be the Labour Party's refusal to serve under Chamberlain. The King, on Hardinge's advice, saw the Prime Minister and offered to speak to Attlee on the need to join the government to help save the country. Chamberlain accepted the offer but advised the King to wait until after the Labour Party conference was held at the Whitsun weekend when he thought the Labour leaders might be more prepared to commit themselves to join the government.

---

[4] Rhodes James, *Spirit Undaunted*, pp 181-2.
[5] Bradford, *Reluctant King*, p 307.

The situation changed drastically as a result of the great debate of 8 May, which went so badly for the government (its majority dropping to 81). It was clear that the government had to be reconstructed immediately. The next day Chamberlain, Halifax, Churchill and Margesson (the Tory Chief Whip) agreed that if the Labour leaders refused to serve under Chamberlain, he would resign and recommend to the King (if asked) that Halifax should succeed him. While the Labour leaders consulted their party executive, Halifax selflessly decided that he could not provide the inspirational leadership which was required in such a moment of peril for the nation.

Although the King offered, if Chamberlain had to resign, to try to persuade Halifax, whom he thought the 'obvious man', to become Prime Minister, he was overtaken by events. On the morning of 10 May Germany invaded Holland and Belgium and the battle for Western Europe began. It was clear to most people that Churchill was the one to lead the country. That afternoon the Labour leaders reaffirmed, after consulting their executive, that they would not serve under Chamberlain, but would be prepared to serve under someone else. Chamberlain then resigned and recommended to the King that Churchill should be appointed Prime Minister. After further deliberation at the Palace, during which it became clear that there was no alternative to Churchill, the King sent for him and asked him to form a government. The dynamic Churchill accepted.

The King had not appointed his new Prime Minister with great personal enthusiasm. Churchill's championship of Edward VIII's cause during the Abdication stood against him in George VI's reckoning — which was of great emotional consequence to the King. The disloyalty shown by Churchill towards Chamberlain as Tory Party leader and Prime Minister over appeasement was also a characteristic which the King disliked. But he had had enough experience of politics to know that there were few politicians — with the possible exception of Austen Chamberlain —who were entirely free from disloyalty to one degree or other. Churchill might indeed be a necessary wartime Prime Minister, as the panzers thundered through Western Europe and Britain licked its wounds from the defeat in Norway; but he did not on his record appear to be wholly a gentleman. He was widely distrusted in Whitehall and Westminster as a political adventurer, who had taken foolhardy risks in the past, such as that which had led to disaster at Gallipoli.

Moreover, the King's self-confidence was a fragile plant. Chamberlain, though older than Churchill, did not really seem quite so grand. The latter, after all, had been a Cabinet Minister in the reign of the King's grandfather, Edward VII. The young King and Queen were worried about being upstaged by a man whose spell-binding rhetoric — whose whole political presence — was clearly ready-made for public consumption.

The King's doubts about Churchill as Prime Minister seemed initially to be justified by the latter's notorious unpunctuality for audiences and by his appointment of Lord Beaverbrook to the post of Minister of Aircraft Production and his insistence that Brendan Bracken be made a Privy Councillor. The King revealed that he had 'a mind of his own' when he registered his disapproval of the appointment of such men, whom his friend Halifax regarded as 'gangsters'. The King eventually grew to appreciate Bracken's qualities but never fully trusted Beaverbrook.

With regard to the other ministerial appointments, the King thought Sir Archibald Sinclair (the Liberal leader and Secretary of State for Air) had an attractive personality but he did not trust his political outlook. He got to know Eden, the new Foreign Secretary, and came to admire his diplomatic talents; although the Queen had doubts about Eden's strength of character. Of the Labour ministers, the King liked best Ernest Bevin, the Minister of Labour, with his strong character, earthy good humour, common sense and forthright manner. He also got on well with that fervent monarchist Herbert Morrison, the Home Secretary. He found the monosyllabic 'Clam' Attlee, the Lord Privy Seal, difficult to communicate with and he positively loathed the bullying, arrogant Hugh Dalton, the Minister of Economic Warfare. But the King had finally achieved the coalition government for which he had long pressed.

As the German war machine rolled through Western Europe destroying all opposition, the King performed a useful role, as head of state, as a rallying point for the continued resistance against the Nazis. He greeted King Haakon of Norway and Queen Wilhemina of the Netherlands after they had fled their conquered countries. He appealed to Leopold, King of the Belgians, to follow the example of his fellow sovereigns and flee to Britain to set up a government in exile. Nevertheless he accepted Leopold's final decision that he should stay with his people. He refused to join in the campaign of vilification waged against Leopold by Churchill and other ministers. As Gort prepared to evacuate the BEF from Dunkirk, George VI broadcast to the Empire, denouncing German aggression and calling for a resolute defence from the British peoples. He sent a message of encouragement to the embattled troops in Belgium.

When France fell, the King sent a message, at Churchill's suggestion, to the French President, Lebrun, urging him to ensure that the French Navy did not fall into hostile hands. It arrived too late to have any influence, and the Royal Navy took the drastic step of crippling the French fleet at Oran on 3 July. The King also welcomed General de Gaulle to Britain, where he formed the Free French movement. George VI gave sympathetic consideration to the position and needs of this difficult representative of the immortal spirit of France, which helped to mitigate the often stormy relationship which de Gaulle was to have with Churchill and Roosevelt.

At such a critical time, the King was again confronted with the problem of what to do with his elder brother. After the Germans had invaded France, the Duke and Duchess of Windsor fled to Spain. It did not seem right to Churchill that the couple should stay in a neutral though unfriendly country. Sir Samuel Hoare, who was then the Ambassador in Madrid, was instructed to tell the couple that the Prime Minister felt they should return to England. A flying boat would be sent to await them in Lisbon. The Duke of Windsor started to lay down conditions (that his wife should be recognised as a member of the Royal Family and that he should be offered an important post), refusing to go until they were met. The Nazis at once saw an opportunity to make use of him. It was a time, after Dunkirk and before the Battle of Britain, when Ribbentrop (now the German Foreign Minister) fully expected the British to seek some accommodation. What better person to use as a lever to make the British see sense than their ex-King, who still would command some respect, loyalty, and above all, legitimacy in the event of Britain's defeat and its occupation by Germany.

So the Germans worked to prevent the Windsors from leaving the Continent. A special emissary, the resourceful SS officer Walter Schellenberg, was sent by Ribbentrop to soften up the Duke, in harness with the German Ambassador to Spain, von Stohrer, and the German Minister in Lisbon, Hoyningen-Huene. Ribbentrop asked the Spanish authorities to see if they could delay the Windsors' passage through Spain to Portugal, while the contacts were made. But the Spanish Foreign Minister, Colonel Beigbeder, made no real effort to prevent the Windsors from leaving for Lisbon on 2 July. In the end, after lengthy bargaining with Churchill and the King, the Duke agreed to become Governor of the Bahamas.

The Germans, however, were not yet ready to abandon their efforts to scare or flatter the Duke into remaining in Europe. Using intermediaries such as Don Miguel Primo de Rivera (the son of the former dictator), they warned of British and German assassination plots if he went to the Bahamas, stressing the need for him to stay in Europe to act as a possible intermediary between Germany and Britain in the event of the latter's military collapse. In London, the Cabinet were not privy to all the details, but were dimly aware that something fishy was going on and must be stopped as quickly as possible by getting the Duke away to the Bahamas. Walter Monckton was despatched to Lisbon to convince the Duke that he must leave Portugal. He succeeded in outflanking Primo de Rivera and Schellenberg and convinced the Duke that there was a greater risk in his staying there than leaving as planned. On 2 August 1940 the Windsors sailed for the Bahamas.

There is little doubt that throughout this unhappy episode the Duke thought that Britain was likely to lose the war and, if so, that he might have a role to play in making terms with Germany. He was not alone among his countrymen in thinking this, but he was indiscreet enough to voice these doubts aloud to various Spaniards, Portuguese and American diplomats. None of this was tantamount to treason. Nor was it likely that, in the event of the Germans having successfully invaded Britain, he would have consented to become a puppet King, ruling over his sullen subjects. He may have been difficult and acted foolishly during the fall of France and his flight to Lisbon but he would not have wished ill upon his fellow countrymen.

The fall of France was followed by the Battle of Britain. As this raged, and invasion seemed imminent, the King suggested to the Prime Minister that they replace their increasingly frequent formal audiences with a regular Tuesday lunch. It was by this means that George VI and Churchill got to know each other better and to discuss the most secret aspects of the war. They not only came to trust and respect each other but to develop a genuine friendship. Churchill, like the other Coalition ministers, came to value the King's common sense and judgement, and admired and respected his moral and physical courage. The King was not only consulted but gave his encouragement and issued warnings. He was given the ability to know. This gave him considerable political influence with the Coalition government. Churchill, a staunch royalist with a strong sense of his own place in English history, compared his relationship with the King as being akin to that of his ancestor, John Churchill, the first Duke of Marlborough, with Queen Anne during the War of the Spanish Succession.

George VI's first Tuesday lunch with Churchill nearly turned out to be their last. On the morning of 13 September 1940 Buckingham Palace was deliberately bombed by a German aircraft and the King and the Queen narrowly escaped serious injury. The actual and symbolic importance of this should not be underestimated. George VI and Queen Elizabeth had had the same experience of being bombed as the residents of London and the other big cities. As the Queen put it: 'We can now look the East End in the face.' But their determination to continue their royal duties in a bombed and boarded up Buckingham Palace, with the royal standard defiantly flying above it, throughout the war provided an inspiring example to the nation and the Empire-Commonwealth, of British resistance to Nazi aggression.

The King chose to make, often in person, weekly investitures at Buckingham Palace. He was responsible for instituting the George Cross and George Medal in recognition of civilian bravery, which had been amply demonstrated during the Battle of Britain and the Blitz. The King's concern for the heroes and victims of the Blitz was not confined to London. George VI and Queen Elizabeth were quick to visit Coventry in November 1940 to comfort the inhabitants of that city following the devastating German raids. Visits to other bombed cities followed. It was through these visits that the King and the Queen came to learn at first hand, and often to share, the dangers and privations that their people were experiencing during the war. It not only earned them great respect but made them very popular in Britain, and also throughout the Empire-Commonwealth and the free world. It also had the effect of entrenching the Monarchy even deeper in the nation's affections.

In his role as head of the nation, George VI personified Britain's dogged resistance to the Axis juggernaut. His position as head of state gave his intervention extra authority, especially overseas. He wrote on ministerial advice, and with mixed results, to other heads of states. He urged Marshal Pétain (head of the Vichy régime in France), rather tardily and therefore unsuccessfully, not to collaborate with Hitler. He communicated with King Boris of Bulgaria, Prince Paul of Yugoslavia and King George of Greece to stiffen their resistance. They held out until the spring of 1941, when the Germans forced Bulgaria and Yugoslavia into the Axis Pact. This precipitated in swift succession a Palace coup in Belgrade (and the brief assumption to power of King Peter), followed by the Nazi invasion of Yugoslavia and Greece.

If George VI's personal contacts with his fellow sovereigns and heads of state in the Mediterranean had mixed results, he had better luck across the Atlantic with President Roosevelt. The King's pre-war Hyde Park talks paid dividends when, at the urging of Churchill, the King and Lord Lothian (the British Ambassador in Washington), Britain secured in September 1940 fifty old but much-needed destroyers in exchange for allowing the United States to use British Caribbean bases for its hemispheric defence. The King was quick to congratulate Roosevelt, whom he regarded as an essential friend of Britain, on his re-election for an unprecedented third term as President in November; a gesture which FDR much appreciated. When Lothian died suddenly in December, the King was instrumental in persuading a reluctant Halifax to take his place (after Churchill appointed Eden to the Foreign Office). When Halifax arrived in the United States, he was welcomed by the President in person. George VI reciprocated when John Winant, the American Ambassador who succeeded Joseph Kennedy, arrived in London. Winant was met personally at the station by the King. This was all part of the King's effort to use his authority to the best effect wherever and whenever he could.

Encouraged by Roosevelt's right-hand man, Harry Hopkins, the King took the opportunity for further correspondence with the President, expressing Britain's appreciation for Lend-Lease and the US Atlantic patrols in his letters to the President (which supplemented the more famous Churchill-Roosevelt correspondence). The King encouraged the idea of a face-to-face meeting between Roosevelt and Churchill which bore fruit in the Allied summit at Placentia Bay, Newfoundland, in August 1941, and the joint declaration of peace aims known as the Atlantic Charter.

Roosevelt confided his fears about Japan's intentions to the King in the autumn of 1941, and George VI rightly concluded that war was imminent. This did not, however, mitigate the shocking effects of the Japanese attacks on Pearl Harbor, the Philippines, Hong Kong and Malaya and the loss of the British battleship, *Prince of Wales*, and the battlecruiser, *Repulse*. The King, writing to the President afterwards, emphasised the 'comradeship of common loss' of Britain and the United States. Worse was to come, as the two island fortresses of Singapore and Corregidor fell and the Japanese forces swept through Burma to the frontiers of India, and through the South-West Pacific to threaten Australia and New Zealand.

The seemingly unending series of British defeats, not only in the Far East but in North Africa, undermined public confidence in Churchill's conduct of the war and led to calls in Parliament and the Press for him to do less. After sounding out the politicians, Hardinge suggested a reconstruction of the government and it was the King who persuaded Churchill on 17 February to agree to this. Out went Sir Kingsley Wood and Arthur Greenwood, and in came Sir Stafford Cripps as Lord Privy Seal and Leader of the House of Commons. But the King failed to convince Churchill of the need for him to rest more and to delegate some of his work to Cripps, Eden, and Oliver Lyttelton minister of Production.

The King was also concerned at the risks Churchill was taking in his frequent journeys by plane and warship across war zones to summit conferences. Indeed Churchill's recklessness became something of an obsession with the King, and in Attlee he found a sympathetic and sometimes amused confidant. However, it would not have been to Attlee, the Lord President of the Council, to whom he would have turned had some catastrophe deprived him of his Prime Minister.

In June 1942, on the eve of Churchill's departure for Washington, the King asked his Prime Minister for advice as to whom he would recommend as his successor in the event of his death. Churchill formally submitted the name of Eden, the Foreign Secretary. Later on the King asked for further advice, when both Churchill and Eden were proposing to be absent together at Yalta in 1945. Churchill's advice then was to send for Sir John Anderson, who was neither a member of the Conservative Party nor a professional politician. His reasons were that Anderson would be more effective in keeping the Coalition together. After a general election, he went on to say, if a Conservative majority was again returned, the Conservatives might then request Sir John to become their leader — he sat as an Independent member for the Scottish Universities — or they might choose someone else. But it would not follow that, even if the Conservatives held a majority after a subsequent election, they would be happy to serve under the Premiership of Sir John Anderson. Certainly, Churchill advised, the King should not send for anyone 'in any way obnoxious to the Party which holds predominance in the House of Commons at the actual moment' — in other words not Attlee.[6]

---

[6] Wheeler-Bennett, *George VI*, p 546.

It is an interesting exchange and, as Wheeler-Bennett noted, it must be the only time a Prime Minister 'should have designated the succession of the premiership as it were to the third and fourth generation'.[7] It would not have bound the King in any way if Churchill and Eden had been killed — but it might have been a useful piece of guidance as to the kind of person he should summon, even if it had turned out to be Anderson. The King's prerogative remained intact, and he could either have acted on Churchill's advice, as though on his initiative, or else summoned the leaders of the parties in the wartime coalition government and discussed it with them. His objective, like his father's, would surely have been to preserve the coalition intact and, in accordance with sound constitutional doctrines, choose the man most likely to achieve that purpose in the minimum time. As it happened, he was saved such difficulties. However, he sought an extra reassurance by asking Churchill and Eden to fly in different planes to the conferences at Malta and Yalta. This they managed to achieve only as far as Naples, from there they had to go on to Malta and Yalta in a single plane, after a bad landing had crucially damaged the undercarriage of the second aircraft.

The Prime Minister and the Foreign Secretary survived their wartime travels but the King's youngest brother, the Duke of Kent, did not. He was killed 'in the line of duty' in an aircraft crash in Scotland in August 1942. In their grief the King and the Royal Family shared the experience of many families throughout the nation and the Empire-Commonwealth. The King arranged with Churchill for the Princess Olga (Princess Paul of Yugoslavia), who was in exile in Kenya, to be flown to England to comfort her sister, the Duchess of Kent.

The death of the Duke of Kent made the question of the employment of the King's only surviving brother in the UK, the Duke of Gloucester, even more pressing. Sir Alan Brooke, the CIGS, was sympathetic towards Gloucester's plight but had to operate with some finesse during the summer of 1942 when the King asked him to find work for the Duke at the War Office. 'From what I had seen of him in France [where he had been liaison officer at Gort's GHQ in 1939], I knew he could not have stood the pace and that used as a permanent assistant he would have acted as a permanent

---

[7] *Ibid.*

drag.' At least the King had given up suggesting a command for his brother and was 'as usual perfectly charming'.[8] The CIGS was able to prevaricate, not only with the King but also with the Duke of Gloucester, who asked to be employed at the War Office. Brooke replied: 'Not an easy job!'[9] In the event the Duke of Gloucester carried out representative duties at home on behalf of the King until he was sent to Australia in November 1943 as Governor-General.

The King and the Queen also shared the wartime austerities of their subjects. On her visit to Britain in the autumn of 1942, Eleanor Roosevelt was much struck by the spartan regime at Buckingham Palace. She thought that George VI and Queen Elizabeth were 'doing an extraordinarily outstanding job for their people in the most trying of times . . .'[10] The First Lady had found it easier to talk to the King than to the Prime Minister, though this might have had something to do with the fact that Churchill was preoccupied with the outcome of the battle of El Alamein. When the Prime Minister brought the King and the Queen the news of the British victory, they could not quite believe it at first, so inured had they become to the long and depressing catalogue of British defeats. But they were as overjoyed as the rest of the nation. The King noted in his diary: 'A victory at last. How good it is for the nerves.'[11] The King was quick to congratulate his Prime Minister on the 'great Victory' and Churchill's efforts to bring it about.

However, the King was not happy about the American deal with the Vichy French commanders Admiral Darlan and General Giraud after the Allied landings in French North Africa in November 1942. The King felt strongly that the United States and Britain should back the Free French leader, General de Gaulle. After the assassination of Darlan in Algiers had solved this particular problem, Roosevelt and Churchill were prepared to sideline de Gaulle if he continued to refuse to reach a compromise with Giraud. It was the King who impressed on Churchill the need to give sympathetic understanding to de Gaulle's revulsion at having to deal with

---

[8]   King's College, London, Liddell-Hart Archive, Alanbrooke MS Diaries, entry for 28 August 1942.

[9]   Bradford, *Reluctant King*, p 347.

[10]   *Ibid*, p 349.

[11]   Rhodes James, *Spirit Undaunted*, p 223.

the Vichy authorities. The King hoped also that when the Allies landed in Italy there would be no attempt to reach agreement with a quisling regime. Churchill took the King's criticism seriously enough to summon the CIGS, Brooke, urgently to help him answer it. Brooke regretted that the King felt it necessary to disturb Churchill at the time, since the Prime Minister was suffering from pneumonia. Churchill rebutted the King's criticisms in a lengthy letter which Brooke helped to draft. Two days later, on 25 February 1943, Brooke was summoned to the Palace to brief the King on the military situation in North Africa (the Americans had just taken the Kasserine Pass). Brooke marvelled at the detailed knowledge the King had about all that was going on. He had 'an excellent knowledge of operations on all fronts, and, what is more, a very shrewd idea of the differences between the PM and Chiefs of Staff.'[12]

The King, as usual, maintained his hold on military authority as much through his attention to detail, as because of his senior rank. He personally designed new medal ribbons; he rebuked the commander of the Eighth Army, General Montgomery, for being improperly dressed; and he visited troops whenever he could, the highlight of this involvement being his visit to North Africa and Malta in June 1943, following the surrender of Axis forces in Tunisia in May. The visit was his initiative, approved by the War Cabinet. In one day he managed to be seen in person by 8,000 troops. This probably fortified his position both in his and their eyes even more than the fact that he also spent time with the Supreme Allied Commander, General Eisenhower, Montgomery, the Commander-in-Chief in the Middle East, General Alexander, and de Gaulle. He took with him Hardinge and Lt Colonel Sir Piers ('Joey') Legh.

The King's lunch for Giraud and de Gaulle, during which he spoke to both men in French, helped to keep alive the possibility of a compromise between the two, as de Gaulle then withdrew the resignation he had tendered that very morning. His talks with Eisenhower, whom he endowed with the Order of the Bath, can only have helped to invigorate the already warm feelings that the General held for the alliance — though he had been somewhat irritated that his office had not been in any way involved in the preparations for the King's visit to the theatre over which he held

---

[12] Alanbrooke Diaries, entry for 25 February 1943, Alanbrooke papers.

the supreme command. Harold Macmillan, who was then Minister Resident at Allied Force Headquarters in Algiers, blamed Hardinge for this omission. Macmillan salvaged the situation by organising a royal garden party for British and American officers and civilians and arranging a royal visit to an American training camp.

The highlight of the King's trip was his visit by warship to Malta, the island fortress that had withstood the Axis air assault for three years. In an imaginative gesture George VI had in April 1942 recognised the bravery of the British and Maltese defenders of the island by conferring upon it the George Cross. Over a year later he was able to pay his own tribute and that of the Empire-Commonwealth to Malta by visiting the island and handing the Governor, his friend Lord Gort, a Field Marshal's baton. The King was touched by the rousing reception he was given by the islanders and did not object to his white naval uniform being stained red by the thousands of geraniums which were thrown at him by well-wishers as he drove around the island in an open-topped vehicle.

The King returned to Britain exhausted but exhilarated by his experiences. Hardinge too was tired out from his travels and, having suffered previously from ill-health, he resigned from his post after arguing with Lascelles. The point of contention was Hardinge's failure to delegate his responsibilities and keep his assistant private secretary adequately informed (eg over the establishment of the Council of State in the King's absence and the appointment of Field Marshal Wavell as Viceroy of India) before his departure overseas. Following the ill-organised trip, the King accepted Hardinge's resignation 'as I was not altogether happy with him and had always found him difficult to talk to & discuss matters with. I knew & felt that he was doing me no good.'[13]

Hardinge was replaced as Private Secretary by Lascelles, who was to have an easier relationship with the King. Although Lascelles had long distrusted Churchill, and it was to take time for them to get on proper terms, it did not really matter since the King had a close relationship with the Prime Minister and did not need a go-between. Lascelles had better contacts than Hardinge in Whitehall and Westminister and his understanding of Attlee was to prove useful to the King after the war. It

---

[13] Rhodes James, *Spirit Undaunted*, p 248.

was Lascelles who persuaded the King in September 1943 that Lord Cranborne would be more useful as Dominions Secretary than as Lord President of the Council, but it was the King who suggested it to the Prime Minister. Churchill rather romantically interpreted it as a command and acceded to it (Attlee becoming Lord President).

By the autumn of 1943 it was clear that the tide of battle had turned against the Axis forces on all fronts although it was plain that their retreat would be hard-fought. It had been decided earlier in the year at the Casablanca Conference that Anglo-American forces would invade Western Europe in 1944 under Operation 'Overlord'. The King was intimately concerned with the D-Day planning from a very early stage. Indeed in October 1943 he arranged a private dinner for Smuts and Churchill, so that his South African Prime Minister could press the case against the Normandy landings on the grounds that the Mediterranean strategy was more urgent and at the same time more rewarding. Smuts was also concerned to prevent the Soviet armies from overrunning the Balkans. The King agreed with Smuts, and at least felt that Churchill, as a result of their warnings, now accepted the need to see that the Mediterranean campaigns were not neglected because of the planning for 'Operation Overlord'.

By the time that Overlord came along he was totally caught up in it, visiting every unit beforehand, attending the final allied briefing, and even for a moment considering a personal appearance at sea to observe the landings. So, too was Churchill. Lascelles intervened forcefully to dissuade both of them. He asked whether the King was prepared to advise Princess Elizabeth on the choice of her first Prime Minister if her father and Mr Churchill were killed simultaneously. Lascelles succeeded with the King; but Churchill behaved more like a furtive schoolboy caught contemplating truancy. Lascelles pressed again: 'It is not going to make things easier for you if you have to find a new Prime Minister in the middle of Overlord,' he told the King.[14] Churchill initially waved those objections aside: 'Oh that's all arranged for,' he said (presumably with his previous exchange on the subject at the back of his mind), 'and anyhow I don't think the risk is 100 to one'.[15] The King, at the urging of General Ismay, the Chief of Staff

---

[14] Wheeler-Bennett, *George VI*, p 604.
[15] *Ibid*.

to the Minister of Defence (Churchill) and Military Secretary to the Cabinet, finally sent his Prime Minister a handwritten note, asking him to desist from his plan. When he received no answer, the King debated whether to journey to Portsmouth to prevent Churchill from boarding HMS *Belfast*. It took a last-minute telephone call from Lascelles to the special train carrying Churchill to Portsmouth finally to get the Prime Minister to comply, albeit reluctantly, with the King's wishes. Churchill subsequently wrote that he 'felt obliged to defer to His Majesty's wishes and indeed commands'.[16] 'Thank heavens the King used his authority to stop it,' noted the CIGS, Brooke, in his diary. George VI had not seen the episode as a constitutional matter, though Lascelles had rather counter-productively pointed out to Churchill that he could not go abroad without the King's permission. The King noted in his diary that: 'I asked him as a friend not to endanger his life & so put me and everyone else in a difficult position.'[17] In the event both Churchill and the King were to visit the beachheads in Normandy soon after they had been established.

The King followed this up with visits to General Alexander's forces in Italy and later to General Montgomery's army after it had advanced into Holland. But George VI was prevented by the Prime Minister from visiting General Slim's 'Forgotten Army' in Burma, as desired by the King and his cousin Lord Louis Mountbatten, the Supreme Allied Commander in South-East Asia.

Churchill feared that the nationalists in India would expect George VI to make some statement on the future of the sub-continent. But Churchill was not ready to make such a declaration. The King resented this restriction of his roles as King-Emperor and head of the armed forces. He much regretted the fact that he was never to visit his Indian Empire before it was dissolved in 1947-8 and independent states were set up in India, Pakistan, Ceylon and Burma.

The King also objected to Churchill's suggestion that the Duke of Windsor should be appointed Governor of Madras or Ceylon, and that he and the Duchess should be restored to full royal status (which would include giving the Duchess the title HRH). George VI realised that he would have

---

[16] *Ibid*, p 606.
[17] *Ibid*.

to agree to both proposals if the Cabinet insisted. Fortunately for the King the matter was never put to the Cabinet (Churchill was in a minority on this) and it never became of constitutional importance.

As the Allied armies advanced towards the German heartland and the end of the war in Europe was in sight, the King gave consideration to the task of reconstruction in Britain. His speeches about the need for the revival of local government showed his awareness of the need to restore the democratic rights of his people, which had been taken away from them by an over-mighty state during the war. He was also keen to revive royal ceremonial and pageantry, such as the State Opening of Parliament, thus emphasising the place of the Sovereign and the institution of Monarchy at the heart of the nation's life. He also made clear to his ministers that he expected to be consulted as to the size, recruitment and uniforms of the postwar armed forces.

The King regretted the effective surrender of Poland by Roosevelt to Stalin, reluctantly acquiesced in by Churchill, at the Yalta Conference in February 1945. George VI looked with considerable apprehension at Soviet advances in Eastern and South-Eastern Europe. The King and Churchill were unable to change Roosevelt's approach to the Soviets before the news arrived on 11 April of the US President's death. The King attended a memorial service at St Paul's Cathedral and ordered a week's mourning at Court. But with the war in Europe in its dying stages, he persuaded Churchill not to fly to Washington for the funeral.

Victory, when it came in 1945, was not quite like the Armistice in 1918, but for the King and the Queen there were moments to be savoured. VE Day (8 May 1945) was a Tuesday so the King celebrated alone at lunchtime with his Prime Minister. After lunch the War Cabinet and the Chiefs of Staff were received and exchanged congratulations — much like the Chairman and his Board. But outside in the great sweep of The Mall, up to Admiralty Arch, and lapping over in St James' Park, the crowds assembled, as they had done at the end of the last great war in 1918; as they did at George V's Jubilee in 1935 — as they do at every Jubilee, and every great national celebration of the British Monarchy. The King and the Queen went out on the balcony of Buckingham Palace eight times during the afternoon (and several times on the following days). On 9 and 10 May they again communed with their people in drives through east and south-east London, and later in a visit to Edinburgh. Illness was to deny George VI a Jubilee; the victory celebrations at least showed him, through his example and his sense of duty, rather than through ceremonial of which in war there had anyway been so little, where he stood in the hearts of his people.

9

A Throne More Stable

The end of the war in Europe was soon followed by the winding up of Churchill's coalition government. The King had known of the possibility of this happening since October 1944, when the Prime Minister had first mooted the idea in Parliament. The war had prevented the holding of a general election (the last one had been in November 1935 and Parliament had been extended annually during the war). Churchill had thought it desirable, as did the Labour leadership, that the country should return to party politics. By May 1945, however, Churchill had changed his mind and wanted to keep the coalition in being until the end of the war with Japan. This was not expected to occur for at least another eighteen months (few knew, apart from Churchill, the King and a small circle of ministers, scientists and soldiers, about the development of the atomic bomb and even fewer believed that it could bring the war with Japan to a swift close). Although Attlee, Bevin and Dalton were prepared to continue the coalition until October 1945, Morrison, more accurately reflecting Labour Party opinion, was not; and his proposal that the party should withdraw from the coalition received the backing of the National Executive Committee.

The King, who had been kept informed by the Prime Minister of developments, regretted the resurgence of party politics. But he accepted that the coalition government had to come to an end. Accordingly, Churchill resigned on 23 May and, as leader of the largest party in the House of Commons, was immediately asked to form a 'caretaker' government until the general election was held on 5 July. The result would not be known until 26 July after time to allow the postal votes of Service personnel serving overseas to be counted. It was difficult, with the

unpredictable Services vote and a pre-war electoral register, to forecast
the outcome. The King and both the Conservative and Labour leaderships
predicted a narrow Tory victory. The actual result, however, came as a
great surprise to the King and to the party leaders. Despite Churchill's
inspiring wartime leadership, the Conservative Party suffered a heavy defeat
(winning 213 seats, though almost 10 million votes), and the Labour Party
romped home (with 393 seats, though only 12 million votes). The Labour
Party actually received a minority of votes, when one counted the 2.2
million that went to the Liberals (but only 12 seats) and the nearly 1 million
(and 22 seats) that went to the other parties. But Labour won the vast
majority of the seats.[1]

It has recently been revealed that, despite his heavy electoral defeat,
Churchill at first contemplated remaining as Prime Minister until
Parliament reassembled. This would have enabled him to return to the
last wartime gathering of the 'Big Three' Powers — the USA, the USSR
and the UK — in the ruined heart of Germany at Berlin (Potsdam).[2] Eden
and the Tory Chief Whip, Margesson, managed to dissuade Churchill
from this. But they found it difficult to persuade him that the correct course
for him to take, after such an overwhelming defeat at the polls, was to
resign immediately. It took a personal intervention from the King, in the
form of a handwritten letter conveyed by Lascelles to No 10 Downing
Street, to convince the Prime Minister that his negotiating position at
Potsdam would be undermined by the obvious fact that he no longer spoke
for Britain. Churchill saw the force of the King's argument and duly
resigned at 7:00 pm on 26 July. George VI felt keenly the sudden loss of
his extraordinarily close relationship with Britain's greatest war minister.
In their parting exchange of letters, they identified what had been
constitutionally important to each of them in that relationship. The King
wrote:

> I regret what has happened more than perhaps anyone else. I shall miss
> your counsel to me more than I can say. You often told me what you
> thought of people and matters of real interest which I could never have
> learnt from anyone else. Your breadth of vision & your grasp of the essential

---

[1]   David Butler and Jennie Freeman, *British Political Facts, 1900-1960* (London, Macmillan, 1960),
      p 124.

[2]   Rhodes James, *Spirit Undaunted*, pp 271-4.

things were a great comfort to me in the darkest days of the War, & I like to think that we have never disagreed on any really important matter.'

Churchill reciprocated by saying that:

The kindness and intimacy with which Yr Majesty has treated me during these ever-glorious years of danger and victory, greatly lightened the burden I had to bear. It was always a relief to me to lay before my Sovereign all the dread secrets and perils which oppressed my mind, & and plans wh I was forming, & to receive on crucial occasions so much encouragement. Yr Majesty's grasp of all matters of State and War was always based upon the most thorough & attentive study of the whole mass of current documents, and this enabled us to view and measure everything in due proportion.[3]

The King wanted Churchill to be made a Knight of the Garter for his services to the nation during the war. Churchill, who was still an active politician, refused the honour. Instead, George VI conferred the Order of Merit, which was in his own gift, upon his former Prime Minister in recognition of his literary achievements. So ended one of the great partnerships in British history. Not since Queen Anne's relationship with John Churchill, the first Duke of Marlborough, had there been one as great as that between George VI and Winston Churchill.

Churchill had at the last minute alerted Attlee to the fact that he was about to resign, which was just as well for the Labour leader since it prevented Morrison from organising a leadership election. Churchill had recommended to the King, when asked, that Attlee should succeed him as Prime Minister. The King had called Attlee to Buckingham Palace at 7:30 pm on 26 July and asked him to form a government. The Labour leader accepted the request but, still recovering from the shock of his stunning victory, admitted that he had not yet had time to discuss with his colleagues the allotment of Cabinet posts. The shock of the transition from Churchill to Attlee was somewhat cushioned by the fact that the King knew most of the leading Labour politicians from the wartime years.

The King was dismayed to learn that Attlee was considering Dalton for the Foreign Office, an appointment to which not only the King, but

---

[3] Martin Gilbert, *Winston S Churchill, Vol VIII: 1945-1965, 'Never Despair'* (Heinneman, London, 1988), pp 114-15.

Eden and the Foreign Office objected, on personal as well as political grounds. Apart from being vain, arrogant and tactless, Dalton was regarded as being anti-German, pro-Soviet and pro-Zionist. With the outcome of Potsdam and the peace settlement yet to be determined, 'Foreign Affairs was the most important subject,'[4] declared the King, echoing Conservative opinion. He, therefore, recommended that the honest, strong-minded and forthright Bevin be appointed as Foreign Secretary. There has been considerable debate about whether the King's intervention was decisive in Attlee's subsequent appointment of Bevin to the Foreign Office. The available evidence would seem to indicate that, when combined with the objections of the Foreign Office and the Opposition, it was to be so.[5] There is no doubt that Bevin's appointment was the right one in the troubled state of the postwar world, and that he went on to be one of the greatest British Foreign Secretaries.

The King was pleased by Attlee's other Cabinet appointments (including Bevan as Minister of Health), though he never altered his unfavourable opinion of Dalton and was pleased when, in 1947, he was forced to resign as Chancellor of the Exchequer after leaking Budget secrets. The King was unsure how he would get on with his new Prime Minister, whom he did not know well and whose long silences interspersed with monosyllabic comments he found hard to cope with. But, with their shared interest in bettering the conditions of the industrial working class, these essentially reserved men had much in common. As they got to know each other better they developed a mutual liking and respect. In the end they forged a surprisingly effective working relationship. Until this happened, however, they relied on Lascelles and the successive Cabinet Secretaries, Sir Edward Bridges and Sir Norman Brook, to bridge the gap.

The King was prevented by security considerations from visiting Berlin and meeting Stalin and the new US President, Harry S Truman. But he managed to secure a meeting with Truman at Plymouth, where the US President stopped over on his return voyage to the United States. The King learnt at first hand from Truman of his impressions of the difficulties

---

[4] Rhodes James, *Spirit Undaunted*, p 275.

[5] See *The Observer*, 23 August 1959; Robert Rhodes James, *Anthony Eden* (Weidenfeld and Nicolson, London, 1986), pp 310-11; Ben Pimlott, *Hugh Dalton* (Jonathan Cape, London, 1985), p 414-22.

that had arisen at Potsdam over British and American resistance to Stalin's gargantuan claims to territory and reparations from Germany. He also learnt from the new US Secretary of State, the talkative Irish-American 'Jimmy' Byrnes, about the inability of his Soviet opposite number, Molotov, to agree to anything without first referring back to Stalin. The King was also pleased to learn that Bevin had shown that he was a skilled, if rather rough, negotiator. The King surprised Byrnes and the Chairman of the Joint Chiefs of Staff, Leahy, with his knowledge of the atomic bomb, and was prepared to wager with a sceptical Leahy that it would work. The King was proved right sooner than he expected. Four days later the first atomic bomb was exploded by the Americans over Hiroshima. Following this, and the dropping of a second bomb at Nagasaki, Japan surrendered unconditionally. On 15 August 1945, while London celebrated VJ Day, the King opened his first Parliament since 1938 with his Speech from the Throne.

Attlee's government was committed to a programme of far-reaching economic and social reform after the war which would transform Britain into a new socially democratic state. George VI saw the Monarchy as being in a similar position in 1945 to what it had been in 1918. Like his father he feared social revolution. During the war George VI had established the Monarchy as a symbol of unified resistance of the nation and Empire-Commonwealth to Axis aggression. His postwar task was to ensure that the Monarchy was not identified with an outdated class structure which the Attlee government intended to sweep away. His wartime experience of government and international politics, combined with his knowledge of industry, had given him an insight into the lives of his subjects which proved invaluable to him in gauging the postwar political mood and making the necessary adjustments to the Monarchy.

George VI was careful to avoid holding any ostentatious entertainments at the Palace which would have been out of place at a time of austerity in postwar Britain. He also decided that there should be no financial grants or excessive conferring of the highest honours to the military as there had been after the First World War. Perhaps the King's most important achievement was to establish good relations with his Labour ministers and to accept, or at least appear to accept, the great economic and social reforms they brought about after the war.

This did not mean, of course, that he did not criticise some aspects of the reforms. His experience and knowledge of Britain's problems was now longer and more continuous than that of his ministers. He made clear to them that he knew what was going on, and expected them to be as well-informed on the subject under discussion as he was. Following Truman's cancellation of Lend-Lease to a bankrupt Britain, the negotiation of the American Loan to keep the country afloat and the deterioration of East-West relations, the King was concerned that it was economically unwise and socially and politically divisive for the Attlee government to embark on such a wide-ranging programme of nationalisation. He was careful to mute his criticism when talking to the Prime Minister. But he made his unease known to Attlee on 20 November 1945 when he said that the Prime Minister 'must give the people here some confidence that the Government was not going to stifle all private enterprise. Everyone wanted to help in rehabilitating the country but they were not allowed to.'[6] He also criticised the slow rate at which new housing was being built (the government was restricting permits to local authorities) and the shortage of clothing. As he was a practical man of affairs, the King thought that these matters should have priority over the abolition of legal restrictions on the activities of the trades unions.

The King was also quick to seek a reassurance from Attlee in the summer of 1947 that Churchill was incorrect in claiming that the government's enactment of emergency powers in peacetime to cope with the economic crisis was an attempt to undermine Parliament and establish a totalitarian government. The 1947 economic crisis, in fact, led Morrison, Dalton and Cripps to challenge Attlee's leadership and to seek to replace him with Bevin. When the Foreign Secretary refused to act with the conspirators, Attlee proceeded to neutralise them by offering Cripps the post of economic supremo.

The crisis had led the Treasury Secretary, Bridges, the Cabinet Secretary, Brook, and Lascelles, to consider what course the King should take if Attlee should resign and be replaced as Prime Minister by a member of his party. Lascelles preferred that the new Labour leader should be elected by his party according to its rules, rather than by the more unreliable method of the Sovereign's having to take soundings among the leadership.

---

[6] Bradford, *Reluctant King*, p 383.

In Lascelles' opinion, it would be an infringement of the Sovereign's prerogative, if the Labour Party were to nominate its leader as the next Prime Minister. The normal assumption was that the King would, except in extraordinary circumstances, invite a new party leader to form a government. In the event, this reasoning was not put to the test. Attlee survived the challenge to his leadership. The whole question, however, was to arise again in the next reign, when two Conservative Prime Ministers, Eden and Macmillan, resigned.

Although he had doubts about the Attlee government's domestic policies, the King was in full agreement with its foreign policy. He approved of Bevin's determination to resist Soviet advances in Europe and the Middle East, and he welcomed the belated American decision to back Britain's strategy with the Truman Doctrine, the Marshall Plan and the establishment of NATO. The King also appreciated Bevin's opposition to the cuts in defence spending demanded by Dalton to fund greater spending on social programmes. George VI used his influence to prevent the new CIGS, Montgomery, from reducing the strength of the Brigade of Guards, traditionally the King's bodyguard, by one-fifth. The Brigade retained its pre-war complement of ten battalions.

The King was generally in agreement with the Attlee government's policy towards the Empire-Commonwealth. The Royal Family's visit to South Africa in 1947 failed to ensure the re-election of the moderate Smuts as Prime Minister. White South Africans returned a nationalist government to power, committed to the imposition of an apartheid regime. Nor did the idea, certainly held by Attlee and Lascelles, of a shift of British imperial power from Asia to Africa amount to anything. But the dream shared by Attlee and the King of the transformation of the Empire into a Commonwealth of Nations, to which the Princess Elizabeth dedicated herself in a famous speech broadcast from Cape Town, did eventually come about after a shaky start.

While George VI had been on tour in South Africa, the most momentous decision had been taken by the Attlee government and Mountbatten, the last Viceroy of India, to dismantle his Indian Empire. The King had warned Attlee that he should give his impulsive, arrogant and bullying cousin clear instructions about what he was to do in India. Instead Mountbatten was allowed to draft his own terms of service and then to disregard them. He cajoled Attlee and the outgoing Viceroy, Wavell, into agreeing to a transfer of power on or about 1 June 1948. After the partition of the Indian Empire into two separate states, India and Pakistan, was decided upon by the Cabinet in May 1947, Mountbatten insisted, in view of rising communal tension, that the date for the transfer should be brought forward to 15 August. The date happened to be the second anniversary of the Japanese surrender. The result of Mountbatten's haste, and the Attlee government's desire to be rid of the problem as soon as possible, was the death of over one million people as Muslims and Hindus tried to flee across the partition lines.

Mountbatten also ignored the King's injunction 'to do what he could to see fair play done for the Princes'.[7] This had been, as we have seen, a particular concern of successive British monarchs since Queen Victoria's 1858 pledge to 'respect the rights, dignity and honour of the Native Princes as our own' in recognition of their loyalty to Britain during the Indian Mutiny.[8] Instead the last Viceroy bullied the 565 Princes into adhering to the Indian Union, for the purposes of defence, foreign policy and communications, by giving a guarantee of their remaining rights and finances which he was in no position to honour after independence. The King was forced to reconcile himself to this melancholy outcome with the thought that the Indian princely states 'could never have stood alone in the world'.[9] Mountbatten also allowed his pro-Congress and anti-Muslim League stance to influence his conduct as the first Governor-General of India towards the adjudication of post-independence border disputes with Pakistan.

It was an inauspicious start to the realisation of the dream shared by Attlee and the King of a British Commonwealth of Nations. It was to be followed by Burma's decision to become an independent republic outside the Commonwealth and Ireland's determination to break the last link with the Crown by repealing the External Relations Act in 1948. The King's plea to the Irish to 'stay in the family' fell on deaf ears.[10] Ireland became a republic outside the Commonwealth in 1949 and India looked set to follow suit.

---

[7]   *Ibid*, p 395.

[8]   *Ibid.*

[9]   Philip Ziegler, *Mountbatten* (Collins, London, 1985), p 415.

[10] Rhodes James, *Spirit Undaunted*, p 313.

In order to prevent the new Commonwealth ideal from being irrevocably lost in the retreat from Empire, the King worked hard, and ultimately successfully with Attlee and the Indian leader, Nehru, at the Commonwealth Prime Ministers' Conference in April 1949 to retain India within the Commonwealth. This was accomplished, and announced in the London Declaration, by agreeing that allegiance to the Crown would no longer be a requirement of membership. The King became 'the symbol of the free association of its independent member nations and as such the Head of the Commonwealth'.[11] The King joked with the Indian High Commisioner in London, Krishna Menon, as to whether he was to be known as 'As Such'?[12] Menon later paid tribute to the behind-the-scenes role played by the King in pressing the Commonwealth leaders to accept the new formula, which was embodied in the conception of the Sovereign as the Head of the Commonwealth. 'As such', he helped to determine the evolution of the modern Commonwealth.

The King had been prevented by his ministers, for political reasons, from visiting his Indian Empire before partition and independence in 1947. But it was ill-health that stopped the King from re-visiting New Zealand and Australia in 1949. After thirteen years on the Throne the King was worn out by the pressures and frustrations of performing his duties during a period marked by successive crises: the Abdication, appeasement, the war and postwar reconstruction. His failing health led to a decline in his political influence and he simply acceded to Attlee's request on 5 January 1950 for a dissolution of Parliament on 3 February with the general election to be held on 23 February.

Everyone, including the King, had expected the Labour Party (which had not lost a single by-election since 1945 and had set up the Welfare State) to be returned to power with a comfortable, though reduced, majority. In fact Labour scraped home with 315 seats and 46% of the vote to the 298 seats and 43.5% of the vote won by the Conservatives (the Liberals won 9 seats and 9% of the vote; 3 seats were won by other parties).[13] With Labour only having a working majority of 5 in the House of

---

[11] Wheeler-Bennett, *George VI*, pp 730-1.

[12] Michael Breaker, 'India's Decision to Remain in the Commonwealth', *Journal of Commonwealth and Comparative Politics*, 12 (1975) 77.

[13] Butler and Freeman, *Political Facts*, p124.

Commons, the King and his advisers had urgently to consider what should be done if Attlee requested another dissolution.

Lascelles concluded, after talking to Churchill and the Conservative leadership, and after the King had seen Attlee on 27 February, that 'it does not seem probable that the government will be faced with resignation during the next few weeks'. He learnt that Attlee planned to soldier on and that the Conservatives were not anxious for another general election in the near future. Even if Attlee resigned, 'the only difficult problem which the King might be called upon to solve is the decision to grant or to withhold a dissolution; in present circumstances the arguments in favour of granting it seem to outweigh those against it'.[14] Lascelles always had in mind the unfortunate Byng precedent which, as we have seen, had caused considerable resentment among Canadian Liberals against the Crown.

Lascelles also took steps to counter the speculative arguments of Lord Simon, a former Lord Chancellor, and Roy Jenkins, a Labour MP and future Home Secretary, contained in letters to *The Times*. The King's Private Secretary himself wrote to *The Times* on 2 May 1950 under the pseudonym 'Senex' that,

> it can be properly assumed that no wise Sovereign — that is, one who has at heart the true interests of the country, the constitution, and the Monarchy — would deny a dissolution to his Prime Minister unless he was satisfied that: (1) the existing Parliament was still vital, viable, and capable of doing its job; (2) a General Election would be detrimental to the national economy; (3) he could rely on finding another Prime Minister who could carry on his Government, for a reasonable period, with a working majority in the House of Commons. When Sir Patrick Duncan refused a dissolution to his Prime Minister in South Africa in 1939, all these conditions were satisfied: when Lord Byng did the same in Canada in 1926, they appeared to be, but in the event the third proved illusory.[15]

With such a slim majority Attlee's second government was vulnerable to the tactics of attrition employed by the Conservative Opposition. In August 1950, following the outbreak of the Korean War, Churchill denounced Attlee for not recalling Parliament immediately and for appearing to give

---

[14] Rhodes-James, *Spirit Undaunted*, p 322.

[15] *The Times*, 2 May 1950.

too little military assistance, too late, to the Americans and the South Koreans. Attlee replied coldly that Churchill was simply bitter at being rejected for the second time in a row by the British people. The King regarded with distaste these bitter exchanges between the party leaders.

The Labour government was then weakened, as Attlee admitted to the King in October 1950, by the resignation of the terminally ill Cripps. He was succeeded as Chancellor of the Exchequer by Gaitskell, much to the chagrin of Aneurin Bevan. The intellectual and ideologically-minded Gaitskell had no true understanding of the King's character, mistakenly regarding him as reactionary when he was essentially conservative by nature and apolitical. Consequently, the King and his Chancellor never really got on. George VI found Bevan, the Minister of Health, much easier to talk to. But he could not understand the ideological motivation which led Bevan, along with Harold Wilson and John Freeman, to resign over Gaitskell's proposed Budget increases in National Health Service charges.

The increased NHS charges were deemed necessary to help pay for the increased defence expenditure to which Attlee had committed the government during his visit to Washington in December 1950. Attlee had, with the King's encouragement, obtained a commitment from Truman, after the latter had seemed to threaten to use the atomic bomb against China, to confine the conflict to Korea. But he failed to get a concrete commitment from the Americans that they would not use atomic weapons without first consulting their allies.

Following the resignation of Bevan, Freeman and Wilson, the Conservative Opposition stepped up its pressure on the Labour government through all-night sittings in an attempt to wear it down. This strategy took its intended toll on Labour ministers, many of whom had served continuously since 1940. Bevin resigned as Foreign Secretary in March 1951 (to be replaced by the lamentable Morrison), and died soon after. Cripps died that same year. Attlee himself was exhausted and he was also aware that it was important for the Commonwealth that the King should make his postponed trip to Ceylon, Australia and New Zealand in 1952. It was undesirable that the King should be out of the country when the political situation was so unstable. Therefore, Attlee decided in June 1951 that he would seek a dissolution of Parliament from the King, and that a general election should be held before the King left on his Commonwealth tour. The King's ill-health was not a factor in the Prime Minister's decision, since neither he nor in fact the King were aware of the seriousness of the

King's condition (he had lung cancer and his left lung was removed in September 1951). In mid-September Attlee requested the prorogation and dissolution of Parliament by the King in the first week of October.

The general election on 25 October 1951 returned the Conservatives and their allies to power with 321 seats and 48% of the vote against Labour's 295 seats and 48.8% of the vote (the Liberals won 6 seats with 2.5% of the vote).[16] Attlee resigned the next day and the King, in gratitude and recognition of the Labour leader's achievements, conferred upon him the Order of Merit. The King sent for Churchill, who accepted the King's invitation to form a government. However, the King objected to Churchill's recommendation that Eden be made 'Deputy Prime Minister' on the arguable grounds that the continuation of this unofficial post (which had been held by Attlee and Morrison) would derogate from his prerogative to choose the Prime Minister's successor. Churchill accordingly withdrew his proposal.

The King's illness prevented him from playing any further part in the formation of Churchill's government, or opening Parliament in person (his speech was read by the Lord Chancellor) or making his Christmas broadcast live (it had to be pre-recorded in stages). But he did manage to persuade Churchill that, for health reasons, the Prime Minister should travel by boat rather than plane to Washington to see President Truman.

The King was too ill to embark upon his long-planned tour of Australasia and sent Princess Elizabeth and the Duke of Edinburgh in his stead. His sudden death on 6 February 1952 came as a great blow not only to his family but to the Prime Minister and the nation after all they had been through together: the abdication, appeasement, the war, and postwar reconstruction and austerity. There was a genuine and general sense of grief felt at the King's passing, not least in the United States, where politicians and the press paid generous tribute to George VI. Perhaps the best summary of the King's achievements and place in history was made by the French Ambassador in London, René Massigli, who as a Free Frenchman had known the King since the war:

> By his simplicity, his goodwill, his courage, and his sense of duty, his respect
> for constitutional principles and the example of his private life, King George
> VI has amassed around the throne a capital of sympathy and loyalty upon

---

[16] Butler and Freeman, *Political Facts*, p 124.

which . . . he could call in case of crisis. Brought to the throne in a climate of dynastic and constitutional crisis, George VI has died leaving to his daughter a throne more stable than England has known throughout almost her entire history.[17]

---

[17] Bradford, *Reluctant King*, p 462.

10

A Seemingly Impossible Task

When George VI died on 6 February 1952, the heir to the Throne, his eldest daughter, Elizabeth, was in Kenya, on the first stage of her tour to Ceylon, Australia and New Zealand. Even before she learnt of her father's death, the Cabinet had met in emergency session and decided to hold an Accession Council that afternoon. For the first time Commonwealth representatives attended, along with the Lords Spiritual and Temporal and Privy Councillors. In her absence she was proclaimed Queen Elizabeth II by the Lord President, Lord Woolton.

In Kenya Queen Elizabeth II had to come terms with the death of her father and the fact that she was now Head of State. She had known since the Abdication that she was destined to become Queen, and she was in some ways better prepared for her destiny than her father had been. She had inherited her father's reserved nature, seriousness and dedication to duty. She was healthier and more intelligent than he had been. She had had a happy childhood and was close to her sister, Margaret, and her parents. She had had a conventionally aristocratic education for a girl, with its emphasis on social rather than intellectual attainments. But she had had a strong sense of the history of her family, the Monarchy and the nation inculcated in her by her grandmother, Queen Mary, and by her tutor, Henry Marten, the Provost of Eton. It was Marten who had made sure she knew her Bagehot, and that she had acquired the ability to appraise a situation from all sides and to develop her judgement.

As Heir to the Throne, Elizabeth had met and conversed with the great and the good, and was used to the extraordinary pomp and ceremony surrounding the Monarchy. She had had some experience of the 'real world', first as a Girl Guide and then in the Auxiliary Territorial Service (ATS) during the Second World War. But it was her visit to South Africa in 1947 which made the greatest impression on her. It was during this tour, in a broadcast from Capetown, that she pledged herself to the service of the peoples of the British Empire and Commonwealth. With her marriage to Prince Philip Mountbatten, RN, in the same year, she took the first step towards running her own life. She had her own Household and access to Foreign Office telegrams. Sir John ('Jock') Colville, a former Private Secretary to both Chamberlain and Churchill, became her Private Secretary. As George VI's health had declined she and her consort had performed more and more public duties, including State visits to North America in 1950 and the ill-fated one to Ceylon, Australia and New Zealand in 1952. Her father's sudden death had cut short the latter tour and she had returned to Britain as Queen.

Looking back on her Accession forty-five years later, Elizabeth II felt that her father's early death had meant that: 'In a way I did not have an apprenticeship . . . It was all very sudden, kind of taking on and making the best job you can. It's a question of just maturing into what you're doing and accepting that here you are and it's your fate.'[1] Yet, though her apprenticeship had been brief, she was a grown woman who had acquired confidence from performing ceremonial duties during her father's illness. In fact, as has been shown, she had more preparation for the Throne than her father and was in some ways better equipped for her new responsibilities. She consciously decided to follow her father's example of strictly constitutional behaviour, thus stressing the continuity of the Monarchy.

As she flew back from Kenya, Elizabeth II was briefed on the protocol and ritual which accompanied the Accession of a new Sovereign. On her arrival at Heathrow Airport she was greeted by a solemn Prime Minister, Churchill, the Leader of the Opposition, Attlee, and other political figures. As Queen the members of her family paid obeisance to her (another unsettling experience). At a formal meeting of the Accession Council on 8 February she read her formal Declaration of Sovereignty and was officially proclaimed 'Queen Elizabeth the Second, by the grace of God Queen of the Realm and of all Her Other Realms and Territories, Head of the

---

[1] Sarah Bradford, *Elizabeth* (Heinemann, London, 1996), p 1.

Commonwealth, Defender of the Faith . . .'[2].

The Queen's titles had been changed by the Cabinet to reflect the recent changes in the Commonwealth and the 'divisibility' of the Crown, which had been recognised in the Royal Titles Bill in 1951 (enacted in 1953). The Commonwealth Prime Ministers were to agree in December 1952 that each state should adopt a title which would succinctly express its own relationship with the Crown. The Cabinet also persuaded the Queen (with the help of Queen Mary, Queen Elizabeth and the Royal Household) that the Royal Family and its descendants should retain the name of 'Windsor' rather than take the Duke of Edinburgh's family name of Mountbatten — much to the chagrin of both the Duke and Lord Mountbatten. The mutual mistrust thus engendered between Mountbatten and the Cabinet might have been avoided had the subject been raised at a later date. Caught between two stools the Queen was too inexperienced to come up with a solution which might have appeased both sides.

The Queen was also not in a position, as her father would have been if he had lived, to persuade her old and ill Prime Minister to resign. Churchill was reluctant to relinquish power. For one thing he was determined to see Elizabeth II crowned while he was still Prime Minister. With his essentially romantic view of the Monarchy and British history, he saw himself playing the same guiding role towards the new Queen as his predecessor Melbourne had done for the young Queen Victoria. He also spoke of the dawning of a new Elizabethan Age. This was a theme which was taken up with alacrity by politicians, pundits and the public in the months leading up to the Coronation on 2 June 1953.

Like Victoria before her, Elizabeth II was seen as 'the Nation's Hope', a symbol of Britain's new-found and fragile optimism for the future. The Prime Minister, the Archbishop of Canterbury and *The Times* all stressed the burdens, duties and the self-sacrifice involved in the Coronation of the Queen. The broadcasting of the ceremony in Westminister Abbey, or at least parts of it, on television for the first time (the Queen overcame her initial opposition to the idea) allowed the nation to participate in this highly spiritual event. The nation's euphoria at sharing in the Coronation of a new Sovereign gave rise to a royal religion which was in the end to prove unsustainable.

---

[2]   *Ibid*, p 168

There was a natural feeling of anti-climax in Britain after the Coronation. Even in the Commonwealth, which perhaps evinced an even stronger desire to renew its association with Britain and the Monarchy, there was a sense of disapointment after the Queen returned from her highly successful five and a half month tour in 1953-54 of her overseas realms. She had visited Bermuda, Jamaica, Fiji, Tonga, New Zealand, Australia, the Cocos Islands, Aden, Uganda, Malta and Gibraltar. People were fascinated by the personalities of the Queen and the Royal Family. They wanted to find out more about them and their lives than the ill-equipped Royal Household, and particularly the Press Secretary, Commander Colville, were able to give them. In the new world of insatiable public curiosity, technological innovation and press economics, the Royal Household, British editors and politicians were to find it increasingly difficult to control the flow of news about the Royal Family as they had done in 1936 over Edward VIII and Mrs Simpson.

The Queen's return to Britain from her Commonwealth tour in May 1954 did not see the immediate retirement of Churchill as some had thought. It was to take considerable pressure from the Cabinet before, nearly a year later, he stepped down as Prime Minister. The Queen was genuinely sad that she would no longer have the enjoyable company at her Tuesday audiences of the man who had led Britain during the war, had become a friend to her father and had served her family since Queen Victoria's time. Churchill recalled this service at his final dinner for her at No 10 Downing Street, when he spoke of 'the sacred causes, and wise and kindly way of life, of which Your Majesty is the young gleaming champion'.[3]

In accordance with constitutional practice, Churchill had not after he had resigned advised the Queen in his final audience as to his successor. But it was clear to him that she had decided to send for Sir Anthony Eden. He was the obvious choice, having been 'heir apparent' for many years. Even in June 1953, Salisbury, Lascelles and Colville had favoured a 'caretaker' government in the event of Churchill's death or permanent incapacity following his stroke. This was to allow time for Eden, who was himself ill, to recuperate and assume the premiership. They wanted to prevent R A Butler, the acting Prime Minister, from succeeding to the top

---

[3] *The Times*, 27 April 1955.

job at all costs. It is likely that any discreet soundings that the Queen had had her new Private Secretary, Michael Adeane, make in 1955 among the Tory Grandees, in the continuing absence of any machinery for electing their leader, would have produced the same verdict: Eden not Butler.

It was Eden who was summoned to the Palace by the Queen and who accepted her invitation to form a government. Shortly afterwards the Queen granted his request for a dissolution of Parliament. After the Conservative Party won the general election on 26 May, with a working majority of 58, Eden again accepted the Queen's invitation to form a government. It was appropriate that one of her first acts during his short and ill-starred administration was to sign a Proclamation announcing a State of Emergency. This was to ensure that public order was maintained and adequate supplies of food delivered around the country during the dock and railway strikes.

The Queen and her Prime Minister were then confronted with a personal crisis for the Royal Family, which rapidly acquired political overtones. This stemmed from the desire of the Queen's younger sister, Princess Margaret, who was third in line of succession, to marry a divorced man, Group-Captain Peter Townsend. Attitudes towards the remarriage of divorced persons were beginning to change in the 1950s. The Cabinet contained three divorced men who had remarried: Walter Monckton, Peter Thorneycroft and Eden himself. But there was a strong High Church lobby who continued to frown upon it. They were represented in the Cabinet by Salisbury, who threatened to resign over the matter. The Cabinet was split and Eden dared not put the issue to the vote. A compromise was worked out and the Prime Minister journeyed to Balmoral on 18 October to put it to the Queen. The Cabinet were prepared to recommend the marriage but only on certain conditions, *viz* that Margaret should renounce her right of succession to the Throne, forgo her provision under the Civil List and exile herself for an indefinite period.

Eden's démarche was followed by a moralistic leader from the editor of *The Times*, Sir William Haley. This placed Princess Margaret in the invidious position of either renouncing her happiness for the sake of the Commonwealth or marrying and forgoing her royal status, thus damaging the image which had taken shape after the Coronation of the Queen as the head of an ideal Royal Family and the Commonwealth Family of Nations. The weight of Establishment opinion against the marriage meant that Princess Margaret, Group-Captain Townsend and the Queen had no choice but to accept that duty and fate must come before personal happiness. Princess Margaret announced that 'mindful of the Church's teaching that Christian marriage is indissoluble, and conscious of my duty to the Commonwealth, I have resolved to put these considerations before any other'.[4] But Margaret's personal sacrifice for the sake of the image of the ideal Royal Family was to put tremendous strain upon her and was eventually to help shatter the image for which she made her sacrifice.

The Queen was again put in an awkward position by the crisis which occurred after the Egyptian leader, Nasser, nationalised the Suez Canal Company in July 1956. The Queen was kept well-briefed on British and Commonwealth policy by the Prime Minister, the Foreign Secretary, the First Sea Lord (Mountbatten) and Commonwealth governments as the crisis unfolded. She was well aware that not only the nation but the British government and her advisers at the Palace were split over the wisdom of using force to make Nasser 'disgorge' the Canal. It is more than likely that she would have discussed this matter at length with the Prime Minister in their regular weekly audiences. But by the autumn of 1956 Eden, who was in a state of nervous exhaustion, was only listening to advice which confirmed his ingrained determination to 'get Nasser'.

It is unlikely that the Queen was privy to the Sévres collusion, whereby Eden and Lloyd, the Foreign Secretary, secretly agreed with the French and the Israelis in Paris on 24 October 1956 to launch an attack against Egypt, with the twin aims of seizing the Canal and bringing down Nasser. But the Queen certainly had to deal with the consequences of the failure of collusion, as the opposition of the United States, the Soviet Union and the United Nations, and the run on the pound, forced Britain and its allies to agree to a ceasefire and the withdrawal of their troops from the Canal.

It was against this background, at a time of great uncertainty for the nation, that Eden informed the Queen on 8 January 1957 that he had decided to resign on health grounds. The Queen regarded this as inevitable, given what had happened. (She later softened the blow for Eden by writing him a gracious letter of thanks for his past, and more illustrious, services to the country. She also offered him an earldom.) However, Eden's intended resignation immediately put the Queen in an awkward situation since,

---

[4] Bradford, *Elizabeth*, pp 212-13.

unlike in 1955, it was not clear who should become Prime Minister. The choice was between Butler and Macmillan. Not since 1923, when Bonar Law had resigned as Prime Minister and George V had chosen Baldwin in preference to Curzon, had a Sovereign been forced to make such a difficult decision. Eden had not been asked at his final audience with the Queen, and therefore did not give, his formal advice as to his successor, although he indicated that he favoured Butler. But Eden had suggested to Adeane that Lord Salisbury, who was not a candidate, should take soundings in the Cabinet.

Both the Queen and Eden had returned to London from Sandringham separately in order to avoid arousing unnecessary alarm. Eden broke the news of his forthcoming resignation to Macmillan, Butler and Salisbury. He also told Salisbury that he was to play a significant part in the succession. Salisbury consulted Kilmuir, the Lord Chancellor, who opposed putting the matter to a meeting of Conservative MPs in case they decided to elect their party leader, thus usurping the royal prerogative of appointing the Prime Minister. Adeane was then informed that Kilmuir and Salisbury would take the necessary 'soundings' in accordance with Conservative Party practice (the exception being Bonar Law's insistence on a party election in 1922 before accepting office from the King).

The Queen's advisers at the Palace thought she should not act until she knew whom the Conservative Party wanted as leader. After Eden held his final Cabinet meeting and then departed for the Palace in order to resign, Kilmuir and Salisbury sounded out their fellow ministers, one at a time, in Salisbury's room in the Privy Council office in the No 10 Downing Street complex. Like schoolboys being summoned to the headmaster's office, they were asked the famous question: 'Well, which is it? Wab or Hawold?' A majority of ministers, as well as Conservative backbenchers sounded out by the Chief Whip Edward Heath, chose Macmillan. In a spectacular miscalculation of the result, the Press predicted that Butler would be the next Prime Minister (only Randolph Churchill, with his inside knowledge, proved right in his forecast for *The Evening Standard*). A confident Butler even prepared his first prime ministerial broadcast.

The next morning, however, Salisbury was summoned to the Palace, along with Churchill, and conveyed the party's view to the Queen. He was backed up by Churchill, who thought Butler indecisive. The Queen then called Macmillan to the Palace and asked him to form a government. He accepted and by 2:00 pm he was Prime Minister. Macmillan's appointment had come as a great shock to the political world, which had expected Butler to succeed Eden. The pundits attributed this to Butler's vacillating behaviour during the Suez Crisis. There was considerable criticism of the procedure by which a young and inexperienced Queen had been forced to make such a choice, and had had to rely on the advice of the Tory Grandees. Ironically, as has been pointed out by a recent biographer of the Queen, Adeane and Salisbury, by allowing the Conservative elders effectively to make the decision, had presided over a delegation of the royal prerogative and thus weakened it.[5] The Labour party made clear that if in the future it was faced with finding a new leader while in office, it would hold a leadership election before accepting a new Prime Minister. This was to avoid putting the Crown 'in the embarrassing position of having to make a choice between rival claimants to the premiership of the same party. This is bringing the Crown into internecine party warfare, which is very bad for the Constitution.'[6] The Conservative Party were eventually to accept this view but only after another succession crisis in 1963.

Eden had not paid much attention to the Monarchy and the Palace had resented his withholding of information. By contrast, Macmillan regarded the Monarchy as being central to his and the Conservative party's electoral fortunes. He went to great lengths to keep the Queen informed. He was conscious that he was the Queen's First Minister and was anxious, at least in theory, to see that her prerogatives were protected. In a revealing misquotation of Bagehot in his memoirs, he said that the Queen had the right 'to advise' the Prime Minister rather than simply, and more correctly, 'to be consulted'.[7]

Both the new Prime Minister and the Queen enjoyed the weekly audiences and the constant exchange of correspondence on the pressing matters of the day. Macmillan was impressed by Elizabeth II's grasp of detail and knowledge of a subject. No doubt the Queen appreciated being taken into the Prime Minister's confidence. They soon established a

---

[5]   Ben Pimlott, *The Queen* (Harper Collins, London, 1996), p 260.

[6]   Cited in D Laird, *How the Queen Reigns* (Pan, London, 1959), p 109.

[7]   Contrast Harold Macmillan, *Pointing the Way, 1959-1961* (Macmillan, London, 1972), p 30, with Walter Bagehot, *The English Constitution*, (Fontana ed, Today 1963), p 113.

rapport. In some ways it bore a resemblance to her father's relationship with Churchill during the war, but it was more like Disraeli's courtship of Queen Victoria. Like Disraeli, Macmillan not only had an emotional need to do this but he sought to harness a popular monarchy to his own brand of popular (one-nation) Conservatism. He struck the right note, on both the personal and the political levels, with the Queen by proposing in February 1957 that Prince Philip should be given the style and the dignity of a 'Prince of the United Kingdom'. He was to be officially known as 'Prince Philip, Duke of Edinburgh' in recognition of his services to the nation and the Commonwealth during his recent tour, and the affection in which he was held by the public. It was a timely gesture by the Prime Minister, which was gratefully accepted by the Queen. It brought to an end the damaging speculation in the Press of a non-existent rift between the Royal couple, following the resignation of Prince Philip's friend and equerry Mike Parker due to the revelation of the latter's marital infidelity.

Macmillan's support for the Monarchy could not, however, shield it from further public attacks. In August 1957, in the post-Suez era of national reassessment, a special issue of the small circulation journal *National and English Review* examined 'the future of the Monarchy', and in so doing caused a furore. In particular the article by the journal's editor, Lord Altrincham (John Grigg, the biographer) attacked the Monarchy for being 'tweedy', or socially exclusive, and the Queen for appearing to have the personality of 'a priggish schoolgirl'. Altrincham called for the abolition of outdated practices, such as the presentation of debutantes at court each Season, and the creation of a 'truly classless and Commonwealth Court'. He thought it important for the future of the Monarchy that the Queen develop a distinctive personality by doing and saying things that people would remember, and that she and the rest of the Royal Family should perform the 'seemingly impossible task of being at once ordinary and extraordinary'.[8]

Altrincham's unprecedented attack on the Queen aroused a storm of protest from his fellow Lords, the Archbishop of Canterbury and the Press. Although the BBC, anxious not to prejudice its special broadcasting

---

[8] Lord Altrincham, 'The Monarchy Today' in *Is the Monarchy Perfect?* (John Calder, London, 1958).

relationship with the Palace, boycotted Altrincham, the commercial television channels gave him full coverage. The outrage felt by many at his attack on the Queen seemed to be expressed by a Mr Burbridge of the League of Empire Loyalists, who struck Altrincham across the face as the latter left Television House with the broadcaster Ludovic Kennedy. But a poll for *The Daily Mail* showed that though a majority (52%) of people generally disagreed with Altrincham, 55% wanted the exclusive Court circle widened.

Altincham's criticisms also had a knock-on effect across the Atlantic, where during the Queen's tour of the United States, *The Saturday Evening Post* published an article criticising the Royal Family by the journalist and broadcaster Malcolm Muggeridge. The latter had already condemned the 'Royal Soap Opera' in an article in the *New Statesman* two years before. He developed these thoughts further in the *Post* piece, implying that the Monarchy, by being identified with an outdated social system, had outlived its usefulness.

Although both Conservative and Labour politicians were careful not to become embroiled in the Monarchy debate in the Press, and in fact downplayed its importance, there was a more positive response from the Palace. The 'modernisers', led by Prince Philip and by Martin Charteris, eagerly grabbed the opportunity offered by Altrincham's criticisms to reform the Monarchy. The Lord Chamberlain announced in November 1957 the abolition of the debutante presentation parties at Court (unnecessary audiences, levees and State balls also went) and the holding of more garden parties to allow more people to go to the Palace. The Lord Chamberlain also invited businessmen, architects, artists and churchmen to attend informal lunches at the Palace. Prince Philip began a dining club in order to garner the views of such people on the issues of the day. Charteris and others revamped the Queen's speeches to give them more point. The Queen also began to make television broadcasts of her Christmas message, which were well-received. The rules for the royal tours at home and abroad were reformed by Sir Michael Adeane, so that the Queen should be seen by as many people as possible. Some of these changes had come about as a result of Altrincham's criticisms; others had already been instituted. The important point to note is that the Monarchy continued to show its ability to reflect the changes in British society and Britain's place in the world by reforming itself.

The theme of renewal was given personal emphasis by a series of births, deaths and marriages in the Royal Family in the early 1960s. These natural rhythms of the Royal Family's life were to become something of an obsession with the media, anxious to satisfy the public's increasing hunger for news. Commentators like Dermot Morrah even began to see the Royal Family as representing an ideal, to be emulated by families throughout the nation and the Commonwealth. The idea of the Commonwealth as a family of nations, with the Queen and the Royal Family at its centre, was given renewed emphasis by the changes to the ideal family during this period.

After the Queen had returned from her gruelling tour of Canada in the summer of 1959, it was announced that she was expecting her third child. The Queen's autumn engagements were cancelled, thus giving the Prime Minister greater leeway when it came to setting the election date. On 8 October the Conservatives were returned to power with an increased majority of 100 seats. The imminent birth of the Queen's third child led to renewed discussion of the family surname. The Queen was anxious to retain the surname 'Windsor' for the Royal House and Family. She wanted also to meet the wishes of Prince Philip and Mountbatten that their name should somehow be incorporated into the surname. She suggested that any members of the Royal Family who were no longer entitled to be styled a Prince or a Princess should take the surname 'Mountbatten-Windsor'. Although the Cabinet had reservations, there was none of the vehement opposition of 1952, which had been largely led by Churchill. The Cabinet approved the change of name much to the relief of the expectant Queen.

On 19 February 1960, the Queen gave birth to Prince Andrew, the first child born to a reigning Queen since Victoria gave birth to Princess Beatrice in 1857. The celebratory mood was somewhat dampened the next day by the sad news that Edwina, Countess Mountbatten of Burma, had died while on a Far Eastern tour. The dissolving of direct links with the past was again emphasised when, on 22 February it was announced that the Marquis of Carisbrooke, the last surviving grandson of Queen Victoria, had died. But four days later it was announced that Princess Margaret was to marry Mr Antony Armstrong-Jones. Despite the fears of the Palace, the announcement of the engagement of the Princess to a commoner, who earned his own living and had divorced parents (though his mother's second marriage was to an earl, and Armstrong-Jones himself was to be created the Earl of Snowdon) met with general public approval. As if to make amends for its censorious tone during the Townsend affair,

The Times declared that the news would be 'authentically welcomed throughout the Commonwealth on the simple assurance that Her Royal Highness is following her own heart and the Queen is delighted with her choice'.[9] The Cabinet was also conciliatory, ruling that in future the Sovereign would not have to seek ministerial advice in advance before giving permission for a person in succession to the Throne, to whom the Royal Marriages Act of 1772 applied, to marry. The Sovereign would only have to tell the Cabinet in advance of the proposed marriage. The marriage of Princess Margaret and Antony Armstrong-Jones took place in Westminster Abbey in May 1960 and was the largest Royal celebration since the Coronation.

The Royal marriage was not only a family and national occasion but a Commonwealth one. It had been watched by over 300 million viewers, many of whom lived in Commonwealth countries. Moreover, the Commonwealth Prime Ministers had met in London in order to represent their countries at the wedding and to discuss changes to that larger family of nations which the Queen, supported by the Royal Family, symbolised. The Commonwealth was under strain as a result of Britain's decision to seek entry to the European Common Market. Britain's bid in 1960 failed because of de Gaulle's opposition. But Commonwealth countries still sought to strengthen ties with Britain. Decolonisation was also changing the nature of the Commonwealth, as African colonies, like Ghana (1957) and Nigeria (1960), followed Malaya (1957) and obtained independence. The opposition of South Africa to these developments led it to strengthen apartheid and to leave the Commonwealth and become a republic in 1961.

The Queen's visit in November 1961 to Ghana, which Kwame Nkrumah now ruled as a one-party dictatorship, provided a good example of the delicate political manoeuvering required in dealing with the new republics if the Commonwealth was not to be irreparably damaged. There was now considerable opposition in Parliament, on both sides of the House of Commons, to the Queen's already postponed visit going ahead in view of the dangerous internal situation in Ghana, where there was resistance to Nkrumah's detention of political opponents and anti-British feeling was running high. The situation threatened to become worse if the new US

---

[9] *The Times*, 27 February 1960.

President, John F Kennedy, carried out his threat to cut off financial aid for the Volta Dam project. Macmillan feared that the combination of cancelling the Queen's visit and stopping the dam project might drive Nkrumah out of the Commonwealth and into the arms of the Soviet Union. Despite vocal opposition in Britain, Macmillan advised the Queen that it was safe to make the trip. Following a bomb explosion in Accra, however, the Commonwealth Secretary, Duncan Sandys, had to be sent out to Ghana to inspect the Queen's proposed route.

The Queen insisted on making the trip. She took her role as Head of the Commonwealth extremely seriously, not least because it helped compensate for her diminished political role at home. In the event, the matter did not come to a vote in the House of Commons, Kennedy did not carry out his threat to cut off aid for the dam and the visit went ahead without mishap. But the Ghana visit is instructive because it showed the Queen's involvement in a diplomatic incident, her coolness under pressure, and her steadying effect on her Prime Minister. In fact, it provided a good example of the Queen's exercising her rights to be consulted, to encourage and to warn. Moreover, there was no clash between the Queen and the Prime Minister on one side and Parliament on the other, as Macmillan had feared. The Ghana visit demonstrated that the Queen took her role as Head of the Commonwealth very seriously and would not be easily deterred from performing it.

In the run-up to the Commonwealth Conference in September 1962, the Queen voiced to Macmillan the concerns of Commonwealth countries that Britain's desire to enter the European Common Market would effectively destroy the Commonwealth as a trading bloc and political association. At the conference itself, though Macmillan tried to calm their fears by denying any incompatability between the two associations, the Commonwealth Prime Ministers made clear their continuing doubts to the Queen. The Queen was put in an embarrassing position by the British government's decision that Britain's future lay in Europe and not with the Commonwealth bloc. Macmillan found it necessary to send her a letter of apology in September 1962. Although de Gaulle refused Britain entry in January 1963, it was clear that Britain would try again when the moment was more propitious and that the Commonwealth countries would have to make their own non-British trading arrangements. It is not surprising, therefore, that the Queen should encounter some resentment against Britain, though it was mitigated by continuing affection for her during her trip to Australia and New Zealand in early 1963.

Macmillan's Common Market entry bid was partly motivated by a desire to boost the flagging fortunes of the Conservative Party after a series of by-election defeats. In a renewed attempt to shake up the government, he dismissed a third of his Cabinet in the 'Night of the Long Knives' on 13 July. The Queen was kept busy comforting sacked ministers and welcoming new ones. But it did nothing to rejuvenate the government. Macmillan was increasingly seen in the country as old and out of touch and representative of a decaying social order, as illustrated by his mishandling of the Profumo scandal.

It was exhaustion and illness which finally forced Macmillan, after much vacillation, to inform the Queen on 9 October that he would have to resign. The situation differed from 1957 in that there were now four contenders for the premiership: the deputy Prime Minister, R A Butler, the Foreign Secretary, Lord Home, the Chancellor of the Exchequer, Reginald Maudling, and the Lord President of the Council and Minister for Science, Lord Hailsham (Home and Hailsham were now able, under new legislation, to renounce their peerages in the event of either of them becoming Prime Minister). The selection process could not be confined to the Cabinet as in 1957. Since Macmillan's resignation occurred during the Conservative Party conference in Blackpool, it was inevitable that the candidates should canvas support among MPs and activists. In fact there was to be a wider canvassing of party opinion both within and outside Parliament than in 1957.

Macmillan has been criticised for orchestrating the selection procedure from his sickbed.[10] Yet it should be pointed out that he only did so after learning that the Conservative Party was not sure how to go about choosing a successor.[11] It seems that Macmillan's method for canvassing party opinion was acceptable to the Cabinet. Macmillan has also been condemned for recommending to the Queen that Lord Home, rather than R A Butler, should be his successor. Yet 'the customary processes of consultation' had indicated to Macmillan that Home was the overwhelming choice of his fellow Conservative peers and had a plurality of votes among Conservative

---

[10] Pimlott, *Queen*, pp 323-35.
[11] *Ibid*.

MPs, the Cabinet and the extra-Parliamentary party.

Macmillan made a conclusive case for Home in the long memorandum which he handed in a large envelope to the Queen on 18 October. The Queen has been criticised for accepting Macmillan's advice, and for summoning Home to the Palace too quickly after Macmillan had resigned in order to head off a revolt by the thwarted candidates. It has been argued that she should have taken further soundings in the Conservative Party which would have indicated that R A Butler was the popular choice.[12] But this would have compromised the Monarchy by involving it in internal Conservative Party politics. It was quite naturally felt at the Palace that it was up to the Conservative Party to decide whom it wanted as leader and to indicate its choice to the Queen. It is significant that Home made sure that he had the support of Hailsham, Maudling and Butler before accepting the Queen's invitation to form a government. So it is clear that Home, Macmillan and the Queen did not act unconstitutionally during the 1963 succession crisis, as some critics have alleged. Yet the tenor of the times demanded that the Conservative Party adopt a more democratic procedure for selecting its leader. This duly occurred in 1965, thus in effect absolving the Queen from any future responsibility for choosing the Conservative leader when his party was in power.

The Queen had been genuinely sad to see Macmillan go. But she felt immediately at home with his successor, Sir Alec Douglas-Home (he had laid his peerage aside). He was a personal friend (the Douglas-Homes and the Bowes-Lyons had long known each other). His view of the world and his own interests were akin to those of the Queen. During the first month of his premiership, the Queen did not appear much in public because of her pregnancy. She gave birth to her fourth and last child, Prince Edward, on 10 March 1964. With Princess Alexandra, the Duchess of Kent, and Princess Margaret also adding new-born children to the Royal Family, it was a happy time for the Queen. It also provided an opportunity for the new Archbishop of Canterbury, Dr Ramsey, to praise the Royal Family for setting a good example to the nation.

The Queen signalled her full return to public duty by embarking on a nine-day visit to Canada on 5 October 1964 to celebrate the centenary of

---

[12] *Ibid.*

the origins of Canadian Confederation. In contrast to her trip to Ghana in 1961, the Queen was visiting Canada as Queen of Canada and would therefore look to the Canadian Prime Minister rather than to the British Prime Minister for advice. The Queen was only required to consult the British government about whether the date was convenient. The British government had considered asking the Canadian government to cancel the visit because the British Prime Minister was considering asking for a dissolution at that time and the Sovereign needed to be in the country. The British government was also concerned for the Queen's safety while she was in Quebec City, where the French separatists were again active and death threats had been received. It was realised both at No 10 Downing Street and at the Palace that any cancellation of the tour, which the Queen was anyway keen to make, would cause a constitutional clash between Britain and Canada and would only enhance the cause of the separatists.

Eventually it was agreed that the Queen's Canadian tour should take place during the British general election campaign. As Parliament was not in session and it was not worth proroguing it, the Queen agreed with the Prime Minister's suggestion that she should dissolve it by Proclamation on 25 September. In order not to infringe the Royal Prerogative it was agreed that this should not be seen as setting a precedent for the future. After the Queen had broken her holiday in Scotland and journeyed to London to make the Proclamation, the Prime Minister would travel to Balmoral to request a dissolution. Sir Alec Douglas-Home and Lester Pearson, the Canadian Prime Minister, also agreed on a face-saving formula whereby the British government announced that it was satisfied that the Canadian government was taking all the necessary precautions to ensure the Queen's safety. In the event the Queen's tour proved a difficult one, not least because of the heavy-handed security measures taken. The Cabinet Secretary, Sir Burke Trend, and the Prime Minister's Private Secretary, Derek Mitchell, had even given consideration to the grim possibility of the Queen being assassinated, and its effect on the British electoral process. They concluded that in this eventuality the general election could be held under Statute, since Counsellors of State had been appointed in the Queen's absence.

The Queen returned safely from her Canadian tour in time for the general election. When it looked in the early hours of 16 October that there might be an electoral deadlock and a hung Parliament, Derek Mitchell had to give consideration to the question of how the Queen should act. He concluded:

> She may (a) press him [Douglas-Home] to stay on until defeated in the
> House; (b) press him to stay on in the hope that he may form a Coalition
> or (c) send for someone who is not the leader of either major Party in the
> hope that some sort of compromise Government could be carried on until
> it were feasible to have another General Election.[13]

In the end the Queen did not have to choose one of these options, because
the new Labour leader, Harold Wilson, won a narrow overall majority of
seats which enabled him to accept the Queen's invitation to form a
government. Despite their different backgrounds and lack of shared
interests, the Queen and her first Labour Prime Minister soon established
a rapport. The Queen appreciated the fact that Wilson treated her as if
she was a member of the Cabinet and sought her advice. He also offered
her a new perspective on northern life and the Labour and Trades Union
movements. For his part Wilson revelled in his audiences at the Palace,
and regarded the Queen as someone in whom he could safely confide
about the matters of the moment. One of his Left-Wing colleagues in the
Cabinet, Barbara Castle, thought Wilson was too close to the Queen and
that this affected his political judgement. Other Left-Wingers, like Richard
Crossman and Anthony Wedgwood Benn (who had renounced his title),
were uncomfortable with the rituals and the symbols of a constitutional
monarchy, which Wilson regarded as sacrosanct. Thus, at the prompting
of the Palace, he intervened to prevent his Postmaster-General, Tony Benn,
from symbolically cutting the Queen's head from British postage stamps.

Wilson also shared the Queen's belief in the Commonwealth. The Prime
Minister recruited her help politically, first to try to prevent Rhodesia's
Unilateral Declaration of Independence (UDI) in 1965 and, subsequently,
to bring the rebellion to an end. At his suggestion, the Queen made it
clear that she would not be the head of state of a rogue regime, and that
she supported the policy of the British government. When Wilson in
October 1965 made his last-minute foray to Salisbury, Rhodesia, to
persuade the Rhodesian Prime Minister, Ian Smith, against UDI, he carried
with him a letter from the Queen reminding Rhodesians of their allegiance
to the Crown. Smith cleverly turned the argument around by making a

---

[13] PRO, PREM 11/4756.

distinction between Rhodesia's continuing allegiance to the Crown, in the person of the Sovereign, and its disagreement with her government. When Rhodesia proclaimed its independence on 11 November, it stipulated that the Queen should remain as Head of State. Thereafter, the Salisbury regime and the British government both continued to invoke the Queen's name in order to legitimise their respective actions. The British Governor, Sir Humphrey Gibb, who remained in Salisbury as a symbol that the Queen had taken over the government, was tolerated by the Rhodesians (The Queen refused Smith's wish to appoint a Rhodesian as Governor-General).

Wilson also obtained the support of the Queen for his plans to send Lord Mountbatten to Rhodesia on another 'End Of Empire' mission. However, they were persuaded, much to Mountbatten's disappointment, by Adeane and Lord Cobbold, the Lord Chamberlain, that such an overt political act by the Queen should only be carried out on the formal and public advice of her government. It was realised that, since Mountbatten would be an official British emmisary, the Rhodesian government would rebuff him, and therefore the idea was dropped. It was not until 1970 that Smith felt strong enough to ignore pro-monarchical feeling in the Rhodesian armed forces (with their oath of allegiance to the Queen) and to cut the direct link with the Sovereign by declaring Rhodesia a republic. The restoration of that link after 1970 was considered to be the necessary step in any settlement of the Rhodesian dispute.

While Rhodesia and other territories in the British Empire-Commonwealth became independent and declared themselves republics, cutting the direct link with the Crown, there were changes to the Monarchy's role at home. While the Queen expressed the spirit of international reconciliation by visiting Germany in 1965, and symbolised the nation's grief by comforting the devastated families of the schoolchildren killed in the Aberfan disaster in 1966, the divorce and remarriage of her cousin, the Earl of Harewood, in 1967 signalled that she was no longer the defender of our morality. The abolition of the Lord Chamberlain's right to license plays, which had barred among other things the portrayal of royalty on stage, signalled that the days of the Sovereign as the Head of Society and the arbiter of public taste had also gone forever. The portrayal of the Queen in plays, on television and in the Press was to become less reverent in tone, in accordance with the spirit of the times. The Queen was even obliged to announce at the Opening of Parliament in 1968 that the government intended to reform the House of Lords, a direct challenge to the hereditary principle on which she had succeeded to the Throne. It was to be another thirty years, however, before another Labour government was able to begin to undertake the reform of the Lords. It was appropriate that the Queen's Press Secretary, Commander Colville, nicknamed the 'Abominable No-Man', should choose this moment to resign. He was succeeded by his assistant, the Australian William Heseltine, who sought to portray a new image of the Royal Family.

It was Heseltine, backed by Prince Philip, who oversaw the making and showing of the BBC film *Royal Family* in June 1969, which for the first time gave the public some idea of what it was like to be a Royal. It was a calculated attempt to court public opinion but, though it was well-received, it only succeeded in whetting the public's appetite for more information on the human face of the Monarchy. Moreover the Palace was, as a result of its own action, no longer in a position to prevent the media from exploiting the commercial potential offered by royal exposés.

The Prince of Wales's Investiture at Caernarvon Castle on 1 July 1969 was also carefully and successfully choreographed for television in order to bring home to the British and Commonwealth publics that the Monarchy was constantly renewing itself. It was a sign of the times that some questioned whether the Investiture should have taken place (and it was held amid tight security in case extremist Welsh nationalist groups carried out their threats to disrupt the event). Some cynics even argued that the conscious raising of the Monarchy's profile at this time (the Queen also went on her first 'walkabouts' in New Zealand and Australia in early 1970) was an attempt to justify an increase in the Civil List provision for the Royal Family. There was no evidence for this, though Wilson was concerned to avert any open discussion of any increase in the Civil List. This was to avoid any public criticism of the Monarchy and the government at a time when it was trying to impose a prices and incomes policy on the workforce and a general election was pending. Wilson solved the immediate problem of the Royal Household running into the red by getting government departments to absorb some of the expenditure. He left consideration of the long-term solution to a Select Committee to be set up after the election. (As a member of this committee Wilson later helped Elizabeth II to obtain a rise in her annual Civil List provision from £475,000 to £980,000, with rises for other members of the Royal Family as well, though there was criticism that her private fortune continued to receive immunity from tax.)

Seeking to take advantage of an upswing in the opinion polls, Wilson requested in May 1970 a dissolution from the Queen. Much to everyone's surprise, the Conservatives won the general election on 18 June and Edward Heath became Prime Minister. He was different from the Queen's previous Conservative Prime Ministers in that he had been elected (in 1965) to the leadership of his party (for the first time since 1921 the Sovereign had not been involved in choosing the Conservative leader). He was also from a working class background and did not have the ease of manner of his immediate Conservative predecessors. He also lacked Wilson's admiration for all things monarchical and had a more matter of fact attitude towards his Sovereign. His preoccupation with Britain's entry into Europe meant that he had little time for or interest in Commonwealth affairs. He was to prevent the Queen from attending the Commonwealth Conference in Singapore in 1971 and only reluctantly agreed that she attend the next one in Ottawa in 1973. Britain's entry into Europe in that year dealt a decisive blow not only to Commonwealth unity but also to the constitutional concept of the Queen in Parliament. While the divergent interests of the Commonwealth nations complicated her position as Head of the Commonwealth and Head of State of some of its members, her future role in relation to Europe had yet to be determined.

The Queen's constitutionally divided personality was exemplified by her opening the Australian Parliament in Canberra during her trip to the South Pacific, and then dashing back to Britain for the general election which Heath had suddenly called for 28 February 1974 (Parliament had been dissolved in her absence). Past Prime Ministers had arranged general elections around the Queen's overseas tours. Not so Ted Heath, who was in desperate straits with a miner's strike which had caused a national emergency. It was as well that the Queen returned in time, for, instead of the predicted Conservative victory, the result was a hung Parliament. Labour had won the largest number of seats but had not obtained an overall majority.

Heath was constitutionally entitled to remain in power to see whether he could form a government in alliance with some of the minority parties. When his attempt to strike a deal with the Liberal Party leader, Jeremy Thorpe, failed, Heath resigned. The Queen could theoretically have invited Thorpe or another leading politician to form a government. In practice, the least controversial course was the one she took, namely to summon Wilson whose party had the largest number of seats in the House of

Commons. Wilson had already indicated that he was prepared to return to power and immediately accepted the Queen's invitation to form a government.

However, the question soon arose whether Wilson, as head of a minority government, would be entitled to a dissolution if he was defeated on the Queen's Speech, or if he tried to obtain an overall majority in the House of Commons by calling another snap general election. Opinion was divided. Some, like Roy Jenkins, argued that the Queen could not refuse a Prime Minister's request for a dissolution. Others, like *The Times*, maintained that the Sovereign had a discretionary right to refusal, if the request came too rapidly after the previous demand for a dissolution, or if there seemed no chance of breaking the electoral deadlock, or yet again, if another party leader could form an alternative government. The Queen indicated to Wilson beforehand, through her Private Secretary, Sir Martin Charteris, that she would be prepared to grant his request for a dissolution if he was defeated on the Queen's Speech. This was made known to the Conservatives who, along with the Liberals, had no wish to force another election so soon after the last one. This was another safeguard, since Wilson did not put anything controversial in the Queen's Speech. The Labour Party certainly did not take the Queen's power of dissolution for granted. The Lord President, Edward Short, quoting constitutional experts, said that 'the Sovereign is not in all circumstances bound to grant a Prime Minister's request for a dissolution'.[14] In the event the minority Labour government survived until October 1974, when the Queen granted Wilson's request for a dissolution. At the ensuing general election Labour were returned to power with a small overall majority.

Although the royal prerogatives were not invoked in Britain in 1974, they were invoked in Australia the following year. In order to break the constitutional deadlock whereby the Labour government could not get its Budget Bills through the Senate, the Queen's representative in Australia, the Governor-General, Sir John Kerr, dismissed the Prime Minister, Gough Whitlam. Kerr appointed the opposition Liberal Party leader, Malcolm Fraser, as his interim successor until a general election could be held. Although Kerr had kept the Queen informed about the constitutional

---

[14] *The Times*, 11 May 1975.

crisis, he had not let her know in advance of his decision to dismiss Whitlam so as to avoid the danger of her becoming involved in the crisis. Nor had he given Whitlam warning of his intention, which effectively prevented the Prime Minister from pre-empting Kerr by advising the Queen to dismiss the Governor-General.

After Whitlam had ceased to be Prime Minister he was in no position to do this. Once he had been dismissed, the Senate passed the Budget Bills and the House of Representatives passed a no confidence motion against Fraser and called for Whitlam to be asked to form a new government. Kerr reacted by dissolving Parliament. The Speaker of the House of Representatives then sought the intervention of the Queen. Charteris replied that she was unable to do this except on the advice of the Australian Prime Minister, and that it was the Governor-General who exercised the prerogative powers in Australia. The Kerr affair only served to exacerbate Republican feeling in the Australian Labour Party. When next in power it ensured, by the 1986 Australia Act, that the Governor-General could never dismiss a government again. It also continued to campaign for the severance of the direct links with the Crown by establishing a republic in Australia.

While the Australian premier had been forced out of office, his British counterpart decided to resign voluntarily. Wilson's resignation on 16 March 1976 came as a surprise to his colleagues and to the nation, but not to the Queen who had known about his intention since September 1975. It was unheard of for a British Prime Minister to go of his own free will rather than after being defeated at the polls, or pushed out by his colleagues. Rumours circulated about plots and an honours scandal. The truth was that Wilson had had his fill of politics. The unprecedented nature of the resignation of a prime minister half-way through his term raised the question of transferring power to his successor and at the same time preserving the royal prerogative. It was eventually agreed between Charteris and Kenneth Stow, the Prime Minister's Private Secretary, that Wilson should remain at No 10 Downing Street until the Parliamentary Labour Party (PLP) had elected a new leader.

After James Callaghan had won the PLP ballot on 5 April, Wilson notified Charteris by telephone of the result and then went to the Palace to resign. Wilson observed the constitutional proprieties and did not directly advise the Queen to send for Callaghan. Instead he merely referred to the voting figures which he had previously sent to her. The Queen then sent for Callaghan, who accepted her invitation to form a government. There was some outcry from the Left about the need to remove the Queen's remaining prerogative powers, and from the Right about any further erosion of them. The solution devised by No 10 Downing Street and the Palace proved a good working compromise. The Queen had regretted Wilson's departure but she soon established a good working relationship with his successor. Callaghan found it useful to discuss the issues of the day with the Queen, who would often indicate her opinion by asking a pointed question or citing another person's viewpoint. Her failure to comment on a policy showed that she disapproved of it. Callaghan's attempt to introduce Prince Charles to the workings of government foundered on the Queen's opposition to his working in the Cabinet Office, and to the Prince of Wales's objection to just being a member of the Commonwealth Development Corporation rather than the head of a Commonwealth body. There were shades here of Queen Victoria's objection a hundred years before to Gladstone's suggestion of government training for Edward, Prince of Wales, and the latter's reluctance to spend time in Ireland as the Viceroy.

The Prince of Wales was not the only member of the Royal Family to concern the Queen and the government at this time. On the very day that Wilson announced his resignation, Princess Margaret and Lord Snowdon announced their separation. Wilson had hoped that his resignation would deflect media attention from the royal separation. It had the opposite effect, as the gossip-mongers in Fleet Street (particularly *The Daily Mail* and *The Daily Express*) gave full coverage to the separation in order to boost their sagging circulation figures. The Snowdons' separation and subsequent divorce, his subsequent remarriage and Princess Margaret's very public affair with Roderick Llewellyn, dealt a serious blow to the Royal Family's image as the nation's 'model family'. Followed as it was by further marital troubles among the younger generation of the Royal Family in the next two decades, it can be seen to have marked the real beginning of the shift away from the 'Happy Family' image which had helped to underpin the Monarchy during the period from the Abdication to the Snowdons' divorce.

Despite fears at the Palace, the break-up of the Snowdon marriage did not ruin the Queen's Silver Jubilee in 1977. After a slow start, and a lukewarm response from a government mired in economic and political problems, the celebrations proved a great success. The lighting of the old beacons around the country, the street parties, and the Queen's visits to all parts of the nation and to much of the Commonwealth, revitalised a sense of community between the Queen and her subjects. It was symbolised by the Queen's reaffirmation of her vows, first given in South Africa in 1947 and again at the Coronation in 1953, to serve Britain and the Commonwealth. The Queen's Silver Jubilee, like her grandfather's jubilee in 1935, demonstrated that there was great residual affection in the country and the Commonwealth for the Sovereign. The celebrations also showed a significant emotional need to identify with a seemingly permanent institution like the Monarchy at a time when other entities, like Parliament, Whitehall, industry, the United Kingdom, Europe and the Commonwealth were changing rapidly. The Queen responded to this need, not only by travelling around her realms but sounding a personal note on the wisdom of Scottish and Welsh devolution: 'I cannot forget that I was crowned Queen of the United Kingdom of Great Britain and Northern Ireland. Perhaps this Jubilee is a time to remind ourselves of the benefit which union has conferred at home and in our international dealings, on the inhabitants of all parts of the United Kingdom.'[15]

Canada, like Australia, was reappraising its link with the Crown at this period. Pierre Trudeau, the Canadian Prime Minister, proposed a new Constitution whereby the British Parliament would relinquish its remaining constitutional powers under the 1867 British North America Act but the Queen would retain her title as 'Queen of Canada'. The Governor-General was to be a Canadian recommended by the Canadian Prime Minister, and with stronger powers of dissolution. The Queen's new Private Secretary, Sir Philip Moore, did not hide the Palace's disquiet over the unnecessarily rough way in which Trudeau, seeking to curry favour with the Quebec separatists, had presented his proposals. There was also concern at the Palace, and among Canadian loyalists, that Trudeau's proposal would lead to the Governor-General becoming the Head of State. This situation gave the Queen an opportunity, with her ability to speak French, to help the Canadians out of their constitutional difficulties. Canadian politicians have testified to the imaginative way in which the Queen handled the delicate constitutional discussions in which she was involved.[16] This helped to ensure that after the Canadian constitution was 'patriated' in 1982 by Westminister under the Canada Act, thus effectively cutting the direct link with the

---

[15] J Parker, *The Queen* (Headline, London, 1991), p 305.
[16] W R Young (ed), *Paul Martin: The London Diaries, 1975-1979* (University of Ottawa Press, Ottawa), pp 387-9, 402-412.

Crown, that the title 'Queen of Canada' actually continued to mean something. *The Times* pointed out that since the Queen was no longer identified with the constitutional issue, it was actually easier for the Canadians to accept her as Queen of Canada.[17]

It was the Queen's understanding of, feeling for, and dedication to the Commonwealth and its peoples which proved to be of assistance to her new Prime Minister, Margaret Thatcher. The Conservative Party, led by its first woman leader, was swept to power in the general election of 3 May 1979 by a wave of disillusionment at the failure of the Callaghan government to cope with the industrial relations troubles of the 1978-79 'Winter of Discontent'. The new Prime Minister's determination to roll back the collectivist state at home was matched by her desire to counter Communism-inspired subversion abroad. She had no time for Marxists, especially those who headed Commonwealth countries. She was prepared to boycott the 1979 Commonwealth Conference in Lusaka and to prevent the Queen from attending, ostensibly on 'safety' grounds but in reality to prevent the Commonwealth leaders from putting Britain in the dock over the continuing impasse over Rhodesia. The Palace acted before attitudes hardened into policy and announced that the Queen would be going ahead with her tour of Central Africa, which was to conclude with several days in Lusaka at the time of the Commonwealth conference. Whether as a result of this announcement or other factors, Mrs Thatcher relented and went to Lusaka. Participants in the Commonwealth Conference have testified to the remarkable change of atmosphere, from recrimination to cooperation, which occurred. This seems to have been partly due to the Queen's encouraging the Commonwealth leaders, who had great respect for her and listened to her, to talk to one another about Rhodesia. The result was that Mrs Thatcher realised that she could do business with some of the African leaders. This led to the Lusaka Accord, and the holding of a new constitutional conference in London, resulting in the Lancaster House Agreement, later in the year, which ended the long guerrilla war in Rhodesia. There followed the holding of elections and the establishment of the independent state of Zimbabwe in 1980.

The Queen's quiet, dignified and efficient performance of her

---

[17] *The Times*, 17 April 1982.

constitutional duties was to be increasingly overshadowed in the next decade by the attention given by the media to the activities of the younger generation of the Royal Family. The public, fed by the media on a steady diet of trivia, went 'Diana-mad' following the engagement and marriage of Lady Diana Spencer to the Prince of Wales in 1981. The subsequent intense public scrutiny of every aspect of an increasingly unhappy marriage was to subject it to intolerable pressures. The private lives of Princess Anne and Prince Andrew were also subject to the prurient public gaze. The Palace's repeated attempts, through moral persuasion or recourse to the law, to protect members of the Royal Family from constant intrusion upon their privacy, proved to have no real effect on a new generation of media tycoons and their minions, who justified their burgeoning profits from royal exposés as being in the public interest.

The media sensationalism was briefly interrupted by the Falklands War in 1982, which reminded the nation of the various roles the Queen performed as head of the armed forces, as mother of a fighting airman (Prince Andrew was a helicopter pilot), as Head of State of a country whose territory had been attacked, and as Head of the Commonwealth. These separate roles were emphasised as appropriate during the conflict in order to mobilise support, not only in Britain and the Commonwealth but also in the United States. They played a symbolic part in Britain's reconquest of the islands.

Not content with prying into the private lives of the Royal Family, the media tried, following the recapture of the Falklands and the Conservative victory in the June 1987 general election, to manufacture a split between the Queen and Mrs Thatcher. Citing unattributable sources at the Palace, or quoting the indiscreet or mischievous remarks of known political opponents of Mrs Thatcher, such as the head of the Commonwealth Secretariat, Sir Sonny Ramphal and the Labour leader Neil Kinnock, the media sought to build up a picture of a Sovereign and her Prime Minister at loggerheads over the American invasion of Grenada in October 1983, the Christmas Broadcast that year endorsing the Brandt 'North-South' Report, the 1984 miners' strike and the issue of sanctions against South Africa at the June 1986 Commonwealth Conference. The campaign was epitomised by the claim in *The Sunday Times* on 20 July 1986, apparently based on remarks by the Palace Press Secretary Michael Shea, that the Queen found Mrs Thatcher's general approach to government 'uncaring, confrontational and socially divisive'.[18] This prompted the Queen's Private Secretary, Sir William Heseltine, to write to *The Times* denying that Shea had ever made such remarks to *The Sunday Times*.[19] The episode, coming as it did after a stream of such revelations, caused much embarrassment both to the Palace (Shea left his post several months later) and to No 10 Downing Street. It stemmed basically from a rather bizarre alliance between the Commonwealth and parliamentary opponents of Mrs Thatcher and her more enthusiastic followers. The former had sought to enlist the Monarchy, along with the Church and the House of Lords, in the attempt to thwart the domestic and overseas policies of the Conservative government. The more gung-ho Thatcherites suspected the Queen of holding Left-of-Centre views on Commonwealth and domestic affairs and, therefore, of being an obstacle (to be ignored rather than removed) to the implementation of radical Conservative policies. The media, with its new sensationalist coverage of the Monarchy, gave full play to such political manoeuverings. That they were not allowed to damage the working relationship between the Queen and Mrs Thatcher owes much to their good sense in failing to respond to such speculation.

However, the Queen's dignified and efficient performance of her multiple roles as head of the nation, Head of State, Head of the Commonwealth and Supreme Governor of the Church of England was largely obscured in the 1980s by the media, which had become increasingly interested only in negative news about the Royal Family. Disproportionate attention was paid to an off-the-cuff remark about the Chinese by Prince Philip, Prince Charles's criticism of modern architects, the state of the Wales's marriage, the activities of 'Fergie' (the Duchess of York) and her father Major Ronald Ferguson, and Prince Edward's unfortunate organisation of an 'It's a Royal Knockout' competition for television. Commentators on both the Left and the Right intoned solemnly about how such activities degraded the Monarchy and could lead to the establishment of a republic. Following the July 1990 increase in the Queen's Civil List (following a reorganisation of the Royal Household by the Lord

---

[18] *The Sunday Times*, 20 July 1982.
[19] *The Times*, 28 July 1986.

Chamberlain, the Earl of Airlie) and the continued exemption of her private fortune from tax, criticism was voiced in the media that the Royal Family was overpaid, undertaxed and did not provide value for money. It was noted that the Royal Family was not involved in the Gulf War in 1991 (as Prince Andrew had been in the Falklands) but was engaged in leisure pursuits. This slur on the Royal Family (the first in wartime in the twentieth century) was emphatically denied by the Palace, which stated that the Queen was kept fully briefed by the Defence Staff and was in close touch, through her Private Secretary Sir Robert Fellowes, with the Foreign Secretary and the Prime Minister.

During the Gulf crisis Mrs Thatcher, who was now regarded as an electoral liability by her party, had stood down as Prime Minister (as Macmillan had done in 1963 and Chamberlain had in 1940). For the first time the Queen was not forced to intervene, since Mrs Thatcher stayed in office until the Conservatives had elected John Major as their leader. The Queen might have had to intervene if Mrs Thatcher had not been persuaded by her Cabinet colleagues that it was folly to stay on as Prime Minister, but not party leader, and request a dissolution.

Major, who kissed hands on 28 November, was the ninth Prime Minister to take office during her reign and the first, at forty-nine, who was younger than she. It was a milestone in another way, for the Queen was no longer receiving advice from politicians and courtiers who were older than she was. In fact her advisers were now able to look to her, with her long experience of domestic and overseas politics, for information about and a perspective on the problems of the day

In fact by 1992, the fortieth anniversary of her accession, comparisons were being made between Elizabeth II and Victoria, especially over the difficulties posed for the Monarchy by a long reign with an ageing Sovereign, a large family and a fickle public. There was talk of scaling down the Monarchy to Scandinavian or 'bicycling' size, and of the Queen abdicating in favour of the Prince of Wales, as Queen Juliana of the Netherlands had done in favour of Princess Beatrix in 1980. The Queen swiftly killed such speculation in her 1991 Christmas broadcast. She was also careful to downplay her few anniversary celebrations in a year which saw further damage to the ideal 'Family on the Throne' image, with the break-up of the Yorks' marriage, the ending of Princess Anne's marriage to Mark Phillips, and further difficulties between the Waleses. There was an attempt to counter this in the BBC television programme *Elizabeth R*, which emphasised the unremitting devotion to duty of the Queen year in and year out. As *The Times* noted on her fortieth anniversary, the Monarchy was 'suffering the effect of the decade of Diana'.[20] The over-concentration by the media on the private lives of the Princess of Wales and other members of the Royal Family, which had sometimes wittingly or not been encouraged by them, had skewed the coverage of the Monarchy and altered the public perception of that institution. This was shown in the revolt of public opinion against paying for the damage done to Windsor Castle by fire in November 1992. It would take more than a television programme to right the balance.

Even the announcement of a major reform of the Monarchy by the Prime Minister in the House of Commons on 26 November, *viz* that the Queen and the Prince of Wales would pay income tax on their private wealth from 1 April 1993 and that the Civil List provision for five members of the Royal Family would be axed, was only grudgingly acknowledged by the media. The 'annus horribilis', to which the Queen had referred in her Guildhall speech on 24 November, continued with the announcement from Buckingham Palace on 9 December of the separation of the Waleses. The Prime Minister made clear that they would not divorce and that, if Charles became King, Diana would be Queen. There were also decisions to be made about raising and educating the children, Princes William and Harry, who were respectively second and third in line to the Throne. The final indignity suffered by the Queen in 1992 was *The Sun*'s publication of her Christmas Day broadcast two days before it was due to be delivered.

The Queen had acknowledged in her Guildhall speech that no British institution, not even the Monarchy, could expect to be free from public scrutiny. She also declared at the Commonwealth Conference in 1993 that she would willingly accept any decision by the people of those Commonwealth countries where she was still Head of State to sever the direct connection with the Crown by becoming republics. There has been no great rush to republicanism. Although Australia, Jamaica and a few other Caribbean islands are on course to become republics, Canada and New Zealand have not gone down that route. Moreover, there has been a renewed interest in the Commonwealth following the readmission of South Africa in 1993. Mozambique (which was a Portuguese colony) has joined

---

[20] *The Times*, 29 January and 30 January 1992.

and Yemen and the embryonic state of Palestine have expressed an interest in joining.

In Britain it is noticeable that politicians, wary of losing votes, have steered clear of the Monarchy debate. Even among intellectuals the argument has focused, not on abolition, but on how to make the Constitution appear more 'republican', in line with Bagehot's analysis of a 'disguised republic'. But the constitutional debate, and even the Queen's performance of her duties (eg the D-Day and combined VE-VJ Day celebrations in 1994-95), were overshadowed by the widening rift between the Prince and the Princess of Wales. Their very public revelations (respectively through the books of Jonathan Dimbleby and Andrew Morton and BBC interviews) of their marital misfortunes led the Queen to persuade them that it was time to divorce. In a remarkable reversal of its position forty years before on Princess Margaret's marriage, *The Times* declared that this had no 'constitutional implications'.[21] Following the Yorks' divorce in April 1996, the Waleses followed suit in August, after a marriage settlement had been worked out by the lawyers. The Princess of Wales lost her title of 'Royal Highness' and became simply 'Diana, Princess of Wales'. She resigned her honorary positions at the head of various British regiments and charities. She concentrated on her humanitarian work, with missions to Bosnia and Angola. She also raised money for the Aids Crisis Trust through the sale of her extensive collection of dresses at an auction in New York. Her increasing tendency to make thinly-veiled political criticisms of the Conservative government on such matters as the timing of a world-wide ban on anti-personnel land mines, along with her erratic private behaviour, led some observers to question not only her judgement but also the state of her mental health. It all ended not only with her death but that of her companion Dodi Fayed in a car crash in Paris in late August 1997.

The outburst of national grief which followed, symbolised by the thousands of bouquets laid by the public outside her former residence at Kensington Palace, clearly demonstrated that the death of a member of the Royal Family was still keenly felt by people, as if they had lost one of their own family. The State funeral in Westminister Abbey and private

---

[21] *The Times*, 21 December 1995.

burial on the Althorp Estate of 'the People's Princess', as Prime Minister Blair dubbed her, was a new blend of the ceremonial and the informal in accord with the mood of the people and the prevailing spirit of the times.

Diana's death can also be seen to have delivered a mortal blow to what has been called 'the cult of royal celebrity', which the Family Monarchy had become largely under her auspices.[22] It is clear that the House of Windsor can no longer play the 'ideal Family' card with any degree of conviction, and the Prince of Wales has admitted as much. But the image of Prince Charles and his sons rebuilding their family life is an enduring one, which has a curious resonance among the public in the age of the fractured, or dysfunctional, family.

The death of Diana also refocused the attention of the media on the activities of the Queen and the Prince of Wales. In an attempt to make amends for their hounding of the Princess of Wales the media gave sympathetic coverage to the tour of Southern Africa by the Prince of Wales and his sons in late 1997. It is not clear how long this will last, as speculation mounts about the future status of his relationship with Camilla Parker-Bowles (the great-granddaughter of Alice Keppel, the last mistress of Edward VII). Despite continuing attempts by some of the media to portray the Queen as remote and out of touch, opinion polls show that the people continue to have considerable respect for her as a woman and as a sovereign. There is a growing recognition that her considerable experience as a constitutional monarch in the second half of the twentieth century is of benefit to the government and the nation. In fact the Labour government of Tony Blair has tried to capitalise on this by taking the rather unusual step of citing her support for the proposed Succession to the Crown Bill, which treats the sons and daughters of the Sovereign on an equal basis. The Prime Minister also persuaded her to state her satisfaction with the way her tour of India and Pakistan was handled in late 1997. It was unprecedented for the Queen to be asked to commend a parliamentary bill or to defend a minister (in this case the Foreign Secretary, Robin Cook) and it could set an unfortunate example for the future. It goes against the

---

[22] David Starkey, 'The Modern Monarchy: rituals of privacy and their subversion' in Robert Smith and John S Moore, *The Monarchy* (Institute for Constitutional Research, London, 1998), p 267.

whole trend of her reign, which has seen the continued erosion of the remaining royal prerogatives (to appoint a prime minister and to dissolve parliament) and the removal of the Sovereign from the arena of political controversy. This has enabled the Queen to make effective use, drawing on her vast experience, of her remaining rights to be consulted, to encourage and to warn. It has also enhanced the dignified role which she has played so well. If the Sovereign is dragged back into the political arena by being forced to make political statements, other than those on the formal advice of her ministers, this will have a dangerously corrosive effect on the politically neutral, and inestimably valuable, position of the Monarchy. The Queen must be seen *not* to be taking sides in the political debate.

The Labour government's pursuit of devolution for Wales, Scotland and Northern Ireland has also raised the question of the future relationship of the Monarchy to those political entities. The future of the United Kingdom is in doubt. If the Monarchy is to continue to play a role in Wales, Scotland and Northern Ireland it will have to associate itself more closely with purely regional activities, to get away from its image as an English monarchy. This regional approach might also determine the Queen's future constitutional position in relation to an increasingly integrated European Union.

As the Queen Mother's 100th birthday in August 2000 and the Queen's Golden Jubilee in February 2002 approach, there is no reason to think that these anniversaries will not see a revival of royal fortunes. If the Queen and the Royal Family continue to adapt the Monarchy to changing circumstances there is no reason why it should not continue to survive. It is well-equipped to do so, having put its finances in order under the efficient direction of the Privy Purse, Sir Michael Peat, and the Way Ahead Group of senior royalty and officials. But they will have to perform a delicate balancing act to accomplish what John Grigg more than forty years ago called 'the seemingly impossible task of being at once ordinary and extraordinary'.[23]

---

[23] Altrincham, 'Monarchy Today'.

Conclusion: Dignified and Efficient

A nation needs its pageantry and its symbols. A political system as old as ours needs to be caparisoned in some tradition, girdled with convention, confident of its past. The question is: does the monarchy amount to any more than this pageantry? Is the Queen merely a symbol, whose importance one can confine to the ceremonial world; merely what Bagehot called a 'dignified' element of the constitution in contrast to the 'efficient' parts represented by Cabinet, Parliament and the Civil Service?[1] The fate of any constitution depends upon the adequacy of the provision it makes for dealing with an emergency: crisis powers, reserve powers, call them what you will. In the British constitutional monarchy, there are still powers not covered by statute that may have to come into play in circumstances which are not conditioned by convention. They concern the appointment of a prime minister and the dissolution of Parliament; and these prerogatives lie right at the heart of the 'efficient' constitution. Unless the constitution is changed, therefore, our monarch may find herself willy-nilly in a situation where she is required either to find a prime minister out of a confusion of all-minority parties in Parliament, or to decide whether or not to dissolve a hung parliament which cannot even agree on the manner of its own extinction.

The important point about the Monarchy, therefore, is that it is not yet constitutionally able to slip back fully into a world of sumptuous, if uncomplicated, ceremonial. At the heart of this old mystery there is still a tiny, critical atom of power, which is a paradox, because its existence both adds magic to the mystery and threatens to destroy it altogether. The Crown once reigned supreme, as a warship does on the high seas, acknowledging

---

[1] Bagehot, *English Constitution*, Chapter 2.

no higher authority, no other law than its own coercive powers. For centuries now that warship has first been challenged on the surface by rival power groups in the area, then pushed further down towards the seabed, sunk beneath fathoms of convention, statute and democracy — in short parliamentary government. From within the hulk, however, there is the sound of tapping; one or two relics of that old *imperium* have survived in the depths of history. Can we risk leaving them there as reminders of an earlier power, in the hope that they will not be called upon again? Or are those very powers hostages to the future of the monarchy for the simple reason that they might have to be used, but, if once used the monarchy might never recover from the fact of doing so?

Let us look at these powers in the twentieth century and see whether, in practice, the monarchy has the capacity to *act* as well as to be; and, if it has the capacity, whether the body politic would accept the monarch's authority to administer such treatment. According to Bagehot, the sovereign has three rights: to be consulted, to encourage and to warn. To that I would add a fourth: the right to know. But these rights carry a major responsibility: to keep the Queen's government functioning. Through all the comings and goings of party politics, the making and unmaking of cabinets, the appointment of prime ministers and their resignation, there is one fundamental goal pursued by the Monarch and her advisers at the Palace. It is to see that the country has a government. It does not matter so much what kind of government, whether it is a good government, weak or strong, peaceful or belligerent. The Palace's purpose is to see that the Queen's business is being conducted, to see that there are ministers to take responsibility collectively for enacting that business, which, although it goes out in the Queen's name is actually the responsibility of those ministers before Parliament.

The Queen's business must go on, and if interrupted it is the Crown which presides over the machinery which masks, or at least mitigates, the pain and uncertainty of political change. It was George V, echoing Bagehot, who said: 'The existence of the Crown serves to *disguise* change & therefore to deprive it of the evil consequences of revolution . . .'.[2] But it was also George V who presided over the greatest change in the monarchy itself, fashioning it into a twentieth-century institution which has, in its essential

---

[2] Nicholson, *George V*, p 62.

character, changed little from the pattern he devised for it.

The man who regarded his first state opening of Parliament as the most awful ordeal he had ever gone through, and who had to have the speech set in extra large type so that he could read it in spite of his trembling hand, emerged into the fulness of his reign, honest, opinionated, correct and immensely fair. He set a standard for his office which has not yet been altered or surpassed.

There was some remodelling at the Palace, of course, but many of the rituals, including that which Richard Crossman used to describe as the 'mumbo jumbo' of Privy Council meetings, still apply today.[3] They apply equally to the highest officers of state — the 'efficient' representatives of government — as to the courtiers. Only the Sovereign stands above it, an object of unchanging reverence. As a Cabinet Secretary once put it to me: 'The monarchy is the one constant factor in politics. Politicians come and go, and it is reassuring to them, when they lose power, to know that they will lose it to someone who may also lose it, and will anyway be subject to the same constraints, the same rituals, the same accountability, as they are.'[4] If senior politicans, civil servants and military men have to perform with such deference, it tends to condition them into recognising that it is not merely a social ritual which restrains them, but a constitutional one. The figure before them, to whom they bow or curtsy, whose name they cannot use, who always keeps her distance, is not just demanding these rituals from them because it takes her fancy to have a people behave like that. The demands are symbolic.

The Queen's experience of government is unrivalled in this country and in the Commonwealth. It is a fallacy to assume that, because she has almost no executive functions to perform, her experience does not have the same dimension as that of the practising politicians who come and go through her ante-chamber. Her role in the political process is primarily a passive one; it is to be there, to be the constant expression of the stability and permanence of our political system. Her political personality, such as it is, is only expressed through the relationship she has with her chief, and

---

[3] Richard Crossman, *The Diaries of a Cabinet Minister, Vol 2, Lord President of the Council and Leader of the House of Commons, 1966-68* (Hamish Hamilton, London, 1976), p 44.

[4] Private information.

only really intimate minister, the Prime Minister. That relationship lies at the very heart of the British constitution; it's the essential core, the mystery which manages to transform the Monarch from being a ceremonial figure, who is expected to take the salute at annual parades, into someone suffused in a certain amount of mystery, with several still undefined prerogatives which lend more than lip service to the expression 'Her Majesty's Government'.

At the bottom of every Prime Minster's box there is a diary of engagements, which is revised on a weekly basis once a day, and on a yearly basis once a week. Through all those endless plans and appointments one immutable, regular, almost importunate entry in the diary appears and reappears with unchallengeable regularity. Tuesday audience. Tuesday audience. Tuesday audience. Every Tuesday, winter, spring, summer, autumn, winter again. In short, if the Prime Minister and the Sovereign are both in London there is an audience at the Palace.

These meetings have no formal agenda, are not attended by anyone else, have no minutes taken of their conclusions. The Prime Minister drives to the Palace with his Principal Private Secretary, who remains in the office of the Queen's Private Secretary, while the latter takes the Prime Minister up the stairs to the royal presence. The audience usually lasts not less than one hour, sometimes stretching to an hour and a half. The Prime Minister reappears and then either stops off in the office of the Queen's Private Secretary for a chat or leaves the Palace immediately. By convention agreed between the Queen's and the Prime Minister's Private Secretaries, no direct attempt is made to discover what went on in the audience. The Private Secretary in the car returning to Downing Street would probably say: 'Did you have a good meeting with the Queen', and then wait for an answer before branching off into other subjects, leaving it to the Prime Minister to unburden himself, or not, of some confidence or another, particularly if action had to be taken. The Prime Minister, for his part, would not feel pressed to do so, if he preferred to preserve the confessional character of the audience. The weekly Palace audience is thus a unique feature of the political process in Britain. It has no statutory validity; the Prime Minister could omit it without breaking the law, or bringing down his government. But such an act would not last long as a mere discourtesy before it acquired the hue of constitutional impropriety.

It is a unique meeting also, because in a Prime Minister's life there is nobody else in the country, outside the Cabinet, who has the right to know what he knows, the right to question him on what he is doing, and who can enforce that right by having seen all the same state documents that the Prime Minister has. On the other hand, apart from the right to know, it is the only meeting in a Prime Minister's diary which will not lead to any political demands being made on the first minister, unless and until the Sovereign allows the Monarchy to make explicit demands of ministers in the way that Edward VIII did, and lived to regret it.

Of course the Queen's relationship with her prime ministers changes very much in accordance with their different personalities, whereas her relationship to the *system* remains unchanged. In that sense she is similar to the Civil Service. Together they have a loyalty to the parliamentary system, and a commitment to see that it is functioning properly. Since civil servants have served the system under governments of both parties, that part of them which is institutionally disloyal to their present masters must be loyal to the monarchy, since it stands for the same thing as they do — a constitution which can accommodate alternating governments.

The dilemma for the monarchy is as follows: the powers that are left to it are either a snare or a delusion. It is clear that, in the matters of choosing a prime minister, and dissolving parliaments, there are conventions and precedents which govern the monarch's decisions for 99 per cent of the time. But what of the one per cent which is left — of the choice of Lord Home for Prime Minister, for instance, or of the potentially confusing parliamentary situation of Edward Heath's government in February 1974?

Supposing the one per cent decision occurs as a result of the next election, with a hung parliament and no agreement about anything; or as a result of devolution creating a new and unconsidered requirement for an arbitrator in disputes between parliaments; or after a reformed and elective House of Lords challenges the Commons? All these possibilities are remote, but they are not too remote to avoid trouble for the monarchy. As our constitution now stands, only the Sovereign, on her own, advised by her private secretary, has responsibility for making these key decisions when they are not governed by any satisfactory case law from the past.

Is it a delusion to consider that these prerogatives, though buried deep in the subsoil of the constitution, still exist against the day that they might have to be dug up? If it is, then some statutory powers must be put in their place, and another, apolitical, permanent, unambitious, symbolic and popular repository found for them. Such is the nature of the monarchy; and it would be hard to find an alternative.

Or is it, on the other hand, a snare? It would be a snare because, although these powers exist, and might have to be used, they might exist only once. Is there any point, therefore, in the monarchy running the risk inherent in having such residual powers, particularly if the royal prerogative to appoint prime ministers and dissolve Parliament is no longer held to be credible or acceptable by the mass of practising politicians?

The point about the Queen's position is that it is one — in the normal course of events — which involves neither power nor influence in any explicit sense. But after prolonged discussion with politicians, diplomats, civil servants, military men and historians, I have reached the conclusion that it is something more pervasive but less identifiable than power or influence. I would call it 'a presence' in the highest reaches of the political process. It is that presence which would underwrite the authority and credibility of the Crown, were it forced to use its reserve powers in the confused circumstances I have described.

But the dangers are manifest, because although this 'presence' has taken the place of many more formidable prerogatives which have dwindled into mere ceremonies, it is something of which the constitution is totally ignorant. The Sovereign's reserve powers remain as tiny promontories jutting into an expanding sea of statutory conventions. To exercise them would require an enormous act of faith by the Monarch, faith that the people would understand the situation and judge accordingly any action by their Sovereign.

Faith therefore lies at the heart of the matter; and how do you test it? However pervasive the presence *within* the political machine, the monarchy is only as strong as its hold on the whole nation's imagination. Its authority is based on an illusion that it is what people want; that, as an aggregate of their wishes, it represents an expression of the power of the people. So be it.

But we have to be careful. Bagehot warned about the danger of letting daylight into magic. Magic it is, but how many magics can you have before they become uncontrollable? We have a Commonwealth of 53 countries, including 16 monarchies ruled by the Queen, six separate indigeneous monarchies and 31 republics. It would thus be surprising if there were not some occasions when this magic, this mystery, appeared to set up intolerable anomalies or became the subject of some confusing political controversy. We have moved a long way from the containable certainties at the start of the Queen's reign.

When the Queen was formally proclaimed, one of her titles was Head of the Commonwealth, though at the time it had no statutory basis. That came later in the Royal Titles Bill, passed into law before her Coronation.

That bill for the first time recognised the divisibility of the Crown, since after its passage the Queen was described differently in each Commonwealth parliament where she reigns. The Statute of Westminster in 1931 had certainly given statutory recognition to the legislative independence of the parliaments of the empire, though with two limitations — concerning their right to alter either the succession or the title. But the Crown had remained one and the same. Yet even then, tensions could arise between Britain and the Dominions as to who should advise the Sovereign when abroad. There were many arguments, for instance between Canada and the British government over which minister should accompany George VI as he crossed the Canadian border in to the USA in 1939.

Though the Royal Titles Bill in 1953 first gave statutory recognition to the title Head of the Commonwealth, its origins lay in the legal device to keep India, though a republic, in the Commonwealth. That device was a law which set aside India's republican status, and which thus preserved intact the status and right of Indian citizens as though their country continued to owe allegiance to the Crown.

At her Coronation, the Queen was seven monarchs in one. By now she is 16. Can such a multiplication retain the original significance of the Crown? Does it need to? Or does this strange simultaneous embodiment of one and many acquire new meanings as it expands? As Patrick Gordon Walker said in the 1953 debate, there was a paradox between the new idea of the divisibility of the Crown and its preservation as a symbol of unity over a Commonwealth of more and more diverse nations.[5] It meant something very important to all parts, but different things in different parts. That is obvious today when the Queen attracts quite as many and perhaps more crowds touring Commonwealth republics than she does in what are technically her own domains.

It is her constitutional position during these tours, however, which remains unclear. It cannot satisfactorily be said to derive entirely and exclusively from her position as Head of the Commonwealth. That is a title, and a symbolic one. But one has to beware of subjecting symbols to the austere stare of the logician, or the jurist. The position of Head of the Commonwealth has no hard substance. There is no hallowed procedure

---

[5] Patrick Gordon-Walker, 'Crown Divisible', *The Twentieth Century* (1953).

to be followed. It has no constitutional foundation based on ritual and precedent. It is an ornament without any plinth of support from ministers or politicians who act in accordance with convention. Without some of those buttresses the title could come to threaten the stability of the monarchy.

The essence of constitutional monarchy is that Her Majesty's ministers are there to accept responsibility for what she says and does. In certain circumstances when parliamentary conventions have broken down, the monarch can still exercise her sole prerogative to accept or withhold a request for dissolution or to find a prime minister from a hung parliament. The person who subsequently accepts the Queen's commission to form a government implicitly assumes ministerial responsibility for the actions taken under the prerogative acts which occurred during the absence of ministers.

In 47 years as Head of the Commonwealth the Queen's stature has increased enormously. She towers over her own ministers. Presidents of former colonies respect the reservoir of knowledge and experience which, combined with a perceptive personality, provide the foundations for great influence. That is all the more impressive for being sparingly exercised, as was shown at the Commonwealth conference at Lusaka in 1979. However, influence operates on the basis of doing good by stealth. It suffers from visibility. It is the visible and audible role of the headship of the Commonwealth which can become controversial. Since the Queen cannot answer for herself, who then is there to answer for her?

In her long reign the Queen has given substance to the role of Head of the Commonwealth in many ways. But it is altogether a different matter to argue that such a role endows her with a distinct and special category of function. Arnold Smith, the first Secretary-General of the Commonwealth, suggested that he had responsibility for advising the Queen on her movements and statements as Head of the Commonwealth. He rejected the argument that it was the job of the British Prime Minister to advise the Head of the Commonwealth on any matter concerned with her attendance at Commonwealth heads of government meetings.[6] Sir Zelman Cowen, Australia's former Governor-General, on the other hand, rejects this argument. In his 1984 Smuts lectures he said that it was really not

---

[6] Arnold Smith, *Stitches in Time: The Commonwealth in World Politics* (Andre Deutsch, London, 1981), pp 236-8.

appropriate to describe the position of the head of the Commonwealth as *an office*. 'It is an expression of a symbolic character' he said.[7] The Secretary-General was not invested with a character and authority analogous to that of a prime minister in relation to a monarch. He had no standing to advise her in any technical and constitutional sense in her capacity as Head of the Commonwealth. He may be received by the Queen to provide her with information and briefings, but that is a very different matter.

Obviously, any of Her Majesty's Commonwealth prime ministers could tender advice to her in the constitutional sense. As Cowen says:

> The test is whether the matter properly relates to the affairs and concerns of the government of that state. When the Queen goes abroad to a Commonwealth meeting or wherever she does not lose her character as Queen of her individual realm and her safety is plainly a matter of concern to her principal adviser in the United Kingdom and, indeed, elsewhere in her several realms. I would suppose that there is a distinctive concern in respect of her office as Queen of the United Kingdom which, in a meaningful sense, is her principal realm historically and since she performs royal functions there in person, and not through a representative.[8]

Consequently, in addition to questions of safety, the Queen is liable to receive formal advice from her UK prime minister wherever she is in the world, and it would not be sustainable to say that she can be regarded as possessing a distinct status as Head of the Commonwealth which allows her to make judgements and to act quite independently of the advice of her ministers. In the matter of a visit to a heads-of-government conference, a British prime minister would obviously think very carefully before tendering advice which would prevent the Queen from attending such a gathering, since her presence there would be expected and acknowledged by every member of the Commonwealth. Let me refer again to Sir Zelman Cowen, who states:

> Were such an issue to arise between Queen and Prime Minister there would no doubt be a very frank expression of views and wishes before formal advice was tendered. The point is, however, that such issues cannot be disposed of by reference to a doctrine that the Queen has some separate

---

[7] Sir Zelman Cowen, 'Crown and Representative in the Commonwealth', unpublished Smuts Lectures, Cambridge University, 1984.

[8] *Ibid.*

standing and capacity as Head of the Commonwealth which has constitutional significance.[9]

Referring in particular to the question of the Queen's broadcasts on Christmas Day and Commonwealth Day, he went on to suggest that, though no Commonwealth officer or officers, or for that matter prime ministers, had any special role or entitlement in advising the monarch on the content or preparation of these broadcasts, their character would always be such that the monarch would have to be concerned to ensure that they did not impinge upon the policies or governmental interests of individual member states of which she is the Head.

We are left, therefore, with a ticklish question. Of all her Commonwealth prime ministers, could any one be singled out to be *primus inter pares*? We cannot risk a situation where the monarch is operating in an environment without the safety net provided by ministerial advice. In the end, I believe, one has to reduce these questions, should they give rise to conflicting arguments, to the question — albeit a narrow one — of finance. That is the fundamental responsibility of all parliamentary governments.

If the cost of the Queen's visit to Commonwealth republics is borne by the British taxpayer, it follows that she is operating within the British political context, regardless of the multilateral nature of the title of Head of the Commonwealth. British ministers cannot therefore avoid the logic of their position, which is that they should accept formal responsibility for Her Majesty's deeds and words on those occasions. The fact that her Commonwealth prime ministers have direct access to the Queen without going through Downing Street, and that she has long-standing personal relationships with her prime ministers, will always put her at an advantage over her British ministers where Commonwealth affairs are concerned. It is no wonder then that the Palace properly cherishes, and indeed cultivates, the Commonwealth connection, since it gives a vast extra dimension to the status of the British Crown compared to that of the other European monarchies.

But when that link comes down from the symbolic to the practical question of accountability, it must, in the final analysis, be for British ministers on behalf of the British taxpayer to answer for the Queen. The only alternative would be for the Commonwealth as a whole to provide a

---

[9]   *Ibid.*

fund for the Head of the Commonwealth to operate on a multilateral basis when she is visiting Commonwealth republics.

Even under such an arrangement, however, the Queen, as sixteen monarchs in one, would be exposed to the danger that, though the title *recognises* what she is, it gives no guidelines about what the Head of the Commonwealth should say or do. On that she would always be on her own with her private advisers. The world being what it is, that is a dangerous position to be in.[10]

Editor's Note

Charles Douglas-Home's acute analysis of the Queen's ceremonial, political and Commonwealth roles is as relevant today as when it was written fifteen years ago. Although modern Britons may lack the taste for the grand imperial pageants of the past, there is still a need for the Queen, as head of state, to open Parliament, receive foreign heads of state, lay the nation's wreath of remembrance at the Cenotaph, and take the salute at such ceremonies as Trooping the Colour. As has been pointed out: 'These are not merely ceremonial roles. They represent long-standing agreements about things which people often find it very difficult to agree upon, things about which people [eg in Africa] frequently kill one another.'[11] The fact that the British Army owes its allegiance to the Queen and not to a political leader (as the Army did in Nazi Germany) keeps it out of politics and averts the danger of a military coup.

As Charles Douglas-Home predicted, the danger posed to the Monarchy if the Queen had to use her crisis or reserve powers to find a prime minister from a minority party, or to dissolve a hung Parliament, has actually increased with the rise of the minority parties and the call for proportional representation, along with devolution for Scotland, Wales and Northern Ireland and the reform of the House of Lords. This danger

---

[10] This section is based on an address by Charles Douglas-Home to the annual conference of the Commonwealth Press Union (CPU) on 7 June 1984. The address was later published in the *CPU Quarterly* and *The Round Table* in 1984.

[11] Charles Moore, 'The Importance of Monarchy' in Anthony Barnett (ed), *Power and the Throne. The Monarchy Debate* (Vintage, London, 1994), p 55.

has been recognised by politicians and commentators who have followed Charles Douglas-Home in calling for statutory powers to replace the remaining royal prerogatives.[12]

It is difficult, as Charles Douglas-Home has observed, 'to imagine the Commonwealth preserving its distinctive character unless its personality included the monarchy.'[13] In fact, it would be impossible, as one constitutional authority has shown, to replace the Queen as 'Head of the Commonwealth' without irreparably damaging this voluntary association of diverse nations, linked by historical ties.[14] However, with the rise of regional economic and political organisations in Europe, North America, Africa and Australasia, the Queen's relationship with the Commonwealth has become less important to Britain and other member countries. It is possible that the Queen's largely symbolic role as Head of the Commonwealth, which gives an international perspective to the monarchy denied to other European monarchies, will continue to erode and eventually to disappear, to be replaced by a continental style of monarchy.

The dash towards European integration might also undermine the Queen's almost wholly symbolic and ceremonial role as Supreme Governor of the Church of England. One historian has postulated a scenario whereby 'a strengthened European Parliament would try to legislate to break the tie between Church and State in England in the name of the harmonisation of constitutional practice in a secular, rational European community. Something similar happened in America when the United States was set up in 1787, the Federal Government deliberately took those powers.'[15] However, he thinks that the more likely route to disestablishment will be determined by the vocal evangelical and liberal elements within the Church of England. By asserting the validity of the ordination of women the Church itself will eventually undermine the episcopacy and the monarchy. After all: 'In the seventeenth century, the equation "no bishop, no king"[16] proved to be true when the Presbyterian attack on episcopacy led to the fall of the

---

[12] James Cornford, 'It's the Civil Service, Silly!' and Jack Straw, MP, 'Abolish the Royal Prerogative', in Barnett, *Power and the Throne*; Peter Hennessy, *The Hidden Wiring* (Gollancz, London, 1995), Chap 2.

[13] Charles Douglas-Home, 'Crown and Commonwealth (II)', *The Round Table* (1984), 292, p 360.

[14] Vernon Bogdanor, *The Monarchy and the Constitution* (Clarendon Press, Oxford, 1995), pp 273-6.

[15] Jonathan Clark, 'The Perils of Disestablishment' in Barnett, *Power and Throne*, p 94.

monarchy. Today the formula is "no priest, no bishop, no king".' The radical secularisation of Britain which would follow disestablishment would endanger rather than preserve religious liberty in this country, as Non-Conformist, Roman Catholic and Jewish leaders (who are not seeking to cut the link between Church and State) are acutely aware. It would also force the monarchy to operate in a secular milieu and to be appraised in a strictly functional manner, for which it is ill-suited. It would only be a matter of time before the Sovereign was replaced as head of state by an elected president (probably a failed politician) as part of a grandiose scheme for constitutional reform. It would also undermine the legitimacy of Parliament which, as has been pointed out, 'could no longer claim to be integral with the monarchy in the historical institutions of government.'[17] It is worth pointing out that whether the monarchy is 'downsized' and secularised will depend, not on the activities of the Queen or the antics of the younger royals,[18] but, as has been made clear, 'on the broader social and international trends from which the monarchy cannot stay aloof.'[19]

The Queen not only performs the role of apolitical head of state, an increasingly important rarity in our assiduously political times, but acts as head of the nation, interpreting the nation to itself. The Queen does this, without compromising the Monarch's political neutrality, through greater involvement in society than in the past. The charitable and philanthropic work undertaken by the Queen and the Royal Family, which has been associated with royalty since the eighteenth century, has, according to one authority, democratised the monarchy, heightened its prestige and served Britain 'by propping up *civil society*' and pinpointing social needs.[20] It has reaffirmed the importance of the monarchy at a time when it has all but retired from the political scene. The Prince of Wales understands and is an effective exponent of this 'welfare conception' of monarchy with his Prince's Trusts and his call for religious and racial tolerance. In fact, as one commentator has noted, the Royal Family seems 'to be playing a far

---

[16] *Ibid*, p 95.

[17] *Ibid*, p 94.

[18] David Cannadine, 'Downsize, Your Majesty', *London Review of Books*, 16 October 1997.

[19] Bogdanor, *Monarch*, p 306.

[20] Frank Prochaska, 'But the Greatest of These — Civil society and the "Welfare Monarch"', *Times Literary Supplement*, 15 January 1993, p 15.

more prominent part in public affairs than George V or George VI or their families would have dreamed of essaying . . .'[21] He attributes this partly to the new mania for self-expression and partly to the decline of the authority of Parliament which, in its ruthless quest for supremacy in the United Kingdom, had neutered the rival centres of power represented by the Monarchy, the House of Lords and the Judiciary.

The future of our monarchy indeed lies in its symbolic influence as a much-needed apolitical institution of state and, therefore, as an emotionally satisfying representative of the whole nation, interpreting itself to itself. As has been observed, this is its main function, its essential justification and rationale; everything else is but embellishment and detail.[22] Far from being a barrier to constitutional and social change, the Monarchy, as has been pointed out, 'offers fixed constitutional landmarks and a degree of institutional continuity in a changing world, so that the costs of change come to appear easier to bear.'[23] In twentieth-century Britain, constitutional monarchy has conferred legitimacy on the actions of a government and cushions the political system from the consequences of failure. It can continue to carry out this role in the next century. It has in the past shown its remarkable ability to adapt itself to changing conditions. Charles Douglas-Home has charted in this book how the modern constitutional monarchy transformed itself from an imperial monarchy at the end of Queen Victoria's reign to being a family monarchy during the reigns of King George V and King George VI. The Family Monarchy has taken a battering during the reign of the present Queen, degenerating as it has done into 'the cult of royal celebrity'.[24] There are encouraging signs of general disenchantment with this dangerously ephemeral image and a desire for something more substantial. It will take time for a new concept of Monarchy to evolve given that we are now living in a society which has lost faith in tradition and deference but has failed to replace it with anything more substantial. But if we value the Monarchy, we should allow it the time and space, as we would any other British institution, to formulate a new rationale for the Millenium.

---

[21] Ferdinand Mount, *The British Constitution Now. Recovery or Decline?* (Heinemann, London, 1992), p 109.

[22] Ferdinand Mount, 'The Sceptred Isle', *The Spectator*, 16 July 1988.

[23] Bogdanor, *Monarchy*, p 301.

[24] Starkey, 'Modern Monarchy', p 267.

Bibliography

MANUSCRIPT SOURCES

Alanbrooke Papers (Liddell Hart Archive, King's College, London).
Altrincham Papers (Bodleian Library, Oxford).
Brabourne Papers (India Office Library and Records).
Buchan Papers (Queen's University, Kingston, Ontario).
Chelmsford Papers (India Office Library and Records).
Charles Douglas-Home Papers (Jessica Douglas-Home).
Esher Papers (Churchill College, Cambridge).
George V Papers (Royal Archives, Windsor).
Hardinge Papers (Cambridge University Library).
Minto Papers (National Library of Scotland).
Murray Papers (Blair Castle, Perthshire).
Phipps Papers (Churchill College, Cambridge).
Rawlinson Papers (National Army Museum).
Salisbury Papers (Hatfield House).
Wigram Papers (Royal Archives, Windsor).
Wilson Papers (Imperial War Museum).

PRINTED SOURCES

Official

Documents on German Foreign Policy, Series C, Vol. IV. (HMSO, London, 1962)
Parliamentary Debates, House of Commons. (Hansard).

Newspapers and Periodicals

The Times.
The Observer.
The Sunday Times.

PRINTED SECONDARY WORKS: BOOKS

Attlee, C R, *As it Happened* (Heinemann, London, 1954).

Barden, Dennis, *Portrait of a Statesman* (Hutchinson, London, 1956).

Barnett, Anthony (ed), *Power and the Throne. The Monarchy Debate* (Vintage, London, 1994).

Beaverbrook, Lord, Men and Power, 1917-18 (Hutchinson, London, 1956).

Blake, Robert, (ed), *The Private Papers of Douglas Haig, 1914-1919* (Eyre and Spottiswoode, London, 1952).

Bogdanor, Vernon, *The Monarchy and the Constitution* (Clarendon Press, Oxford, 1995).

Bradford, Sarah, *The Reluctant King* (St Martins Press, New York, 1989).

Bradford, Sarah, *Elizabeth* (Heinemann, London, 1996).

Brook-Shepherd, Gordon, *Uncle of Europe. The Social and Diplomatic Life of Edward VII* (Collins, London, 1975).

Butler, David and Freeman, Jenny, *British Political Facts, 1900-1960.* (Macmillan, London, 1960).

Churchill, Winston S, *The World Crisis, 1916-1918. Part II* (Thornton Butterworth Ltd., London, 1927).

Churchill, Winston S, *Great Contemporaries.* (Thornton Butterworth Ltd, London, 1937).

Clynes, J R, *Memoirs, 1924-1937.* (Hutchinson, London, 1937).

Crossman, Richard, T*he Diaries of a Cabinet Minister, Vol. 2, Lord President of the Council and Leader of the House of Commons, 1966-68.* (Hamish Hamilton, London, 1976).

Donaldson, Francis, *Edward VIII.* (Weidenfeld and Nicolson, London, 1974).

Esher, Oliver, Viscount (ed.), *Journals and Letters of Reginald, Viscount Esher.* (Ivor Nicolson and Watson, London, 1938).

Fergusson, Sir James, *The Curragh Incident.* (Faber, London, 1964).

Fraser, Peter, *Lord Esher.* (Hart-Davis, MacGibbon, London, 1973).

Gilbert, Martin, *Winston S. Churchill, Vol. VIII: 1945-1965, 'Never Despair'.* (Heinemann, London, 1988).

Gooch, John, *The Plans of War. The General Staff and British Military Strategy, c. 1990-1916.* (Routledge and Kegan Paul, London, 1974).

Gore, John, *King George V. A Personal Memoir.* (John Murray, London, 1941).

Hardie, Frank, *The Political Influence of the British Monarchy, 1868-1952.* (Batsford, London, 1970).

Hardinge, Helen, *Loyal to Three Kings.* (William Kimber, London, 1967).

Harvey, John (ed), *The Diplomatic Diaries of Oliver Harvey, 1937-40.* (Collins, London, 1970).

Heffer, Simon, *Power and Place. The Political Consequences of King Edward VII.* (Weidenfeld and Nicolson, London, 1998).

Inglis, Brian, *Abdication* (Hodder and Stoughton, London, 1956).

Jones, Thomas, *A Diary with Letters.* (Oxford, University Press, 1954).

Lacey, Robert, *Majesty: Elizabeth II and the House of Windsor.* (Hutchinson, London, 1977).

Lee, Sir Sidney, *King Edward VII.* (Macmillan, London, 1927).

Lockhart, J G, *Gordon Cosmo Lang.* (Hodder and Stoughton, London, 1949).

Mackay, Ruddock F., *Fisher of Kilverstone.* (Clarendon Press, Oxford, 1977).

Magnus, Sir Philip, *King Edward VII.* (John Murray, London, 1964).

Marder, Arthur, *From the Dreadnought to Scapa Flow. The Royal Navy in the Fisher Era, 1904-1919, Vol. 1.* (Oxford University Press, London, 1961).

Marder, Arthur, *Fear God and Dread Nought. The Correspondence of Admiral of the Fleet Lord Fisher of Kilverstone. Vol.II. Years of Power, 1904-1914.* (Jonathan Cape, London, 1956).

Middlemass, Keith, *The Life and Times of Edward VII.* (Weidenfeld and Nicolson, London, 1972).

Middlemass, Keith and Barnes, John, *Baldwin.* (Weidenfeld and Nicolson, London, 1969).

Minney, R J, *The Private Papers of Hore-Belisha.* (Collins, London, 1960).

Mount, Ferdinand, *The British Constitution Now. Recovery or Decline?* (Heinemann, London, 1992).

Murray, Bruce K, *The People's Budget 1909-10: Lloyd George and Liberal Politics.* (Oxford University Press, London, 1980).

Nicolson, Harold, *King George V. His Life and Reign.* (Constable, London, 1952).

Nicolson, Harold, *Diaries.* (Collins, London, 1966).

Pimlott, Ben, *Hugh Dalton.* (Jonathan Cape, London, 1985).

Pimlott, Ben, *The Queen.* (Harper Collins, London, 1996).

Rhodes-James, Robert, *Chips: The Diaries of Sir Henry Channon.* (Weidenfeld and Nicolson, London, 1967).

Rhodes-James, Robert, *Anthony Eden.* (Weidenfeld and Nicolson, London, 1986).

Rhodes-James, Robert, *A Spirit Undaunted: the Politcial Role of George V.* (Little Brown, London, 1998).

Roberts, Andrew, *Eminent Churchillians.* (Weidenfeld and Nicolson, London, 1994).

Rose, Kenneth, *King George V.* (Macmillan, London, 1983).

Smith, Arnold, *Stitches in Time: The Commonwealth in World Politics.* (Andre Deutsch, London, 1981).

Spender, J A, and Asquith, Cyril, *Life of Herbert Henry Asquith, Lord Oxford and Asquith.* (Hutchinson, London, 1932), 2 vols.

Templewood, Viscount, *Nine Troubled Years.* (Collins;London, 1954).

Thompson, J A and Mejia, Arthur, Jr., *The Modern British Monarchy.* (Doubleday, New York, 1971).

Wheeler-Bennett, John W, *King George VI: His Life and Reign.* (Macmillan, London, 1958).

Wilson, John, CB. *A Life of Sir Henry Campbell Bannerman.* (St Martins Press, New York, 1973).

Windsor, Duchess of, *The Heart has its Reasons* (Michael Joseph, London, 1956).

Windsor, Duke of, *A King's Story.* (Cassell, London, 1951).
Woodward, David R., *Lloyd George and the Generals.* (Associated University Presses, London, 1983).
Young, G M, *Baldwin.* (Rupert Hart-Davis, London, 1952).
Ziegler, Philip, *King Edward VIII.* (Collins, London, 1990).
Ziegler, Philip, *Mountbatten.* (Collins, London, 1985).

PRINTED SECONDARY WORKS: ARTICLES AND COLLECTIONS

Altrincham, 'The Monarchy Today' in *Is the Monarchy Perfect?* (John Calder, London, 1958).
Breaker, Michael, 'India's Decision to Remain in the Commonwealth', *Journal of Commonwealth and Comparative Politics*, 12 (1975).
Cannadine, David, 'Downsize, Your Majesty', *London Review of Books*, 16 October 1997.
Douglas-Home, Charles, 'Crown and Commonwealth (II)', *The Round Table* (1984).
Gooch, John, 'Adverserial Attitudes: Servicemen, Politicians and Strategic Policy in Edwardian England, 1899-1914', in Paul Smith (ed), *Government and the Armed Forces, 1856-1990.* (Hambledon Press, London, 1996).
Gordon-Walker, Patrick, 'Crown Divisible', *The Twentieth Century* (1953).
Mount, Ferdinand, 'The Sceptred Isle', *The Spectator*, 16 July 1988.
Prochaska, Frank, 'But the Greatest of These — Civil Society and the "Welfare Monarch"', *The Times Literary Supplement*, 15 January 1993.
Spiers, Edward M, 'The South African War', in his (ed), *The Army and Society, 1815-1914.* (Longman, London, 1980).
Starkey, David, 'The Modern Monarchy: rituals of privacy and their subversion', in Robert Smith and John S Moore, *The Monarchy.* (Institute of Commonwealth Research, London, 1998).

UNPUBLISHED MANUSCRIPTS

Cowen, Sir Zelman, 'Crown and Representative in the Commonwealth', unpublished Smuts Lectures, Cambridge University, 1984).
McLean, Roderick, 'Monarchy and Diplomacy in Europe, 1900-1910'. Unpublished PhD thesis, Sussex University, 1996.

INDEX

NOTE: Ranks and titles are generally the highest mentioned in the text